# Developing Skills with People

Training for Person to Person Client Contact

# Developing Skills with People

## Training for Person to Person Client Contact

SHEILA DAINOW AND CAROLINE BAILEY

**WILEY**

Chichester · New York · Brisbane · Toronto · Singapore

*Library of Congress Cataloging-in-Publication Data:*

Dainow, Sheila, 1937–
  Developing skills with people.

  Bibliography: p.
    1. Helping behavior—Study and teaching.
  2. Interpersonal relations—Study and teaching.
  3. Professions—Psychological aspects—Study and
  teaching. 4. Helping behavior—Problems, exercises,
  etc. 5. Interpersonal relations—Problems, exercises,
  etc. 6. Professions—Psychological aspects—Problems,
  exercises, etc.  I. Bailey, Caroline.  II. Title.
  BF637.H4D27 1988        158'.3            88-27693
  ISBN 0 471 91726 5

*British Library Cataloguing in Publication Data:*

Dainow, Sheila, *1937–*
  Developing skills with people.
  1. Interpersonal relationships. Communication:
  For professional personnel
  I. Title      II. Bailey, Caroline
  302.

  ISBN 0 471 91726 5

Printed in Great Britain at the Alden Press Oxford London and Northampton

# Contents

# SECTION 3:   CONTINUING TRAINING

# Preface

The purpose of this book is to help those who are responsible for training people to become good, or better, helpers. It is intended as a guide for training officers, teachers, trainers, managers, team leaders, lecturers—in fact anyone involved in the training of client contact skills.

When people cannot manage or resolve a problem on their own, they will very often seek out someone to help them. As soon as they make contact with someone, each person involved takes on a role. The person who has the problem becomes a client, a customer, a student, a petitioner or a patient. The other becomes the helper who may have information which would help the person to understand the situation better; or control over resources which the person needs; or a set of skills which the client lacks; or be in a position of power which can be used on the person's behalf. Helpers may be lawyers, teachers, nurses, doctors, counsellors, salespeople, accountants, social workers, advisors, counsellors, priests—in fact may be doing any job which requires them to be in contact with other people.

Helping people to deal with the problem areas of their lives requires a range of skills over and above the skills and knowledge that go with the specific competency which the client will have identified as potentially helpful. These are the accomplishments which we have labelled as *client contact skills*.

The book is arranged so that the reader can progress logically through theory and practice or dip in to different sections when appropriate.

The first section provides an introduction to the theoretical foundations related to the training style we have adopted.

Sections 2 and 3 comprise a complete basic training course in client contact skills and with suggestions for follow-up training. Each chapter in these sections contains the training objectives, identification of any issues for the trainer to consider when planning the session, lecture inputs where appropriate and group exercises. Trainers can select from the sessions to make up courses to meet their particular needs. For example, one-, two- or three-day courses; courses in introductions to different skills; courses to deal with particular aspects of the helping process; skill-based practice sessions, and so on.

The fourth section describes a range of training techniques and audiovisual aids.

Section 5 provides some ways in which the sessions can be selected in order to make up different kinds of courses, and the book ends with a comprehensive resource and reference guide.

We have drawn from the rich and ever-increasing collection of theory and practice to which many people of talent and skill have contributed, as well as from our own experience as trainers. We have provided source references which make up a large part of the resource guide. However, alas, it is not possible to provide all the acknowledgements that are due for the practical exercises described in Sections 2 and 3. Many of the exercises we now use are modifications of those we have learned from gifted and generous colleagues, who themselves may have gone through the same process. The actual origins of some of them have by now been lost in the mist of time! So we would like here to acknowledge all those people from whom we have been privileged to learn, and have been generous enough to share their material with us.

# SECTION 1
## The Rationale

# Chapter 1
## How Can Skills Be Taught?

### WHAT IS LEARNING?

In this first chapter we will explore the way that current ideas about training have developed, and describe a systematic approach to the design and presentation of training.

There have been many attempts to understand exactly how the learning process works. Theories range from the highly specific approach of Pavlov, Watson and Skinner and others who continued their work who concentrated on the idea that learning was a matter of stimulus and response. At the other end of the spectrum were theoreticians like the Gestaltists, Lewin and Tolman, who were more concerned with the influence of individual perception and the way people organized their internal world.[1]

These differences in approach have led to many definitions of learning. However, there is common agreement that learning is a change in a person's behaviour resulting from experience. This means that it is not enough for people to *say* they have learned something—there has to be something that they *do* which is evidence that the learning has taken place.

Knowledge, skill and attitudes are the three areas in which learning can occur. For instance, providing someone with some information they did not have before may change how they perceive that particular issue; showing people how to do something and then letting them practise may increase their dexterity in a particular skill; providing a new experience may modify someone's attitude. If these changes lead to different behaviour, then we can say that learning has happened.

The methods that educators use depend on how the objectives are related to these three areas. For example, *knowledge* is something one has. It can be obtained through reading, listening to experts, observing skilled practitioners and so on. It provides a context within which skills can be used appropriately.

*Skill* is something one does, and which is mastered through practice and feedback. Some skills take a long time to learn; some are acquired quickly if the person has a particular talent, or is practised in similar skills. The process of learning a skill inevitably means making mistakes which can be disheartening for a learner who has no support during the learning process.

*Attitudes* arise from the set of beliefs which come from each person's individual history and experience and which inform that person's particular view of the world. Whether deep-seated attitudes can be changed through training is a matter of debate. Most trainers can describe the attitudes they wish their participants to display; and have little problem in identifying those they do not—how to change the latter into the former is more problematic.

## HOW DO PEOPLE LEARN?

It has been contended that people generally remember 10 per cent of what they read, 20 per cent of what they hear, 30 per cent of what they see, 50 per cent of what they hear and see; 70 per cent of what they say and write, and 80 per cent of what they say as they do something.[2] If that is true then effective education requires a mixture of information inputs and active participation.

As early as the 1930s, John Dewey was advocating 'learning by doing': his approach involved active experience which provided the focus for learning.[3] Ideas about how people learn best changed dramatically as a result of the introduction of experimental learning—a concept which developed in America in the late 1940s. Sensitivity groups, T groups and encounter groups began to offer learning based on participants' own experience rather than on an expert's ability to impart information. Kurt Lewin's research, based on his work in T-groups, demonstrated that learning is best facilitated in an environment where there is a tension between immediate, concrete experience and analytic detachment and reflection.[4]

Although, in the main, psychologists and psychiatrists developed these ideas, the ideas quickly spread into the spheres of education and industry as evidence grew of their effectiveness as educational techniques. Increasingly adult education has moved away from the classic passivity of 'chalk and talk', placing more emphasis on the importance of awareness of process and active participation.

Here are four examples of people who have exerted an important influence on thinking regarding this field of educational development:

## 1. George Kelly

George Kelly developed a theory of personality based on personal constructs. He writes about people as 'scientists' who generate hypotheses about life based on their interpretation of reality as they experience it.[5] People categorize the thinking by which they 'order' their world. Kelly calls these categories 'personal constructs': they are developed through experience and constantly adapted in the light of ongoing events. Kelly's belief is that we all learn how to order our individual worlds in the light of our experience. Learning which creates experiences can therefore develop and enrich the individual's constructs.

## 2. Carl Rogers

Carl Rogers, too, was concerned with how people could change and learn. He also saw that an individual's self-concept was a social product, shaped gradually through interaction with the environment. His theory was that, in order for people to develop a healthy self-concept, they needed to experience unconditional acceptance, positive regard, empathy and congruence from 'significant others'.[6] He created a form of therapy known as 'client-centred', in which the therapist provided these qualities. As well as being a respected psychotherapist, Carl Rogers was a talented and creative educationalist and transferred his ideas into the field of teaching.[7] A colleague of his who participated in an early student-centred class wrote: 'I have taught for many years but I have never experienced anything remotely resembling what occurred. I, for my part, never have found in the classroom so much of the whole person coming forth, so deeply involved, so deeply stirred.'[8]

Rogers led educationalists and therapists to reconsider their role in the learning process, encouraging them to see themselves as offering experience and resources to others, rather than direction and leadership.

## 3. Abraham Maslow

Abraham Maslow emphasized subjective experience as the most significant way to understand human behaviour. He wrote: 'The basic coin in the realm of knowing is direct, intimate experiential knowing . . . there is no substitute for experience'.[9] He described life as a progress towards self-actualization, that is the process of becoming everything that one is capable of. He introduced a pyramid model which distinguishes different levels of human need which have to be met in order to gain the peak of self-actualization. He identified the tension between the basic need for safety and security (the base of the pyramid) and the need to change and grow. Growth requires courage and involves risk-taking, a willingness to break away from old patterns of behaviour, making mistakes and being open to new ideas. These elements can be provided by experiential learning structures, which if skilfully designed, will also meet the basic safety needs. In such a structure, people can feel free to use their new experiences to learn and change.

## 4. Marshal McLuhan

Another of the important influences on modern educational thinking is described in the work of Marshal McLuhan, who in the 1960s pointed out that the impact of communication comes more from the medium it employs than its content.[10]

Relating the idea that the 'medium is the message' to teaching means that *how* the teaching is experienced by the student is crucial. Information relayed by experts, passively received by participants, will confirm the message that in order to develop yourself, you have to be dependent on an expert, who will read your mind in order to determine your needs

## EXPERIENTIAL LEARNING

As the name implies, the basic principle of experiential learning is that the learner's actual experience plays a significant role. It involves the learner being directly involved in an event and then drawing learning from it. It is essentially active, with the learner *doing* rather than *receiving*.

David Kolb devised a theoretical model of experiential learning to describe this process.[11] There are four parts of the cycle:

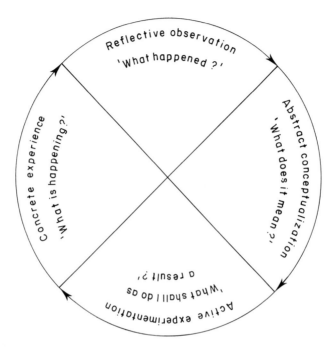

Figure 1. David Kolb's theoretical model of experiential learning.

(a) *Concrete experience: 'What is happening?'* The personal involvement in ex-
    periences.
(b) *Reflective observation: 'What happened?'* The understanding of the ideas and
    situations by observing them, and reflecting on that observation.
(c) *Abstract conceptualization: 'What does it mean?'* The use of logic and a syste-
    matic approach to problem solving.
(d) *Active experimentation: 'What shall I do as a result?'* Practical application in
    order to achieve goals.

For example, a learner is involved in a role-play which requires her to interview a
'client' (a); she reflects on the experience and through feedback sessions realizes that
she did not get all the information she needed from the 'client' (b); she relates her
observations to 'real life' and realizes that she tends to ask closed questions rather
than open, and does not listen carefully enough (c); finally she experiments by
consciously asking more open questions during her interviews and actively listening to the answers (d).

In an experiential learning structure all four sectors have to be involved. For
example, an observation exercise which does not involve the participant in a
concrete experience is not sufficient; a role-play which is not related to practical
application is unlikely to lead to a substantial change.

This cycle is a useful tool in the design of experiential learning and can be used
rather like a compass. Wherever you are in your design process—the compass
points to where you should go next!

Skill training which is based on lectures and presentations by experienced and
talented experts can be amusing, interesting and stimulating—and, if so, it will in
all likelihood add to the listeners' knowledge. But unless it can be integrated into
the participant's own practice it remains an intellectual exercise. People who want

to increase their level of skill will only do so through practice, and experiencing the results of that practice. It is not enough to be stimulated into new thinking, if the new thoughts do not lead to action! The trainee's employers and clients who, are, after all, the people who have most invested in the results of the training, are not able to read the new thoughts—they just experience the results!

## CONDITIONS NECESSARY FOR LEARNING SKILLS

In order for skills training to be effective there are some basic conditions which should be met.

## 1. Connecting links

There must be a link that the learner can understand between the training and his or her perception of the present situation. If the things that people are asked to learn do not logically connect with what they already know, or if there is no logical framework which explains the purpose and benefits of the training, then the training is likely to be discounted by the participant.

Take for example the bereavement counsellor whose understanding of her job is that the best way to help clients is to 'get them over' their grief as soon as possible. As a result of this belief she spends the counselling sessions cheering up the client. She believes that the right thing to do is to take the initiative and not let the client dwell on emotions. Imagine this counsellor in a training course where the assumption of the trainer is that the best way to help people who are bereaved is to encourage them to express and discharge their feelings. If the trainer is unable to make connections that the counsellor will understand between those two beliefs, then there is a high likelihood that the counsellor will reject the training.

## 2. Practice and feedback

The opportunity to practise a skill is a crucial condition if the skill is to be mastered. You cannot learn how to interview a client by reading books or by watching other people do it. Books and observation will give you useful information about how you could interview—but it is only by doing it, receiving feedback, and then doing it again that gradually the new skills become natural.

## 3. Follow-up and/or support

Learning means change, and any change is difficult to maintain without support and an opportunity to evaluate the results. Many trainers structure follow-up sessions into their training programmes, so that people can build on the learning which has taken place. If, however, the training is provided by people outside the learner's place of work, it is more difficult for them to provide ongoing support.

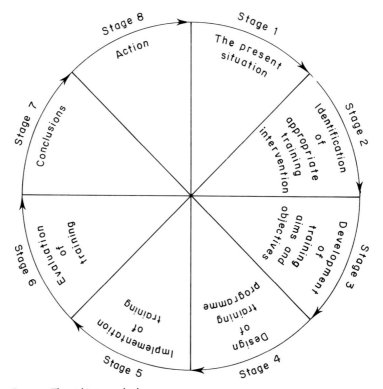

Figure 2. The eight-stage wheel.

## DESIGNING THE TRAINING

## The training wheel

This model is a useful tool for the preparation, design and evaluation of training programmes (see Figure 2).

STAGE 1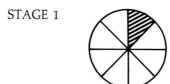

Present situation

Training is usually requested because some problem is being experienced either by an organization or by an individual. The process of diagnosing the nature of the problem and deciding whether training will help is often known as 'training needs analysis'. Many organizations have a systematic process for collecting this information. They may do it through regular questionnaires to staff members, asking them to identify the problem areas in their work; through individual appraisal or supervision sessions; through regular discussions with groups of staff; or through the recommendations of a training consultant.

The trainer needs to be able to use this information to decide what kind of training intervention is most appropriate. The kind of questions which are useful in this exploration are:

What is actually happening?
What is not happening?
How are you affected by the situation?
How are others affected?
What do you want to be different?
What would you and/or the organization have to do to make the required changes?
What are you and/or the organization prepared to do?
What barriers to change exist?

The answers to this kind of question will help the trainer to discover the nature of the problem that the training is required to addresss. They also will create the foundation of the contract between the trainer and the organization or individual (see page 37, 'Making a Contract', Chapter 3).

## STAGE 2

Identification of appropriate training intervention

Can the problem be traced to some lack of information or skill? If so, then training can probably be devised to fill the gap. If not, some other solution needs to be found. This analysis is a crucial part of the process because some problems cannot be resolved by training interventions. However, it is tempting to fall into the 'knight in shining armour' approach to training—that is the belief that the 'right' intervention will magically solve the problems. Trainers are often faced with expectations from a group or an organization which are unrealistic. For example, some problems in meeting organizational objectives can be traced to faulty procedures or unrealistic policies. In situations such as these, although training sessions might highlight and clarify the problem, it is managment decisions that are needed in order to change the situation.

Here the trainer needs to ask:

'What are the gaps in knowledge or skill which might resolve the problem, or make it easier to manage?'

'What appropriate experience, skills or knowledge do I have to offer?'

STAGE 3

## Development of training aims and objectives

When the nature of the problems is understood, and it is confirmed that training interventions are likely to be useful, training aims and objectives can be formed. This is the starting point in the design process. If we are to travel somewhere or buy something we need to know where we are going and what we want. Without this information we may not get to wherever we are going, or not know when we have arrived, nor get what we want. Trainers, too, need to know where they should be going with a person or a group of people before they can decide on a plan of action. They need aims and objectives.

Aims and objectives are not the same thing; an aim is a general statement of intent, whereas a training objective is more specific.

*Training aims*

Aims can be expressed either as something the trainer wants to achieve, or as something the learner should be able to do. For instance, here are some examples of trainer-oriented aims:
(1)  To improve managers' selection interviewing techniques,
(2)  To enable advice workers to use counselling skills in their work.
(3)  To enable training officers to carry out a training needs analysis of their departments.
If these were expressed as learner-oriented aims, they would state:
(1)  At the end of the training the managers will be able to plan, prepare, implement and check their own selection interviews for new staff.
(2)  At the end of the training the advice workers will be able to recognize and understand the purpose of counselling skills and decide how and when it is appropriate to use them in their work.
(3)  At the end of the training the training officers will be able to carry out a training needs analysis in their department through the use of questionnaires and interviews with staff.
As you can see, the aims expressed as learner behaviour are more specific than the training-oriented aims, but neither are as precise as training objectives. Deciding on the aims is, however, a good starting point. They tell us *what* we want to do.

*Training objectives*

Training objectives tell us *how* we can get it. They should be clear, precise, and much more detailed statements of what the participant will be able to do at the end of the training. An objective can be formed around these three elements:
(1)  *Performance.* A description of what the learner will or could be able to do at the end of the training period. In stating this it is important to use *doing* words rather than *being* words.

For instance words like list, solve, write, question, calculate are better than happy, understand, appreciate, value. There is no way of quantifying 'under-standing' or 'appreciation' so the learners will not know precisely what they are to do to demonstrate enough understanding or appreciation. Either the trainer does not know either—which will make it difficult to design a programme; or is not telling—which is underhand!

(2) *Conditions*. States what the learners will be able to use or what they will be denied; under what conditions will you expect the behaviour to occur? There are usually five types of conditions for consideration

(a) the range of problems the learner must solve

(b) the tools, equipment and clothing to be used

(c) any special job aids and manuals provided

(d) environmental conditions

(e) any special physical demands

For example, 'Given a list of . . . ', 'Without the aid of . . .', 'Using a calculator . . .', 'In a role play situation . . .'.

(3) *Standards*. States how well a learner must be able to perform in order for practice to be the only requirement for improvement? How competent must a learner be in order to be ready for the next stage? Standards can relate to speed, accuracy, quality.

Here are some examples of unclear training objectives:

(a) To understand the principles of good counselling. (How can 'understanding' be quantified? Which principles need to be understood? What is 'good' counselling?)

(b) To know the needs for nursing care associated with the stresses of life situations and with common aspects of illness. (This is an example of a good aim, but the objective is not measurable; e.g. How many needs? Which particular life situations? Which aspects of which illnesses?)

(c) To be able to *really* understand the theory of Rogerian counselling, Italicizing something does not make it specific. (How will the understanding be demonstrated?)

(d) To be able to demonstrate a knowledge of the symptoms of stress behaviour. (Demonstrate is a word that seems as if it is specific but actually isn't. *How* will the knowledge be demonstrated?)

All of this may seem very picky and unnecessarily detailed. However, you will find that clarifying your aims and objectives is an extremely helpful discipline in planning training courses—if they are thought out and stated clearly enough the design of the course is much easier to tackle.

Here are some examples of clear training objectives:

(a) (*For a tutor training course*)   Using any chosen visual aids, and with reference to the course notes, be able to design and deliver a 30-minute input to a group of up to 20 participants on client contact skills.

(b) (*For a counselling course*)   Be able to switch the roles of the observer, client and counsellor in a simulated exercise lasting 45 minutes, and be able to (as 'counsellor') summarize their understanding of the 'client's' problem; (as 'client') describe in discussion the experience of being counselled and (as 'observer') identify and list helpful and unhelpful strategies used by the 'counsellor'.

STAGE 4

## Training design

When the aims and objectives have been identified, the process of design can begin. To a large extent designing courses is as much a creative art as designing fashion, or a new dish or the decor for a room. The designer uses his or her resource of knowledge, experience and intuition to produce the required result.

### Knowledge

It goes without saying that trainers must have the knowledge relating to the content of the session. What may not be so obvious is that an understanding of learning theory is also essential. It will ensure that structures can be planned to allow for anxieties and fears to be diminished to a manageable level; that new learning can be established and consolidated before moving on; that a variety of approaches are used; that time is allowed for physical and mental relaxation and so on. Their knowledge of the experiential learning cycle will ensure courses which take their learners through the complete process.

Knowledge of a range of training techniques is also useful; for instance information can be delivered via lectures, visual aids, questionnaires, programmed learning, seminars, trainee-prepared assignments, reading and testing, and so on. Skills training can be organized with case studies, role play, video and audio feedback, simulations, observing a skilled practitioner, discussions, and so on. Training structures include large groups, small groups, pairs, trios, individual work, seminars, fishbowl discussions, games, and on-the-job supervision (for more detailed description refer to Section 4). The list is only limited by the trainer's imagination and creativity.

### Experience

Experience is probably the greatest contribution to a trainer's confidence. We do not know any way of actually getting experience other than by living through it! Every trainer we know, including ourselves, has lived through disastrous training experiences as well as wonderful ones! Each situation has added to our experience and knowledge. Being willing and able to evaluate and learn from experience is a great skill (see Stage 6, Analysis of Experience).

One way of building up confidence is to co-tutor with someone more experienced.

Another kind of useful experience is to be a participant. It can be very salutory to attend a course, and see someone else do all those things that you recognize in yourself, and experiencing the result! Returning to a course after a heavy lunch and desperately trying to keep your eyes open during the two-hour lecture that follows is probably the most effective way of learning: (a) never to have a heavy lunch in the middle of a training course, and (b) never to deliver a long lecture just after the lunch break. Experiencing your own rising panic at the thought of revealing yourself in a role-play is likely to lead to your developing sensitive ways of introducing these kind of activities into your own courses.

## The practice of designing a course

Here are two designs for a one-day course entitled 'An introduction to interviewing skills'.

*Course No. 1: objectives*

(a)  To help people to be better interviewers;
(b)  To explore skills necessary for good interviewing;
(c)  To practise interviewing techniques.

| | |
|---|---|
| 9.30–10.00 | Introductions |
| 10.00–10.30 | Lecture: 'The process of interview'. |
| 10.30–11.00 | Questions and discussion. |
| 11.00–11.30 | Role-play: participants take it in turns to role-play a counselling interview. |
| 11.30–12.30 | Small group discussions. |
| 12.30–1.30 | Lunch. |
| 1.30–2.30 | Film and discussion: 'How to conduct a good interview'. |
| 2.30–3.30 | Small group discussion: 'What skills are needed for good interviewing?' |
| 3.30–4.00 | Report back to large group. |
| 4.00–5.00 | Second role-play; exercise in trios; participants briefed as 'client', 'counsellor' and 'observer' taking it in turns to play each role. Feedback in large group. |
| 5.30 | Course ends. |

*Course No. 2: aims*

This course is concerned with helping participants to get the most out of the interviews they conduct as part of their work. Examples of types of interviews that the course will relate to include:

Assessment/appraisal; grievance and disciplinary; recruitment and advice interviews.

The course will adopt a workshop approach, and participants will have the opportunity to identify and practise the skills required to manage an interview effectively.

*Course No. 2: objectives*

(a)  The tutor will present the theory of a three-part interviewing process model, and through discussion participants will relate it to their own situations.
(b)  To identify and list relevant interviewing skills.
(c)  To provide structures for practising: (i) active listening; (ii) explorative questioning; (iii) goal setting; (iv) evaluation/summarizing.

| | |
|---|---|
| 9.30–10.00 | Introductions: Course objectives and structure; personal introductions and learning objectives. |
| 10.00–10.30 | Group exercise: 'What is an interview?' (see page 40 for description). |
| 10.30–11.00 | Feedback from exercise (large group brainstorms plus small group work) (see page 177 for description); identification of: objectives, barriers, skills. |
| 11.00–11.15 | Coffee break. |
| 11.15–11.45 | 'The process of managing an interview' (tutor input). |

11.45–12.30    Interview skills: exercises to demonstrate the importance of active
               listening (see page 51 for description).
12.30–1.30     Lunch.
1.30–3.00      Interview skills: a series of exercises to demonstrate different
               phases of the interview process: (a) exploration; (b) action; (c)
               evaluation (see pages 51–71 for description of exercises).
3.00–3.15      Tea break.
3.15–4.15      'Putting it together': a role-play in trios, each participant taking
               roles of 'interviewer', 'interviewee', and 'observer'.
4.15–4.45      Structured feedback in large group comparing experience of first
               morning interview exercise and the afternoon exercise.
4.45–5.15      Evaluation: individual work; then general discussion.
5.15–5.30      Course ending exercise.

Clearly, in any 'spot the mistakes' competition, Course No. 1 is the loser! Let us
explain why:

In Course No. 1 the objectives are too general to be useful; of course, the point
of an interviewing skills course is to help people become better interviewers—but
the statement as it stands does nothing to enable the trainer to judge how
successful the training is.

For Course No. 2 the aims and objectives are separated, and the objectives more
specific.

Course No. 1 begins with a lecture, followed by questions and discussion. This
means that, for the first hour, participants will be in a fairly passive role. Course
No. 2 begins with an active exercise, which sets the scene and is intended to focus
people's minds on the process of interviewing, through experience rather than
listening.

The active part of the morning in Course No. 1 comes after the lecture. No break
has been programmed here, so there will be no natural movement from one type
of session to another. Three hours is a long time for people to concentrate without
any break, and it is likely that people will begin to flag later on in the morning.

The active session is a role-play. It seems early in the course to introduce an
activity which often puts people under some pressure (anxiety is often expressed
by people who fear taking part in role-play activities). It is a big jump from the
passive listening and discussion, into playing clients and counsellors.

The role-plays are followed by a lengthy small group discussion. The programme does not indicate the objectives of this session; and there is no attempt
to bring the whole group together to share the learning which comes from the
experience. Unless feedback is skilfully structured, reflective observation can drift
into an unfocused chat.

In Course No. 2 the tutor lecture input comes after the exercise, and is intended
to draw together the feedback from the exercise and relate it to the theory of the
interview model. This is followed by a set of exercises which demonstrate an
important skill.

After lunch, the participants on Course No. 1 will watch and discuss a filmed
interview. Apart from the temptation to have a nap as the lights go down,
especially after a heavy lunch, there is also a problem with showing an example
which presents the 'right way'. Helping other people is as much an art as a science.
Imagine that you were learning to paint, and watched one of the great masters.
You would be interested and admiring—maybe even amazed at the ease with
which this person produced a painting. However, when you came to take up your
own brush you would not be able to emulate, except very superficially, the master

you watched. There are two dangers: you might go on trying to copy the painting or style of the master you admire, and suppress your own style and talent; or you might get so depressed at the gap between your performances that you give up altogether.

Course No. 2 follows the experience–reflection–conceptualization–experimentation cycle with a series of exercises intended to demonstrate aspects of the theory model presented in the morning.

The participants in Course No. 1 are again given no break in the afternoon, and after a long session in small groups take part in another role-play exercise. Notice that very little time is given for feedback from this.

Course No. 2 provides a similar role-play exercise, which is clearly linked to the work that has been done so far. A substantial time is given for the feedback, which is structured in such a way that participants will be able to observe any change in their performance from the morning session.

This course ends with an opportunity for people to identify their next step in their continuing development. This means they are back to the beginning of the training cycle and can seek or design for themselves training experience which will enable them to learn more. This course is like a miniature model of the training wheel in that it begins with people setting their learning objectives, moving from aims and objectives through action to evaluation and future planning.

STAGE 5

*Implementation of training*    So far the training wheel has been concerned with *what* the training will be; now we are concerned with *how* it will be done.

## 1. Information-based training

We have emphasized already the importance of distinguishing between knowledge- and skill-based training, and although this is primarily a skill-training manual, we have included some considerations related to knowledge-based courses. The training needs analysis may show that problems are caused by a lack of knowledge. For example, advice workers need to be updated about changes in the law. Their interviewing skills will be wasted if they do not have (or know where to obtain) accurate information about, for instance, time limits which operate in the appeals system. Knowledge gaps can be filled with teaching methods like lecturing, reading, case studies, films, and individual programmed learning. Each of these is examined in detail in Section 4 (Training Techniques); however, there are a few general points to make about this type of training.

### (a) Testing knowledge

Since the main point of a knowledge-based course is to fill gaps, it seems sensible to start any session with some kind of assessment of the participant's present knowledge. A quiz; a series of short case studies; brainstorming answers to questions like. 'What happens when . . .", 'How many types can you think of . . .?'

are all ways of checking how much participants already know. There are two advantages in doing this; one is that it engages the participants actively from the beginning, and the second is that it enables the trainer to avoid losing their attention by talking at too low or too high a level.

### (b) Change the pace

If at all possible mix the formal instruction with some activity; or if this is not possible use a variety of visual aids. Even in a large group it is possible to allow participants some time to form small 'buzz groups' with their immediate neighbours to discuss some point that has been made.

### (c) Control the physical environment

If you have the opportunity check that there is a good supply of fresh air in the room—nothing is more depressing to a lecturer to see people nodding off half-way through the session. They may actually be feeling drowsy not as a result of boredom—but lack of air! On the other hand, check also that the temperature is not freezing—it is difficult to concentrate, however riveting the content, if one's feet are becoming numb!

Make sure that everyone will be able to see and hear you, and if you have any doubts give people an opporutnity to move around at the beginning so that they can.

### (d) What makes people forget?

It is useful for a trainer to understand the mechanisms which cause people to forget information they have been given.

 (i) *Long- and short-term memory.* Short-term memory covers the first few seconds after information is received. There is a limit to the amount that can be taken in—it is generally reckoned at seven digits. Any overloading of the short-term memory means that only a small amount of information is actually processed. This means that long lists of facts are unlikely to be retained by the listener. If you read a long list of items to someone—what that person will probably recall are some items from the beginning and some from the end. The brain needs time to transfer the information from the short- to the long-term memory. If you are giving a lecture do not read out long lists or present flip charts or slides with a lot of information written on them, and do allow time for the information you are giving to be transferred from the short-term to the long-term memory.

 (ii) *Too much material.* People find it difficult to remember several different, but equally important, points if they follow on from each other. For instance, if a trainer who is giving information on supplementary benefit follows it with information on housing law, the two are likely to interfere with each other. The trainer should make certain that separate points should be dealt with separately, so that there is time for the content of one to be digested before the next subject arrives.

 (iii) *Trying too hard.* If a course participant is over-anxious to get everything at once, and to do it as quickly as possible, it is unlikely that their short- and long-term memory will be able to cope. 'I don't know why we're wasting three days on this course, if we did away with the breaks we could finish in two!' is the kind of reaction for the trainer to resist. Another way that participants can try too hard is to get every single word down in their notes. They concentrate so hard on the notes that they miss large chunks of the content. Informing them that you are providing memory notes in a hand-out to be given at the end of the session, and that they need only to note down points they want to explore later, may help.

People tend to remember beginnings and endings rather than middles; items which are linked in some way rather than disconnected and anything which is strange, unusual, out of context or outstanding. Recall is often easier with anything which is reviewed than with items which are simply skimmed over[12]

## 2. Skills-based courses

As in information-based training, the environment is a crucial factor in how effective the training will be. For learning skills people need to feel safe and to have opportunities for practice and feedback. Skills training can take the form of:

(a) *Individual exercises*, where trainees work through a series of tasks alone, then maybe sharing their thinking in pairs or a larger group.

(b) *Structured group exercises*, where trainees work in groups through particular tasks, and then share feedback.

(c) *Unstructured group experiences* are sometimes used in management or self-awareness training. The principle is that participants learn by being in a group which has only the task of studying itself. There is usually a facilitator or consultant who provides some interpretations, but who gives no direction to the group.

(d) *General discussion groups*, where a topic is presented for discussion and ideas shared.

(e) *Action learning*, where participants are given a task to perform outside the course, perhaps at work placement, and then review the experience.

(f) *Role-play*, in which participants take on the role of someone else and play out some situation related to the skills they are learning.

(g) *Audio and video exercises*, where participants are recorded practising the skills they are learning, and then watch their performance.

All of these are described in detail in Section 4 (Training Techniques); the point we want to make here is that whatever methods you decide on, you need to be clear how that particular method will fulfil your objectives and to give consideration to the three conditions: safety, practice and feedback. If, for instance, a group of participants have never taken part in experiential learning structures before, they may need a more gentle introduction than those who are in the middle of a three-year course where these methods have been used frequently.

Before we leave this stage, we would like to suggest a few more general points about the setting in which the training is taking place.

(1) *Punctuality*. It may seem an obvious point, but trainers should be on time! Ideally, you should have arrived early and organize the room appropriately. Arriving with five minutes to spare, and discovering that the circle of chairs you wanted is actually serried ranks set out for a lecture, leaves you with little time to do anything but panic! This kind of start may well decrease the amount of safety which participants need to feel in order to benefit from experiential learning.

(2) *Respect*. Another obvious point to make is that the communication between trainer and participants should indicate respect. Attempts to put participants down because they are nervous, display unacceptable attitudes, are too quiet

or too noisy, too clumsy or too clever will not create the kind of atmosphere which is conducive to learning. Acknowledging contributions, using people's names, sharing information about the process are all ways of showing respect.

(3) *Working rooms.* Check that the rooms are big enough for the size of group and the type of activity which is planned. Small offices where the desks have been moved back, and where people have to fit themselves around the furniture, are not good training venues. There should also be a guarantee of no interruptions —this is particularly important where the training is taking place in the participants' usual work place. People being called out to take phone calls or answer enquiries is disruptive to the whole group as well as the individual.

(4) *Equipment.* Make sure the equipment works—and that you know what your are going to do if it fails! Some of our most frustrating moments have been when we have designed a sessions around the use of video and then dis- covered that the machine doesn't work. Unless you are very confident that you will be able to repair the fault, move into a contingency plan rather than fiddle around trying to get the machine going. It is also useful to take a supply of portable items like flip chart pens, 'Blu-Tack', a roll of paper, etc., just in case the venue at which you are working does not supply them.

STAGE 6

## Evaluation of training

Evaluation is the process of measuring results in order to decide whether to go on in the same way, change or stop altogether. It is important because:

(a) If the problem situation responsible for the training intervention is not progressing, you need to find out why.

(b) If the training itself is not going well, the question to ask is: 'What is going wrong and what can I do to correct it?'

(c) If your success is not as complete, efficient or speedy as expected, ask 'What can be done to improve the situation?'

(d) If success is absolute, evaluation will be based on 'What other problems can these strategies, skills and techniques be used for?'

(e) If there is no product that can be seen and touched at the end of the day which would give evidence of your effectiveness, then evaluating how your inter- ventions help people manage their problems better, will help you know whether your objectives are being achieved.

(f) Evaluation makes it easier for you to present your work to the outside world in such a way that it will be valued. Just telling people that training is useful is not enough to prove that it is in fact so.

Training evaluation is usually undertaken in two stages:

*End-of-course evaluation based on feedback*

Here the trainer asks for immediate feedback from course participants, using one of these methods:

(a) *Open-ended evaluation,* where course participants write their answers to questions such as 'What I have learned during this course is . . .'; 'What I would like to have been different is . . .', 'The session I most enjoyed was . . .' and so on.

(b) *Multiple-choice questionnaire,* where participants mark their choice of answer:

---

e.g.   This course has enabled me to understand the principles of active listening (very clearly) a little better/not much better/not at all.

The practice sessions were (very well organized) well organized/difficult to understand/chaotic.

---

(c) *Scaled evaluation,* where participants mark their opinion along a measurement scale:

---

e.g.   This course has enabled me to understand the process of inter-viewing,

Very clearly 1 (2) 3   4   5   6   7 Not at all.

---

(d) *Visual representation,* where participants are asked to draw a line between two points of a spectrum of opinion to represent their view:

---

e.g.   This course fulfilled the training objectives:

Completely . . . . . . . . . .Not at all.

---

These immediate feedback evaluations are a useful temperature gauge for the tutor, but they have obvious disadvantages. The only real test of whether someone has learnt something is if that person can demonstrate some change as a result. This will not usually become evident until the person is back at work dealing with the problems which caused him or her to take the training in the first place.

*Evaluation based on change in performance*

Serious training evaluation depends on effective training needs analysis. If that analysis has pointed out what people need to be doing differently in order to solve or manage problems, then it will be easy to evaluate the training.

The questions which need to be answered are:

(a)   *What are people doing differently as a result of the training?* For some types of training this can be tested during the course, participants can be given a quiz or a task to perform at the beginning, and then again at the end. Evaluation like this can often be actually woven into the fabric of the course. Another way of providing a measure of how people are progressing is to pace the course so that relatively easy tasks are given at the beginning, building up to more difficult ones.

Evaluation can also take place soon after the participant's return to work. Demonstrating increased skills during the relatively safe and unpressured training course may be quite different to the participant hanging on to these changes in the light of the real-life pressures which may be experienced. Participants, too, may have to contend with their staff's or employer's resistance to change. 'But we've done it this way for years—why should we change it?' is not an uncommon reaction to someone returning from a course with fresh energy and ideas. It may be possible to make it part of the training contract that some structured evaluation will be organized in the work-place, by arranging for a follow-up questionnaire, or assessment by the participant's manager which can then be discussed.

A longer-term evaluation can also be helpful some time after the person has returned to work. Questions like 'Are you handling problems any differently, and are the results better?' can be asked of the participants; the employer or manager can be asked, 'Are the staff who attended the course managing more effectively?'

Another way of helping people evaluate their own learning is to encourage them to keep a journal, which will demonstrate their progress. Especially in areas like time management, it will be easy for someone to monitor progress through keeping a record before and after the course. Clients will be able to see immediately whether they are succeeding in managing their time better.

(b)   *Are the results of the training worth the time, energy and money invested in it?* This is a difficult question to answer because often the types of results desired are not measurable in concrete terms. Members of staff who attend an assertiveness training course may feel more confident as a result—but how can that confidence be converted into a currency which can be measured?

Although it is difficult, it is an important consideration. A great deal of money, time and energy goes into providing training—it follows that some of that should go into finding out whether it is worth it.

Again, the key to ongoing training is analysis. If a particular problem crops up again and again, even though training is directed towards it—then the training is not working! There is no point repeating the training over and over again in the hope that it will work this time. An example of this is how in the training needs analysis for an advice-giving agency the workers pinpointed their difficulty in advising on new housing benefit law. The organization provided lots of courses on the new law—and the problem still kept arising in the three-monthly training needs analyses. So, more courses in housing benefit law were organized—and still the problem remained. On investigation, the training officer identified that the problem was not ignorance of the law, but a much more practical difficulty in computing the extremely complex calculations; the problems were compounded by much confusion in the local government agencies responsible for paying out the benefit. The programme was changed to provide training based on practising calculations —rather than more information about the law. Assertiveness courses which the organization was already running, included a new session on communciating and negotiating with local authority staff.

After training, changes should be noticeable. For instance if a high stress-related sickness record has led to stress management training, then one would look for a decrease in that sickness record.

After a course on interviewing skills, record cards should show that interviewers have followed the process of exploration, action and evaluation with their clients.

After a course on running meetings more effectively, check whether they now run to time, the agenda worked through and decisions made and kept.

STAGE 7

## Conclusions

When the information provided by evaluation is gathered the next part of the process is to decide what conclusions can be drawn. For the trainer, these conclusions will relate to questions such as:

'What do I need to change?'
'What can I repeat?'
'How should this be followed up?'
'Were the objectives appropriate?'

For the organization and/or individual participants, these are the considerations:

'Does any action need to be taken as a result of the training?'
'What actions are appropriate and possible?'
'What are the options for carrying out the action?'

STAGE 8

## Action

If the conclusions show that some change and/or development is required then the next stage is planning and executing whatever action is necessary to effect the change

When the action is taken the present situation needs to be reviewed and so we are back for another turn of the wheel.

# Chapter 2
## What are Client Contact Skills?

## WHAT ARE CLIENT CONTACT SKILLS?

Client contact skills are the abilities which ensure a helper relates to the client in such a way that they can work productively together on the management of the client's problems.

It is not enough for a lawyer, for instance, to know a great deal about legal solutions and implications; the lawyer needs also to be able to communicate this understanding to a client. It is not enough for a doctor to have all the information about a disease unless that information can be passed on in such a way that the patient understands what is necessary to effect a cure.

A helper has several options as to the kind of help to offer a client; the helper can, for instance:

(a) *Act*— which means doing something for, or on behalf of, the person requiring help (e.g. physiotherapist giving a massage; a welfare benefits adviser telephoning the local authority; a plumber mending a burst pipe).

(b) *Instruct*— telling people what they must do (e.g. a doctor prescribing treatment; a teacher giving rules about school uniforms).

(c) *Teach* — passing on information which the other person may need; or demonstrating and coaching a skill which the other wants or needs to master (e.g. a games coach; a nurse showing a patient how to inject; an advice worker explaining the law).

(d) *Advise* — telling people what in your opinion is the wisest course of action for them to take (e.g. a lawyer explaining the best option; a careers teacher telling a pupil which job will be best for him or her).

(e) *Counsel*— helping individuals to a greater understanding of the situation they are in and the options available to them (e.g. a manager helping a staff member who has personal problems; a teacher aiding a pupil to understand the possible reason for learning difficulties; a friend).

(f) *Mediate*— assisting parties with conflicting interests to communicate with each other (e.g. a social worker dealing with a neighbour dispute; a department head dealing with staff in disagreement).

(g) *Negotiate*— bargaining with someone, or on behalf of someone, in order to reach an acceptable agreement (e.g. a union official transacting with management).

(h) *Support* — being with people while they work through emotions or issues, or take action, in order to encourage or sustain them (e.g. a nurse helping bereaved relatives; a friend talking about emotional problems).

(i) *Supervision* — providing support and challenge to someone with the focus on work objectives and issues.

## Objectives

While all of these ways of helping people are useful, some are more appropriate than others in different situations. For instance if one of the main objectives of the helper is to assist the other to develop more autonomy, then giving instructions, or taking action, or advising, may not be as effective as counselling or supporting. If speed is of the essence to the best management of a problem, then counselling or teaching may not be as helpful as taking action or instructing.

So clearly one of the first considerations for the helper is clarity regarding the main objectives for themselves and for the client with regard to the best management of the problem.

## Power balance

Another crucial element to take into account is the difference in the balance of power between the helper and the helped. Each type of helping which we have identified involves a certain distribution of power between the parties involved.

Whenever one person approaches another for a help he or she is accepting that the helper will have some power—that is the opportunity to influence thought, feeling or behaviour to some extent. The helper has a responsibility to use that power for the benefit of the client, and in the wisest possible way. Different helping situations provide different opportunities.

The helper who acts on behalf of the client, or orders the client to take action, will take most of the power at that moment; the counsellor helping someone to discover insights into his or her behaviour is able to share the power; the helper who is supporting an individual through a difficult period can leave most of the power with that person.

Helpers' styles will be heavily influenced by their approach to these two elements—objectives and power. For instance people who have the *solution* of problems as their main objective are likely to adopt a style in which the emphasis is on the content of the problem rather than the person in the problem. The difficulty for helpers with this as their main objective is that some problems do not have solutions! This situation can lead to a sense of failure and may lead to the discounting of the help that might be given to clients even though their problem cannot be solved. It is probably wiser to identify as the main objective the desire to help people *manage* their problem situations better. With this objective there is always something that can be offered. For instance time to listen to a client is no longer wasteful; having someone who is prepared to pay you close attention and give you support and sympathy can in itself be therapeutic, and may indeed help you manage just a little bit better. The helper whose only motive is to solve problems will not be easily able to offer this kind of listening, since it will not in itself lead to a solution and will seem like a waste of time.

Another example of an objective which will influence helpers' attitudes is the desire to encourage as many clients as possible to become less dependent on others. In this case what is offered will include more teaching, counselling and supporting and less action taken on behalf of the client.

The objectives will determine how the power between the helper and client is distributed.

These issues provide the foundation for the transactions which take place between helper and client, and so are also of crucial importance to the trainer. Most trainers engage in some form of discussion with their prospective trainees or their representative before the training contract is drawn up. These discussions can be used to clarify how the training is intended to help the organization or individual to meet his or her objectives.

This example shows how lack of clarity on the trainer's part can create an unhelpful and unhappy experience for both parties.

A well-known national voluntary organization concerned with the provision of generalist advice to the public put much more emphasis on skill-based rather than on information-based training, which had up to that point been the main focus. They employed an experienced counsellor–trainer who ran several courses in which the emphasis was on communication and counselling skills. The courses were not well received by the trainees, most of whom were experienced advice-givers. At this point in their development most workers did not see that listening and empathizing (two of the skills focused on the training) were of very much use to them when their main concern was to solve people's problems as quickly as possible in order to keep the waiting rooms from overflowing. The trainer was use to operating in a field where the ability to listen and empathize in order to help a client through the counselling process was accepted without question. This acceptance was based on the fact that time was not a problem to the counsellors being trained since each of their clients had a 50-minute appointment; and people were in the main working on emotional problems rather than on practical crises. The advice workers, on the other hand, were working in situations where people did not make appointments and so just queued until they could be seen; where it was not possible to predict how long each person would need the interview; and where often the clients were in crisis situations like having no money if their Giro had not arrived, or no reasonable housing for their children.

The trainer ran very well-designed and creative courses which were very effective in teaching basic communication skills. The problem was that they were not linked to the main objectives of the trainees. The situation improved when the trainer and the organization explored together how basis counselling skills training needed to be modified for advice work.

## PRIMARY CLIENT CONTACT SKILLS

There are a set of primary skills which every helper needs, regardless of the type of situation in which they are involved with others. Rather like the primary colours from which each painter will make up individual palettes, helpers will use these skills differently according to the situation they are in at any particular time.

These primary skills have been very well defined by Carl Rogers, the American psychologist who pioneered the client-centred approach,[1] and can be described under the titles of genuineness, acceptance and empathy.

Genuineness is self-awareness which comes from the ability to relate to the client as a real person and not to hide behind a uniform, a clipboard, a white coat or an organization. It means being honest about one's thoughts and feelings; to be oneself without front or facade. Whereas it is inappropriate and sometimes unwise to be totally self-revealing, the genuine helper is committed to being as open and honest with the other person as possible and practical.

Accepting others means being willing to be non-judgmental and non-possessive with regard to them. It does not necessarily mean liking or approving of what everybody does. In fact there will always be some people whose behaviour you do not approve of or like, but this need not stand in the way of a willingness to value the other person as an individual. One way of defining this is an attitude of neutrality towards the other. The helper who is accepting is offering communication largely uncluttered by judgements on the thoughts, feelings or behaviour of the client.

Empathy is the ability to understand other people's worlds and themselves in it as they experience it. Robert Bolton[2] places empathy along a continuum that ranges from apathy to sympathy (Figure 3). Apathy is a lack of feeling or concern; to be apathetic is to be uninvolved and detached from other people and their feelings ('I don't care', 'That's your problem'). The other end of the continuum is sympathy, which is an overinvolvement in the emotion of other people. Sympathetic people feel for the other person and those feelings can easily become sentimental. It is a mixture of pity and patronage, and can be extremely destructive if it deprives its object of autonomy ('Oh! You poor thing', 'I feel so terrible for you').

APATHY              EMPATHY              SYMPATHY

Figure 3.

Empathy lies in the middle of this continuum; it has been defined as trying to get inside another's skin in order to share his or her experience of the world.

Empathy involves experiencing the feelings of another without losing one's own identity, and responding accurately without being overcome by them. The empathic helper will sense the feelings of the other but not be disabled by the pain or distress of the client. ('It looks like you're feeling really low today', 'It seems as if you were hurt very much by that').

It was Rogers's contention that if helpers created relationships with the characteristics of genuineness, acceptance and empathy, then the people they were attempting to help would understand aspects of themselves hitherto hidden from them; that they would become better integrated and more able to function effectively; more self-confident and autonomous; more able to understand and accept others and more able to cope with their problems adequately.

There is much research to support this claim. For instance a study in 1950 by D. V. Bergman[3] showed that there was significant interaction between a counsellor's response and the client's subsequent progress. Where the counsellor reflected feelings, the client would continue self-exploration and develop insights. When the counsellor responded with evaluative and interpretive responses, the client would abandon self-exploration. Bergman concluded that self-exploration and insight, both undisputed positive aspects of the therapeutic process, appear to result more often from reflective and empathic responses on the part of the helper. This is just one of many investigations into the best way of helping people through therapeutic interventions.

In emphasizing the importance of empathic listening, Robert Bolton draws from research which shows how each person's own emotional conditioning affects that person's perception. Some members of a group of executives were asked to leave the room. Those remaining were asked to study a picture of an incident involving people in a fight. After the group had time to study the picture, which was projected on a screen, the projector was turned off. One of the people was asked to return from outside the room and listened to a description of the picture by someone who had studied it. Then the next person was asked to return to the room and had the picture described by the person who preceded him. This procedure was repeated until everyone was back and had had a description of the picture. The last person was asked to face the group, back to the screen, and relate what the picture contained. At the same time the picture was projected, so that the accuracy of the description could be matched with the original. The distortions which occurred in those descriptions were considerable. For instance, people described weapons which were not actually in the picture; the verbal argument got turned into a fight which was described in detail; people who were observers in the picture were described as taking part in the fight; and so on. The executives heard the descriptions through their own emotional fiters, and this had resulted in gross misunderstandings. We all have emotional filters which influence our perceptions and inhibit our listening ability[4].

# HELPING SKILLS

We can break down these basic ideas into groups of helping skills, as follows:

## 1.   Communication skills

These are skills which enable someone to understand and be understood. They include:

(a)  *Creating rapport.* Welcoming, explaining and managing boundaries such as time and limitation of helper's resources, negotiating a reasonable contract between the client and the helper; controlling the environment are all elements in creating the kind of relationship which enable the work to be done in the most effective way.

(b)  *Active listening.* Listening in order to understand the significance of what the other person is communicating, rather than to evaluate the worth of the contribution against one's own value system.

(c)  *Body Language.* An understanding of the significance of posture, eye contact, gestures, tone of voice, etc.

(d)  *Empathy.* Empathy is demonstrated by the ability to reflect feelings and meanings, to paraphrase and to summarize reflectively.

(e)  *Questioning.* Understanding the distinctions between open, closed and leading questions and the importance of using them appropriately.

(f)  *Challenging.* An ability to offer the clients new perspectives on their situations.

## 2.   Assertiveness skills

These are skills which enable people to maintain respect, satisfy their needs and defend their needs and defend their rights without manipulating, dominating or abusing others. They include:

(a)  The ability to distinguish between assertive, passive and aggressive behaviour.
(b)  The ability to both give and receive criticism constructively.
(c)  To say 'no' without feeling guilty.
(d)  To express feelings appropriately.
(e)  To be able to identify causes of and manage stress.

## 3.  Cooperation skills

These are the skills which enable the person to work together with others towards the fulfilment of shared objectives and the solution or management of problems. They include:

(a)  Team building.
(b)  Negotiation.
(c)  Problem management.
(d)  Conflict resolution.
(e)  Group work.
(f)  Leadership.

## 4.  Decision-making skills

This is the group which enables choices to be made and action to be taken in order to accomplish whatever the desired objectives are. They include:
(a)  The ability to gather information and then prioritize and focus.
(b)  Summarize and set goals.
(c)  Create options for action.
(d)  The ability to decide which communication skills are the most appropriate to use in any situation.

# THE HELPING PROCESS

Although we have identified many different kinds of helpers and client groups, the process of helping can be seen as having three distinct phases: INVESTIGATION, DECISION and ACTION.

## Investigation

Whatever the problem, the first task of the helper is to discover what the problem is, to find out as much as possible about the client in relation to the problem, to clarify what kind of help is needed and so on. Helpers are rather like detectives searching for clues; observing, checking their understanding encouraging the client to communicate and so on.

The helper must be able to give attention, listen, empathize and understand. The skills they need include the ability to set up a positive and collaborative working relationship. At this stage the client will be encouraged to talk about the problem and the helper will be listening and clarifying. This phase ends with the helper and client focusing on the most important or pressing aspects of the problem so that they can decide what needs to be worked on first. At this stage the helper will need the ability to summarize and present options.

# Decision

Then the process moves into the phase of deciding what action to take. These decisions ideally are taken in the light of new thinking that the helper and client have been able to generate with regard to the problem. So at this point the helper needs to be able to introduce new insights, perhaps by giving information that may be new to the client or suggesting a different way of seeing the situation. For this helpers need a range of skills as well as the basic listening and empathy which they will have been using up to now. They need to be able to challenge the client's present view of the problem; to help the client to set goals which are practical and realistic; to give complex information in an understandable way.

# Action

The third stage is concerned with the action which the helper or client (or both) will take. Here the helper will assist in the generation of as many options for the achievement of the goals set as possible; will support the client through whatever action is decided upon, if appropriate, and will evaluate with or without the client what the situation is once the action has been taken.

This third stage ends with the final part of the process which is evaluation. This is important because if not undertaken the process in unfinished. Without stopping to evaluate the situation once action has been taken (or not been taken) the client and helper may find themselves stuck in unproductive or unrewarding courses of action instead of finding out what the trouble really is. In some circumstances the helper will be in the position of assessing how effective his or her interventions have been without the presence of the client.

Much of what we said in the previous chapter about training evaluation relates to this phase of the helping process. The helper will be asking the same kind of questions as the trainer at the end of a training session. For example:

(a)   If things are not progressing well, decisions not carried through, expected results not emerging, it is important to consider 'What's going wrong, and what can be done to correct it?'

(b)   If the success is not as efficient, speedy or complete as expected, the question to ask is 'What can be done to improve this course of action?'

(c)   If the problem is being managed absolutely successfully then the question to pose is 'What can be learned from what has been done and how can that learning be transferred to other situations?'

THE MEASUREMENT OF EFFECTIVENESS.

A big problem for many helpers is that there is no product that can be seen and touched at the end of the day that would provide evidence of competency. A disciplined approach to evaluation ensures that helpers know if and how their goals are being reached.

This notion of a three-stage logical process through which the helper works is of great value to the trainer as it enables the identification of the skills which are necessary for the accomplishment of each stage, and provides a logical and flexible framework which to present training.

For instance, training can be provided on the process as a whole, with the training programme moving through the various stages identifying each set of skills. Or training can be provided on separate parts of the process, particularly if specific weaknesses have been identified by the trainees or their employers.

The advantages of approaching problem management in this way, that is seeing it as a logical process, is very helpfully described by Gerard Egan in *The Skilled Helper*.[5]

# SECTION 2
## Basic Training

# Chapter 3
## Beginnings

### SESSION 1: STARTING THE COURSE

### Training objectives

(a)  To introduce participants to the tutor.
(b)  To introduce particpants to each other.
(c)  To provide experience of learning methods.
(d)  To negotiate a contract.

ISSUES FOR THE TRAINER

Beginnings are exciting, although sometimes they can be difficult, nerve-racking and full of tensions. At this stage the trainer's main task is to set the scene and create the climate which will inform the training to follow. The need to 'get it right' by getting things off to a good start can be extremely stressful for the trainer.

Participants, too, will be experiencing a gamut of emotions which might include joyful anticipation, relief at being away from work for a while, apprehension about how much they will reveal of themselves, resentment at being made to attend and maybe even boredom.

In some circumstances information about the levels of experience and skills of trainees is available in advance. While it is useful for the tutor to have this information, it is often academic if the trainer is from outside the organization, and the task of getting to know the participants as individuals still remains.

If the training is in-house, most of the participants may know each other. If this is the case although some introductions are necessary they will be different to the 'getting to know you' variety needed where the group is made up of strangers. Where participants are unknown to one another the immediate concern is to recognize and work with the isolation which participants may be feeling and move towards creating a working group.

Trainers and participants who have gone through countless beginnings may experience a creeping sense of 'Oh, not again!' at the start of a new course. Far from being a challenge, there may be a tedious sense of having to go through what are essential but bothersome preliminaries before the real work of the day can begin. Beware, though of falling into the temptation of ignoring them, for that would be like starting to build a house without foundations. The tutor will provide a model of interpersonal skills from the outset; establishing a clear beginning, whatever the circumstances of the group, is fundamental to the course and to the well-being of the participants. In other words, 'In the beginning is my end.'

## TUTORIAL INPUT

So, where and how do you start? The focus is most usually concentrated on the here-and-now, for the sooner everyone in the group has heard their own and other people's voices, the sooner the sense of the void disappears, Group participation from the very beginning produes a sense of group 'lift-off'.

You need to assess how much information participants might want to know about your taining, professional background, experience and so on. Having welcomed everyone to the course and shared your name it is probably comforting at the very least for the participants to learn something of your experience in the field. The notion of 'the expert' or 'the specialist' is strong in our culture and no-one likes to feel that they are being practised or experiemented on (unless that is one of the stated aims of the course) so a couple of sentences about your experience as a trainer can lay this ghost at the outset. Having shared your differences with the group by virtue of your experience, it is then important to share your similarities with them. For example, by sharing how you feel at that moment you are demonstrating that you are not expecting something of the group which you are not prepared to offer also. You are providing by example the way towards developing a climate of trust, honesty and openness. An invitation to participants to begin to share something of themselves then flows naturally from this brief introduction.

For some participants even the simple request to 'Introduce yourself and say a bit about what you want to get from the course' can be extremely stressful. One way of reducing this is to give participants an opportunity to think over for themselves what their learning objectives for the day are, and to write them down as a private list. This helps people to focus their thinking, and means that if they are nervous about speaking in a group they can refer to their list if they want to.

There are usually some administrative details like mealtimes and arrangements, starting and finishing times, and so on which need to be clarified. These can be dealt with at the beginning, although it is dubious at this stage whether participants will remember any of this sort of information while they are anxious or impatient to get some sense of what the day holds for them. Don't forget them altogether, though. Clients who are worried that they don't know where the loos are, or who has a lunchtime appointment, and so needs to know exactly when the break will occur, will not give their full attention to the content of the course until they know.

Issues around smoking and non-smoking need to be negotiated early on, and may form an exercise in negotiating skills. Identify where needs and wants lie and focus on the *issue* of smoking rather than the smokers. This allows the group to come up with a workable solution. It may also form part of the *group contract* which will need to be negotiated in the opening session.

# Introductory and warm-up exercises

*For participants who do not know one another*

### Exercise 1a:    Introductions

Ask participants to find a partner (suggest that the group stands up and chooses someone to work with) and find out about one another for 5 minutes.

They then team up with another pair and each person introduces his or her partner to the others (5 minutes).

*Variations*    Each pair can introduce each other to the group; each group of four can produce a flip chart list of the experience or needs of that group; if the group is a very large one, the groups of four can move into groups of eight and these may become working groups for the course.

### Exercise 1b:    Name games

Go round in the whole group and ask each person to share the name he or she would like to be known by during the course, and then to offer an image which describes how he or she is feeling at the moment.

*Example*:    My name is Julia and I feel terrified as if I'm standing on the edge of a five-storey building.

*Variations*    Participants can be asked to share something nice that has happened to them recently; a sound that reflects how they are feeling; one word that describes what they most want from the course; to say their name and briefly describe the story behind how they were given it and so on and so on.

*For groups of strangers, or participants partially known to one another*

### Exercise 1c:    Bean bag

Ask group to stand in a circle. One person with a ball or a bean bag throws it to another saying, 'I'm Caro and this is Michael'. Repeat this until there is a general sense that most people know most names.

*Variations*    Sitting in a circle, one person starts by saying 'I'm Gerry'; person sitting next to him says, 'He's Gerry and I'm Sonia'; next person says 'He's Gerry, she's Sonia, and I'm Angela', and so on around the circle.

Stand up and mill around for two minutes and introduce yourself to as many people as possible saying no more than, 'Hello, I'm Caro'. The tutor joins in and encourages circulation and keeps time. this is a useful preliminary for the Name games above, if very few people know one another.

### Exercise 1d:    Quick on the draw

Organize participants into pairs, preferably with someone who is relatively unknown, each with a sheet of paper and pens, draw six objects which describe you. (Assure the group that artistry is not an essential!) Let each partner guess as much as possible about the other while the person who is being described remains silent. In the whole group, each partner introduces the other.

## TUTORIAL INPUT

By now if there has been ice it will have begun to thaw and the group will be feeling more relaxed and able to hear any administrative details. These may include coffee and lunch breaks, when the day will end, and the location of the lavatories. Always invite questions and comments at 'natural' break points, which encourages those who find it harder to participate without a little prompting. It is useful at this point to invite participants to let you know if they are getting uncomfortable —if the room is getting too hot or too cold for instance; or if none of their learning objectives seem to be met. As the day goes on, your energy will probably be focused on other things and you may not be so aware of the actual environment. By pointing this out you are reminding the group that training is a shared enterprise and that they don't have to abdicate all their power to you. You may be in charge of providing the structure and content, but you will also respond to their needs as far as possible as long as they make them known.

## Hopes, fears and expectations

### ISSUES FOR THE TRAINER

The emotional well-being of the group will be adversely affected unless there is an opportunity early on its life to check out its emotional content. Giving participants time to assess how they are feeling, and the strength of their investmant in the training at the start, provides the possibility of airing hidden agendas and also a yardstick on progress at the end. Introducing self-evaluation from the beginning demonstrates the value and need for monitoring in training.

*Exercise 1e:   Hopes, Fears and Expectations*

Suggest that the group works in pairs for five minutes answering the questions: 'What do I hope will happen on this course?' 'What am I afraid of happening?' and 'What expectations do I have of meeting my hopes and fears?' Ask them to write down key words and phrases. Asking the group to reconvene, the tutor then collects suggestions on a flip chart, dealing with each question separately. It usually becomes obvious that most participants share a range of feelings. Some contributions may need clarification and so need to be pursued; but all will indicate the affective nature of the group. (15 minutes).

*Exercise 1f:   Best and Worst*

Ask the group to brainstorm answers to 'What are our best hopes?' and 'What are our worst fears?'; collect responses directly on to flip chart (5 minutes). Participants then work in pairs or small groups on questions. 'How can we ensure our hopes are realized?' 'How can we deal with our fears?' (15–20 minutes).
Group reconvene and share results.

# Group contracts

ISSUES FOR TRAINER

There are two parts to a training contract. One is the *group contract* and is related to the atmosphere in which the work takes place and the expectations of participants upon each other. The other is the *learning contract* and clarifies the content and nature of the work to be achieved.

Participation will thrive best in a group which is clear about the boundaries in which the work will take place. Negotiating a contract with the learning group may also bring to light some of the underlying tensions which may inhibit progress if left unattended.

Confidentiality is a key issue, and any training which involves individuals sharing their own thoughts, feelings and experiences should take place in an environment in which people known that they or their contributions will not be talked about outside the session. Other issues include smoking rules, respect for each other's contributions, no 'put-downs' or personal vendettas, individuals taking responsibility for their own learning, and punctuality. Any particular concerns of the tutor can also be added.

It is difficult to time this activity, since occasionally deep disputes are uncovered by the process. The tutor needs to judge how much time needs to be given—for instance in a one-day course, to spend half of it negotiating this kind of contract will leave many people frustrated. In that case it may be necessary for the tutor to set parameters such as confidentiality and punctuality, and check that everyone is in agreement. In a longer course the negotiation process is important. Blurred edges to the structure of training can lead to a dissipation of creative learning within the group.

Having already split into pairs or small groups, it is probably more effective to work in the whole group—unless it is too large to contemplate. This final session in the introduction also needs to be seen and felt as a whole group activity to round off the opening.

*Exercise 1g:  Group Contract*

Tutor offers a brief description of the concept of contracts, i.e. a contract is an agreed exchange of needs and resources. Suggestions are invited and written on a flip chart headed 'Group contract'. Each item is then dealt with by the tutor asking 'Is this agreed?' and requiring a response from each person. It is important to avoid items being included 'on the nod' or by the assumption that silence means assent. Participant should say either 'Yes' or 'No', or raise their hands, or indicate in some other way that they are taking responsibility for their decision. Any item which is the subject of disagreement can be left to the end for negotiation.

*Variation*  Each individual is asked to make a private list (5 minutes) participants then work in small groups and produce a group list (10–15 minutes); the groups come together for the final agreements.

*Exercise 1h:  Learning Contract*

This exercise is useful for clarifying a learning contract. After a brief explanation about contracts, the group are asked to write down privately the answers to the following questions (which could be written up on a flip chart):

(1) What do you want to achieve as a result of attending this course;
(2) What would you have to do in order to ensure you do achieve it?
(3) What will have changed if you do achieve what you want?
(4) What might stop you achieving what you want from the course?

After giving people about 5 minutes to jot down their thoughts on these questions, ask them to make up pairs and exchange their answers to the first question with each other. Emphasize that they need only talk about the first question—the other three questions are more for their private consideration and constitute a contract they will be making with themselves (10 minutes).

When time is up, ask the group to reconvene and each person to introduce his or her partner by relating what they want from the course. As each person does this, the points will be written up on a flip chart so that at the finish of the exercise there will be a record of the participants' main concerns.

## TUTORIAL INPUT

At this stage it is appropriate for you to clarify exactly what you are offering as a tutor to the group. You may need to negotiate with the group if they have expectations which are not within your capability or brief for this particular training. It may be necessary to refer the group to any printed publicity about the course, if they seem to have needs which are not related to it. You will probably find it useful to define some of the key terms or concepts you will be using. Words like 'management', 'counselling', 'assertion', etc., hold a very wide range of meaning for different people, and so it is important that the group understand you from the very beginning.

Before you take a break it is useful to point out to the group that the thoughts, feelings and processes they have experienced during the opening session are similar to those experienced by a client on first contact with the helper. Remembering this may encourage participants to be more aware of the needs of clients when they come to a strange place, meeting strange people and feeling full of uncertainties.

By now your teaching method will have become apparent to the group. They will realize that the course will be a mixture of tutorial input, experiental learning, exercises in pairs, small groups and in the whole group. Above all, it will be clear that each participant is responsible for his or her learning; the tutor is responsible for the means of that learning.

# SESSION 2: CLIENT CONTACT SKILLS

## Training objectives

(a) To clarify the purpose of client contact.
(b) To identify the necessary skills.

## ISSUES FOR THE TRAINER

Beginnings have a double function: the first is to establish the climate and conventions in which learning is to take place, and the second to explore the purpose of that learning. While the onus initially falls on the tutor for the first, the second should build on the achievements of the introductory sessions. The session can be structured to enable the group to 'see for itself' what issues are involved in client contact, rathe than stating or imposing them.

It is tempting to assume that people who work with clients are aware of the fundamentals in practising this skill. The reality for most workers is that there is little time for assessment or review. Furthermore, job descriptions do not always match job realities. So establishing clear objectives about the nature of client contact from the start leads to an understanding of the relevance of training and to effective action planning.

On the other hand, it is important for the tutor to value the existing experience and knowledge of the participants. Many people attending training courses of this type are already doing the job. They may be doing it very well, or very badly, but however they are doing it they have developed some level of skill. If this is ignored, participants may feel resentful and patronized and resist the tutor's attempts to create learning opportunities.

### Exercise 2a:   *Why Do They Come to Me?*

A useful method of answering this and other open ended questions is *Brainstorming (see Section 4: Training Techniques)*. If the group consists of people working in different fields, the exercise will probably reveal a range of client groups which in itself may provide individuals with a wider perspective (5 minutes).

*Variations*   Participants work in pairs to produce a list and then share in the large group, with the tutor collecting ideas on a flip chart (15 minutes).

Participants produce a private list, and then write up their two or three most important points on blank flip charts posted on the wall. This method has the advantage of providing some movement for people who have been static for a long time (10 minutes).

### Exercise 2b: *What Kind of Help is Needed?*

Participants in small groups share their knowledge and experience in answer to the question 'What kind of help is needed?' Each group elects someone to record the different categories of help they identify (15 minutes).

Debriefing may produce a variety of responses. One group, for instance, may concentrate on examples rather than categories. Both are important and it would be useful to divide the flip chart in two, heading one side 'Categories' and the other 'Examples'.

*Example:*   Client attending Women and Health Advice Centre asking for help. The helper discovers there are problems related to stress, her husband drinks, the marriage is going through a rough patch, there are debts, children are in trouble at school, neighbours complain . . .

The flip chart relating to this problem might look like:

| Category | Example |
| --- | --- |
| Counselling | Exploring the whole situation; providing relief and support; seeking solutions. |
| Advice | Legal rights; welfare rights. |

Practical help      Legal rights; welfare rights
Mediation           Dealing with neighbours
Representation      With DHSS, etc, re. debts
Befriending         To help with feelings of isolation
Education           As a means of raising self-esteem
Information         Resources

*Exercise 2c:    How Might Client and Helpers' Expectations Differ?*

Invite participants to share their expectation of clients and collect on a flip chart. People then share their beliefs about the expectation of their clients (10 minutes).

This can be followed by a discussion on gaps, contradictions and conflicting expectations.

*Variation*    Divide into two groups. Tutor gives each group a flip chart page already headed. One group gets 'Clients are . . .' and the other 'Clients expected . . .'. They have 5–10 minutes to complete the sentence in as many ways as possible; then both flips are displayed and discussed.

*Exercise 2d:    What Skills are Required?*

Ask participants to work in pairs making a list between them of all the skills they think are necessary for helping clients (5 minutes), When the group reconvenes write up contributions from each pair.

*Variations*    Participants are asked to work with someone they have not yet talked to, and the exercise continues as above. Ask small groups to work together and produce a flip chart which is displayed.

*Exercise 2e:    What Happens in an Interview?*

Ask participants to pair up and find out as much as possible about their partner in 5 minutes; when that 5 minutes is up everyone is asked tochange partners and the process is repeated. This can be repeated two or three times more.

When the group reassembles, ask them to note down their immediate responses to the exercise. What was easy? What was difficult? Were some people more difficult to talk to than others? How did they find out information? Did they find out what they wanted to know? What did it feel like to have to be giving information about oneself to a stranger? . . ., and so on.

A general discussion can then take place about the situation they have just experienced—relating their feedback to the interviewing situation with clients. The tutor can then focus the discussion on the skills which they have identified.

*Variation*    Participants can be given written instructions which they are told to keep secret from their 'interviewer'; e.g. 'You are worried that you have parked on a double yellow line'; 'You are anxious because a very close friend is in hospital having an operation'; 'You have just learned that you have won £25,000 in a competition' and so on. The task of the partner is to discover what instruction they have been given without directly asking.

TUTORIAL INPUT

In this session there is little direct tutor input. The focus is on the participants discovering and ordering their knowledge. Your main task is to draw together the various exercises and feedback sessions, always connecting what is being discussed with the objectives of the course.

At the end of this session the group will have explored why they have clients, the categories of help available, differences in expectations between helper and client and the types of skills necessary to affect good client contact.

## SESSION 3:   THE THREE STAGE PROCESS

## Training objectives

(a)   To introduce the concept of a three-stage helping process.
(b)   To provide exercises to demonstrate the process.

ISSUES FOR THE TRAINER

Defining how the helper can help is often a problem in itself. It is invaluable to have a model that can be shared by client and helper alike, and one which provides guidelines at all stages.

Some people become habituated to seeking help from others and get used to abdicating personal responsibility for resolving their problems. They may have become accustomed to expecting answers to their problems. This is usually unhelpful in the long run for while the immediate difficulty is taken care of, the client has not undergone any behavioural change or acquired any new skills which could enable him or her to tackle similar problems in the future.

The helper also has a problem when faced with this demand. Some problems do not have answers, and if the helper's main objective is to solve people's problems then on occasions like these the helper will fail. One cause of stress often quoted by helpers is that because they cannot solve many of their clients' problems they feel like failures.

The problem management model on which we have based this manual, and which is adapted from the problem solving model which Gerard Egan describes in *The Skilled Helper* (Brooks/Cole, 1975) provides a framework for helpers within which they can help people manage their problem situations better. There is always something a helper can to do assist someone manage better if a solution cannot be found. For instance, just spending a little time listening empathically to a troubled client will help that person to feel not so alone, or misunderstood. For the helper who believes that success only lies in the solution of problems this will seem like a waste of time; the helper who is aiming to assist the person to manage better will know he or she spending time productively.

The model makes it clear that the client takes ultimate responsibility for seeking solutions to current difficulties. The helper enables the client to develop a sense of personal responsibility and self-reliance which will have a more lasting benefit than simply resolving the immediate problem.

The main focus of this session is the input during which the tutor describes the three-stage model. There are practical exercises to support the ideas. It is a matter of choice whether the tutor gives the information first and then organizes the exercises to demonstrate the ideas; or runs the exercises first and fits the input around the outcome and feedback.

## TUTORIAL INPUT

One of the things that seems to happen to us when we have a problem is that we lose our ability to be logical. As anxiety and confusion increase, our perceptions become distorted, and as stress builds up we feel more and more helpless.

### Exercise 3a:   Seeing Red

An interesting way in which you can demonstrate this to participants is to ask them for a moment or two to look around the room and focus on all the red things they can see. When they have done this ask them what they notice. They will tell you that (a) there was more red than they thought; and (b) all the other colours receded into the distance. This is what it is like to have a problem—everything is seen in relation to the problem and consciousness of everything else, for instance, the strengths and experience which would help in dealing with the problem, fade into the background.

One of the advantages of a systematic process for managing problems is that it encourages the helper and client to approach the situation logically.

If an enabling process is to be effective then the client needs to know what is going to happen. To assume that clients will found out in due course or 'know' intuitively what is happening can lead to feelings of resentment and manipulation through lack of understanding. It is important that wherever possible the helper explains the process he or she is using. This is one way of ensuring that the power balance between helper and client is as equally shared as possible. Not to explain what you are doing, and why, is a way of covertly retaining the power in your hands.

The three-stage process starts with Investigation, moving to Decision which in turn leads to Action.

In the chaos which a problem or difficulty brings, it can seem impossible to known where to start. Problems can seem like tangled skeins of wool—how and where can the thread be found that will unravel the muddle? Personal problems are very similar and a good deal less tangible.

## Stage 1:   Investigation

One way of looking at the beginning of the process is to compare it to starting to paint a picture. Rather than concentrate on completing one small part perfectly, your aim would be to block out the broad canvas to get a sense of the whole.

So it is with the helping process. Start with the here and now. Gather information—what is the problem all about? What is the context in which it has occurred. What resources does the client indicate he or she has to deal with the situation? As a helper your role is to enable the client to stay with the problem which is causing the malfunction through the use of questions, prompting and encouragement so that a clear picture begins to emerge. Listening is of paramount importance here. At the end of this stage you should be able to summarize and paraphrase the problem fairly accurately to the client. It is important that at this stage as the helper you avoid making your own interpretation of the situation—it is not your problem! Your main job is to understand the problem and what it means to the client. If you move into providing solutions or interpretations too early, you may miss important information.

The ability to be empathic is of the utmost importance at all stages; it is absolutely crucial for effective investigation. For clients to feel that their world-view is accepted and understood, helpers need to demonstrate through reflection and paraphrase that they are on the same wavelength. This is what will encourage clients to explore, to feel at ease and see ways forward. Noticing the client's body language will enable the helper to be more atuned to the client's state of mind and feelings. Sharing hunches and clues given by the client will help elucidate the situation further.

Sometimes, having articulated the difficulty, the client sees a way forward. For others the problem may be too great; some clients may lack confidence in their own assessment of the situation and their abilities to solve it, or they may be habituated to allowing others to take control. Then it becomes necessary to move on to the second stage. This kind of exploration may take some time, particularly if the client is confused or distressed. It is worth spending time at this stage because this stage forms the foundation for the rest of the process, and if it is done well will save time in the long run.

Most people who are engaged in helping others have experience of clients who do not take the advice given; who do not return when they need to; who three-quarters of the way through a long session suddenly reveal a piece of information which invalidates the work done so far. Some of these hazards can be avoided through careful and empathic investigation.

## Stage 2:  Decision

If it becomes apparent during the exploration that there are a number of factors contributing to the problem, the next task is to prioritize and focus on the elements which will be concentrated on first.

The client will probably have offered various interpretations and explanations for the difficulty. Before any decisions are taken, it is useful for the helper to provide opportunities to explore the situation in a new perspective. Seeing things in a new light often replaces the lethargy and depression which arises from feelings of helplessness with a new energy and willingness to take action.

The next task for the helper is to clarify exactly what the client wants to achieve, and what is possible.

Although it may be tempting for you to decree what should be done, it is important that the client shares the decision about what to do next. The helper should guide the client in the process of converting general statements into specific goals.

Goal setting is a crucial preliminary to making decisions regarding action. The helper uses his or her skills to ensure that the goals the client is setting are realistic, adequate, within the client's control, valuable, measurable and with a reasonable time limit.

In deciding which goals to pursue the client will have some notion of *how* they may be pursued as well as the possible outcome. The danger at this stage is that the client may be feeling such relief at finding a way out of the maze that he or she may devise unrealistic resolutions. Stating the way forward is often a good deal simpler than actually pursuing it.

## Stage 3:  Action

Contained within the goal-setting process there will probably be some ideas about *how* to achieve the chosen goal.

In many ways the beginning of this final stage links with the beginning of the whole helping process, for the client is now ready to explore the action inherent in the process. Here *brainstorming* (see Section 4) can be useful. What are the possible causes and effects of various alternatives? In effect a balance sheet is being drawn up with a number of courses of action being set down.

As this stage is being undertaken it is helpful to explore gently, with the client, any barriers which may exist that could hinder a successful outcome. For example, is the client afraid of taking risks? Change will be harder to achieve if this is so. Equally important, what resources, the client's own and others, will help in the pursuit of the goal?

Your final task at this stage is to summarize the process which has taken place, and encourage the client to recognize what accomplishments have been achieved. You can help the client to assess progress and point out, if necessary, that the process which has been undertaken can be applied to other problems and difficulties.

It is useful to check out how the client will evaluate the success of this programme. For example, will the achievement of this goal determine how next to go forward? Will the client need or want to return to the helper to confirm progress? Are there other resources available to the client which could be employed to do this—partner, friend, member of the family.

The input on the three-stage process should finish with a brief summary, and with the suggestion that this process can be used by the participants themselves to guide them through the management of the problems they are faced with—both when they are helping others and for their own benefit.

*Exercise 3b:    Problem Solving*

> The group divides into small groups of not more than four or five participants each.
>
> The tutor suggests that each group spends a little time (about 5 minutes) finding out whether one of their number has a problem he or she is willing to share.
>
> Clarify with the groups that they each have a 'client' who will share or role-play a problem. The rest of the group will be 'helpers'.
>
> Allow about 20 minutes for the groups to work through the problem bearing in mind the stages of the helping process. Remind them that a contract for time has been agreed and it is important to stay with this. At the end of the time, de-brief in the whole group.
>
> *Variations*    Topics such as: 'A recent strong emotional experience which shocked me'; 'What causes me to get angry is . . .'; 'A goal I have problems in achieving is . . .', are written on pieces of paper and given at random to the small groups, then the exercise can proceed as above.

*Exercise 3c:    Identifying Helping Skills*

> Organize participants in small groups of five or six and ask them to list skills they think are necessary for each of the three stages (10 minutes). These are shared in the whole group. Participants then individually rank themselves on a scale 1 = not competent/10 = extremely competent for each of the skills identified (5 minutes).
>
> Participants then work in pairs discussing their thoughts and feelings about the exercise (10 minutes). This can be followed by a discussion in large group focusing on the training implications. Participants then work firstly individually, and then in pairs on a personal learning plan (20 minutes).

# Chapter 4
## Helping the Client: Phase 1

## SESSION 4: THE FIRST CONTACT

### Training objectives

(a)  To clarify the importance of the first contact between client and helper.
(b)  To practise interpretation of verbal and body language.
(c)  To define the skills of assessing the client's emotional state.

ISSUES FOR THE TRAINER

The concerns which participants bring to a training course are in many respects shared by clients when they first seek help. It may be helpful to re-emphasize this with the group as was suggested previously at the end of Chapter 3, Session 1.

The first contact is fundamental to the helping process as it quite literally lays the foundations of everything that follows. Helpers and clients are likely to come to the first session from different backgrounds and with different viewpoints and perspectives. Clients will come with a problem about which they want guidance or solutions and will be expecting some sort of help. On the other hand the helper has no idea of the client's difficulties, but must seek to understand the client enough to be able to provide genuine and practical aid.

Just like the participants on a training course, clients will bring with them a set of hopes, fears and expectations of the process. For example, a client may never have sought professional help before, and may be feeling timid, nervous and overwhelmed. Or the helper could be confronted with an 'assistance junkie'—someone who habitually turns to others to solve personal problems, rarely attempts to take responsibility for problems or difficulties, and who may exhibit an air of defeat implying that nothing changes.

Whatever states of mind and emotion clients bring to the session they communicate by their bodies, as well as their words, what this may be from the moment of meeting. In order to be able to communicate fully with the client, the helper needs to have a sensitive awareness and an ability to interpret body language.

TUTORIAL INPUT

At least three dimensions influence the laying of the foundations for the helping process. The first is concerned with the social aspects and affect the 'setting of the scene'; the second relates the personal dimension brought by the client and the third is the assessment of the client's emotional state by the helper.

# 1. Setting the scene

Participants know for themselves the difference between an encouraging welcome and one which can amount to a grudging acknowledgement of their presence. It is probably most useful for the group to rediscover and experience for themselves the pros and cons of effective first contact through exercises.

> *Exercise 4a:    Discouraging Introductions*
>
> Ask everyone to find a partner and choose who will first be helper and who first be client.
>
> Helpers are asked to be as discouraging as possible during this first contact exercise. Quickly go through the process of first contact from the time the client comes through the door. Check out whether the helper is behind a desk, where the 'client' will sit and so on.
>
> 'Clients' are going to bring real though minor problems to the helpers. The content will not matter because there is going to be little opportunity for the 'clients' to share it.
>
> Allow a couple of minutes for the pairs to check out the scenario. Have a few suggestions up your sleeve—e.g. doctor and patient, teacher and parent, income tax inspector and taxpayer. Allow 3–4 minutes for the first practice and then change roles for the same length of time.
>
> After both partners have tried being a discouraging helper and an unfulfilled client ask each pair to share with one another how they felt when they played both roles. Allow about 5 minutes each way for this. (20 minutes total).
>
> *Variations*    Have instructions for 'client' and 'helper' which you hand them in an envelope (or folded so that the partner can't see them). Instructions for the 'helper' might be: 'Don't listen to your partner, just keep trying to tell her something important to you'; 'Appear to listen to your partner, but be thinking of something else'; 'Smile every time your partner says something'; 'Keep a deadpan expression while your partner is talking'. The instruction for the 'client' is always the same, 'Tell your partner about something that has been on your mind lately. Do not choose anything deeply intimate or troubling for you as this is only a short exercise.'
>
> In pairs, with one partner playing client and the other helper, sitting back to back, the client presents a problem to the unseen helper and is constantly interrupted. The helper insists on telling his own story rather than listen to the problem of his client.
>
> Again, allow 3–4 minutes for each partner and then change roles. Allow

5 minutes each way for the pair to exchange how they felt in their respective roles. Allow 20 minutes.

Whichever variation is used spend time with the whole group, exchanging what it feels like to be ignored and rejected.

*Exercise 4b:     Welcoming Introductions*

Having looked at the negative possibilities in first contacts, ask the whole group to brainstorm a positive contrast. Write up a list on the flip chart. It will probably include points like:
(a)   meeting, greeting and seating the client;
(b)   saying hello and exchanging names;
(c)   being aware of seating arrangements—are there barriers like desks and chairs which can indicate powerful and powerless positions?;
(d)   is the client facing the sun and unable to see the helper's face?;
(e)   confidentiality and possible limitations on this;
(f)   listening to, rather than grilling, the client.

*Variations*   In the same pairs role-play an effective introductory session reminding participants of their experience in the previous exercise and the discomfort it caused. Ask them to structure the session in a way which will encourage the client to share his or her problem. Take 5 minutes each way so that each partner has experience of being both helper and client.

Allow 5 minutes for debriefing in pairs.

Out of this exercise, ask the whole group to brainstorm a list of points around establishing effective first contact.

## 2. Verbal and body language

TUTORIAL INPUT

Encourage participants to think of themselves as helpers with all their antennae working at top receptivity. They are using all the skills we talked about in describing the first stage of the helping process in Chapter 3, Session 3—listening, reflecting, being genuine and accepting, asking appropriate questions, paraphrasing and attending. *How* the client responds will enable the helper to assess his or her emotional state, which in turn will begin to indicate the nature of the help that is being asked for and the nature of the help that can be offered.

Sheer familiarity with words as one of the two most usual ways of communicating may cloud our ability to hear their meaning. The danger of assumption looms larger here. For example, a client may be thoroughly distraught but also highly articulate. It would be relatively easy for the helper to assume the client is coping emotionally simply because she is in command of words.

Plunge straight into exercises and use them as the means of explaining your point.

*Exercise 4c:     Client Clues*

In the whole group spend about 15 minutes discussing the 'clues' which clients offer to the helper through their verbal language. Points arising will probably include:

(a)  Level of articulacy-is the client hiding behind a facility with words?
(b)  Does he or she have problems describing facts and/or feelings?
(c)  Use of the third person; client talks about 'you' or 'it' and avoids saying 'I'—who takes responsibility for the meaning behind the words?
(d)  Silence—does the client want to be there? Has he or she been brought unwillingly to you? Is the client unaccustomed to having the spotlight on her? Does the client have a speech impediment?
(e)  Questioning rather than making statements; is the client inviting you to make guesses or join in a conspiracy?
(f)  Tone and level of voice—is the client nervous? aggressive? frightened? Is there a visual or a hearing difficulty?

*Variations*  Alternatively the group can mini-brainstorm in pairs or small groups and produce their own lists for an exchange in the whole group. Spend about 5 minutes in a pair or small group and allow 10 minutes for an exchange session after.

Which variation is chosen will depend on group cohesiveness at this stage. Sometimes participants are more inclined to share in the whole group if they have broken the ice with just one or two people over a period of time.

## TUTORIAL INPUT

But for most of us verbal language is only half the equation. Again it is important for participants to be aware of the possibility that their clients may have poor hearing, and so rely heavily on the signals given out through body language. By looking first at the words we use, participants will be more aware of the way they are emphasized—or not—in the body 'speak' of the client.
    Allow the group to find out the truth of this by using the following exercises:

*Exercise 4d:    Mixed Messages*

Ask the group to form pairs, then ask them to stand and face one another. Decide who is A and who B. The tutor may choose to take part in the exercise and, if so, would take up position among the pairs while giving out the instructions.
    Ask the pairs to *say* one thing but *demonstrate* another through their body language. Offer a few examples but encourage the pairs to find their own; e.g.:

say you are angry—but with a smiling face;
say you're feeling very happy but look as if you're about to cry;
say you'd like to help but indicate that's far from the truth.

Spend about 5–10 minutes on this exercise. Make sure that each partner is having a turn so that everyone has the experience of receiving two messages. It usually provokes laughter and encourages group participation.
    In the whole group spend a further 5–10 minutes talking about giving and receiving mixed messages and the confusion it causes. The examples given are extreme but demonstrate how much we rely on receiving two modes of communication in order to assess messages.

## TUTORIAL INPUT

By now the importance of body 'speak' is hopefully becoming more obvious. One final exercise will establish the way in which we consciously or unconsciously communicate our feelings as much through our bodies as through the words we use. Additionally it may be worthwhile to mention that clients without speech or hearing, or with partial speech and hearing, may rely more on body than on verbal speak for clues in communication.

*Exercise 4e:    Body Speak*

Have prepared as many cards as there are participants in the group, each card will have a mood word printed on it such as *angry, desperate, fearful, anxious, excited, tired, jubilant, depressed, happy,* and so on. Ask the group to divide into threes or fours and form a circle with that group.

Distribute one card to each player but ask participants to keep what is written on the card to themselves.

Ask the groups to take turns and allow each of its members to role-play the mood written on the card using only body speak. The rest of the group guesses the mood being enacted using verbal speak to which the 'actor' can respond only using body language.

Encourage lots of participation from the groups.

Allow about 10–15 minutes before a whole group debrief.

*Variations*    Use the cards described in Exercise 4f but play the game more like charades. Every player will be describing a mood so you can leave out whether the action describes book, film or play. But the actor needs to hold up as many fingers as she is going to break the word into, in order to act it; for example, she would hold up two fingers to describe 'depressed' which she is breaking into two sections—'deep' and 'pressed', and so on. If the group fails to recognize the word being described in the two describing playlets, then the actor has to move on to playing out the whole word in a mime.

Considerably more time needs to be offered for this variation on the exercise, probably about 20–30 minutes if each group member is to have a turn. Choosing this option depends too on the tutor's assessment of whether the group as a whole is ready to be so extrovert.

Discuss the experience of playing this exercise in the whole group and check out as many individual experiences as possible.

## 3. Assessment of a client's emotional state

## TUTORIAL INPUT

Assessment has taken place throughout the previous exercises, and it is now a matter of tying up the first two components of making first contacts. Again the tutor more usefully facilitates the process through exercises rather than delivering a set speech. (There is, after all, nothing new in the content of this session; it is more a matter of emphasizing what is known and drawing the group's attention to that fact.)

*Exercise 4f:   Practising Assessment*

Ask participants to find a partner, ask them to decide who will be helper and who client for the first round.

The object of this exercise is to practise assessment of the client's emotional state, something which everyone will have done—and it may be helpful to point out that we often do this away from work as well as at it. Ask the pairs to work out a scenario between them, preferably one that one or other has experienced but failing that, have a few suggestions on hand like:

'You have just been knocked off your bicycle and are shaken but not hurt. Unfortunately you were unable to get the number of the offending car so are unclear about your rights and whether you can make a claim and there were no witnesses. You are articulate and the advice worker at the CAB concentrates entirely on the event and does not mention how you might be feeling.'

*Or:*

'You've just bought an expensive piece of electrical equipment, have tested it and part of it fails to work. You dislike making a fuss but have spent a lot of money so take back the offending part to change it. The assistant is unbelieving and unhelpful.'

*Or:*

'You are at the end of your tether with the noise level of your neighbours. They repeatedly ignore your requests to turn the level of their television down. You are seeking help about what you can do and, as is your habit, you lose your temper and become aggressive.'

Remind participants of the importance of the setting so a little time will need to be given to set the scene and for each player to be clear about the part being played (10 minutes).

After the first player has acted client, give each pair 5 minutes to debrief amongst themselves. Ask them to explore what it felt like to play the role, how easily or not it was to identify with the client's difficulties, what emotions did the client display—did the helper pick these up and did her own emotions become involved or not?

When this is done, change roles and then debrief as before.

Debrief in the whole group and encourage participants to share how they felt—were there factors which encouraged or inhibited clients from getting what they wanted; what's it like being on the other side and not knowing what to do?

## ISSUES FOR THE TUTOR

In this session the tutor has acted largely as a facilitator of games and exercises which enable the group to explore issues which are likely to be both well known and well rehearsed by them in their work.

This underlines the importance of knowing something about the level of expertise shared in the group so that exercises can be chosen according to the group needs—rather than the facilitator's assumptions. Your role as facilitator is to ensure that participants connect the object of the exercises with the content of this session. By the end of this session the group will have explored the reasons for establishing a firm basis for the work between client and helper which continues after the initial contact between them.

# SESSION 5: LISTENING

## Training objectives

(a)   To clarify the difference between passive and active listening.
(b)   To look at helpful responses in active listening.
(c)   To explore briefly barriers which may get in the way of active listening.

ISSUES FOR THE TRAINER

Paradoxically what appears to be one of the least complex training issues is made problematic by its sheer familiarity. Most of us from the cradle to the grave *listen*. This session poses all the problems which a producer of, say, *Hamlet* must face —how to present anew something which is both well known and about which many people feel they have some degree of expertise; using this undoubted expertise which is shared in the group is the best place to start.

> *Exercise 5a:   Active Listening*
>
> Having introduced the subject of the session, ask the members of the group to make themselves comfortable and close their eyes. Ask them to listen to the sounds around them and within them. Suggest that they do not analyze or try to explain what they are hearing, but accept that these sounds are there.
>
> After 5 minutes invite participants to open their eyes and rejoin the group.
>
> Ask participants to share their experiences within the group; what did they hear? What got in the way of hearing? What are the differences between hearing and listening? (5–10 minutes).
>
> As the discussion gets under way, write up points on the flip chart. They are likely to include items like:
>
>> *Inner* sounds, ranging from tummy rumbles to private thoughts.
>> *Outer* sounds, like those outside the training room, shifting on chairs within it.
>> What is it like to hear but not to see? How much of listening is involved with bodily as well as vocal messages?
>> To what extent do we interpret in our own world-views rather than quietly accept the sounds we hear?
>> If so much goes on within ourselves when we are *passively* listening, how then do we engage in *active* listening with other people?
>
> This opening exercise allows participants to renew acquaintance with the complexities of listening. The tutor may now usefully share some input with the group.
>
> *Active* listening is a two-way process involving both *receiver* and *sender* skills. Effective listening can only be assessed by the recipient: that is, if I as listener have not managed to convey that I have done so, communication has not taken place. (It's interesting to note that when communications are

failing within a relationship often one or both of the parties concerned complain that the other hasn't *listened* properly).

For most people except those with hearing impediments, listening is a *natural* activity. We learn to hear and listen from the moment of birth; alongside sight and touch this is how we begin to assess the world around us. This assessment or interpretation of the sounds we hear has to be learned and acquired, and is not in itself natural. In being listened to, we accept ourselves and at the same time assess that we are acceptable to others. One of the most essential aspects of the socialization process is to develop the ability to listen to the *inner* voice within ourselves—our thoughts and feelings—as well as developing the capacity for *outer listening*—to others.

Perhaps one way of describing active listening is to think of it as *disciplined* listening—the reverse of 'in one ear and out the other'. Another may be to remind the group of the ratio between ears and mouth—two to one! It is hackneyed but true that communication is a two-way process: developing ability in one way is no guarantee of developing the other half of the equation. Highly articulate talkers may be poor listeners: alternatively, passive listeners may be defensive and cautious about taking the risk of communicating their thoughts and feelings. This may cause the other party to feel manipulated if communcation lacks reciprocity of some sort.

After this brief input, check out to see whether there are any questions or comments in the group. Then move on to the next exercise.

*Exercise 5b:    Listening as a Four-level Activity*

Ask participants to form into small groups of about four or five. While this is being negotiated, write up on the flip chart: '*Listening as a four-level activity*' (This is the title of a paper written by John Rowan, a humanistic psychologist, in 1984.) Invite the groups to discuss what this means to them and suggest it may be useful to jot down a few notes for later full group discussion. Allow 10 minutes for this part of the exercise.

In the whole group check out the findings of the small groups. Given the deliberate lack of direction by the tutor, numbers of possibilities may arise. As tutor you are aiming for the group as a whole to recognize that listening involves communication on a level of intellect, feeling, body and soul. With this in mind you may need to structure the group discussion to work towards this recognition. Allow discussion time for this idea to be fully assimilated —or rejected! You may need to allow about 20 minutes for this part of the exercise according to how much discussion it generates.

## TUTORIAL INPUT

You may find that most people are more comfortable about listening on a primary level; that is with their intellects. This is, after all, what much of our learning at school is all about. It may be appropriate at this stage to assure the group that *body* listening is another way of describing the non-verbal or body speak which we looked at in the previous session. The third *feelings* level is the emotional context within which what is heard is experienced. The *soul* or *spirit* level of listening perhaps more properly belongs to an advanced level of empathetic listening more likely to be aimed for in counselling or therapy sessions. It is mentioned here to accentuate the enormous implications of what active listening is all about. For the purposes of this session we will concentrate on body, mind and feeling ˌstening, and how to convey this to the recipient.

After this, it is hard to imagine that listening can be anything other than a strenuously active occupation. Allow the group to find out for themselves what it feels like not to be heard and listened to.

*Exercise 5c:   Passive Listening*

Ask participants to make up groups of three and to decide who will be talker, listener and observer. Align chairs so that talker and listener are facing one another with the observer being able to see and hear both. Ask the talker to talk about something interesting, perhaps a hobby, how I like to spend my weekends, what I'm looking forward to. The topic should be emotionally involving to some extent so that it can be talked about with some feeling. The listener on the other hand, should evince no interest whatsoever and convey this in whatever way possible. The observer watches the pair and makes notes if this is helpful. Allow 5 minutes for this.

Debrief by asking the talkers to describe how they felt when they received no encouragement, what did the observer observe about the 'client' . . . and the 'helper', what body language was present, what did the talker feel like doing to the helper, did she feel like giving up? Allow 5 minutes for debriefing in the group and then swap roles. Debrief after each person has played the speaking role. Allow no more than 30 minutes in total for this exercise.

In the whole group allow a brief time for discussion. Comments about this not being the 'real thing' may come up, or that it is only a game and therefore by implication is not relevant. While arguing the pros and cons of what is real and not real is not appropriate here, it may be useful to point out that all the exercises in the manual are 'real' in the context of this training, and the feelings which they arouse are genuine.

## TUTORIAL INPUT

Conclude this input on the differences between passive and active listening by noting that listening is more than a matter of lying back and letting something happen. If it remains the former, the only thing that is likely to happen is that the speaker gives up.

*Exercise 5d:   The Cocktail Party*

This is a fairly light-hearted exercise which can be introduced to lighten the atmosphere, or to begin an after-lunch session. Ask participants to sit in pairs, facing each other. Then ask them to tell each other, in as much detail as possible, what they have done since they woke up this morning. Their instruction is to speak at the same time as each other and to try to get their partner to listen to them (3 minutes).

The effect of the exercise is usually to demonstrate how impossible it is to listen and talk at the same time—as soon as people find themselves listening to their partner, they have to stop talking themselves.

## TUTORIAL INPUT

It is already more than apparent that active listening involves *response*. While the intention to respond might be there, many things can obstruct the process. It is probably more useful at this stage to look at barriers which can get in the way of active listening before turning to responses (some of these are in any case dealt with in more detail in other sessions within this chapter: Session 7: getting information and Session 10: clarifying).

Allow the group to recognize how selective all our listening can be until we learn how to achieve discipline in the skill.

### Exercise 5e:   Chinese Whispers

This exercise is a good one for generating a sense of group cohesiveness —not to mention providing an opportunity for getting out of chairs.

Ask all the participants to form a line, preferably not a straight one, and have ready a paragraph to read to the first person in the line—out of earshot of the rest of the group. Subject matter is immaterial, ideally not too weighty. Do not spend more than about 2–3 minutes on the reading matter. The first person then repeats the passage to the next in line . . . and so on until everyone has had a turn.

As you have gathered by now, this is a form of Chineses whispers. Ask the group to discuss what they heard, assess what was left out and added or changed. When you have asessed that all who are going to contribute have done so, read out the passage which you started with.

Allow some time for observation, after the game as such has finished, for the group to bring up issues about selective listening. This may include matters like not hearing exactly and making sense of what is left thus making new history—we all attempt to make familiar the unfamiliar, by processing information through our existing belief systems. Check out with the group what implications this may have for our clients. Allow 10–15 minutes for this debriefing after the game itself has been completed.

The previous exercise could be seen as one which draws the group's attention to internal barriers to listening actively. The following exercise expands on this.

### Exercise 5f:   Barriers to Active Listening

Ask participants to form into small groups. Have ready something to write on and with. Suggest that one person in the group writes *Helper* in the centre of the page. Invite the small groups to brainstorm all the different types of barriers or obstructions which could get in the way of the helper listening actively. You may like to suggest broad categories if there appears to be a slow start; e.g. organization pressures, those exerted by the client, or by the helper.

Allow 10 minutes for this and then debrief in the large group for about 5 minutes.

## TUTORIAL INPUT

To a great extent *disciplined* or *active* listening embodies the idea that the medium is the message. In this context the listener needs to demonstrate attentiveness and interest with *bodily* as well as verbal messages. We all know people who we label 'good listeners'. The following exercise encourages participants to use their expertise as users as well as recipients of good listening skills. In the language of counselling skills training these are called *attending skills* and are relevant to all interpersonal skills training.

*Exercise 5g:    Attending Skills*

Divide the group into pairs, A and B. Suggest that each pair creates a space for itself sufficiently far away from other pairs so that some sense of privacy can be engendered.

Person A talks for 3 minutes about any issue or topic of interest; B demonstrates attention by means of bodily attention *only*. Talking is not allowed. While talking, A should be aware of how encouraging B's body messages are. After 3 minutes, call time and allow A to give feedback to B for a further 3 minutes. Reverse roles for the same length of time.

In the whole group, debrief findings ensuring that participants offer positive suggestions. Write these up on a flip chart; the list will probably include the following items:

(a)   space: too close (crowded), distant (rejecting), approximate arm's length;
(b)   movement: towards the client, rather than away;
(c)   posture: relaxed and attentive rather than either rigid or slouched;
(d)   eye contact; focused but not staring or absent;
(e)   feet and legs, arms and hands: unobtrusive, avoiding mannerisms that get in the way of concentration;
(f)   facial expression: is congruent with attentiveness;
(g)   energy level: constant and alert.

*Variations*   These can include the use of video, which is invaluable for trainees to see themselves as others see them. It can be quite a salutory shock to discover mannerisms which were unsuspected. The video itself provides the feedback; clearly more time needs to be allowed for this.

*Alternatively,* when video or time is not available, working in triads allows the observer to add her comments to those of the client when giving feedback.

## TUTORIAL INPUT

Hopefully it has become increasingly obvious to the course participants that listening skills have a very 'chicken-and-egg' flavour to them, for if listening is to be a truly participatory and active skill it clearly involves more than absorbing the recipient's words. So far we have looked a great deal at *receiver* skills and briefly at *sender* skills in terms of *body language*.

The next three sessions focus on empathy, an essential requirement of listening; using questions as a means of encouraging or clarifying information and clarifying complex information. These are usefully used in conjuction with this session.

For the remainder of this session we shall confine ourselves to verbal responses used in conjunction with bodily ones to demonstrate active listening.

*Exercise 5h: Feeling Comfortable with Feelings or Facts*

This exercise has two linked parts:

**A**:   Ask participants to find a partner they would like to work with and to decide who will be helper and who client.

Allow clients a few minutes to decide on a topic they would like to share with their partners, but specify it should be one which has some emotional content—i.e. not a shopping list.

Give clients 3 minutes to talk about their chosen subject and ask helpers to reflect back only factual content; i.e. either at the end of the session or where appropriate during the 3 minutes, the helper is asked only to comment on or reflect back to the client factual details. Allow 3 minutes debriefing time between the partners and suggest that the helper explores the effect of concentrating only on 'things' on the client. Reverse roles for the same length of time and debriefing.

**B**:   For the second round ask helpers to reflect back only the feeling content and debrief as before (the topic can be the same or different to the first round). Reverse roles as before.

The whole exercise should be contained within 30 minutes and should be rounded off with the whole group sharing thoughts and feelings about their comfort in listening to facts and feelings. Some participants may discover that they concentrate on factual content and do not hear the emotional context in which these facts are contained, or the reverse. Whatever the situation it is important for individuals to recognize their own patterns of listening and to know which specific areas require further work.

## TUTORIAL INPUT

The notion of reflecting back, which ocurred in the previous exercise, is one way of describing *paraphrasing*. Perhaps another way of describing this activity is to think of the helper/listener as a looking glass, someone who reflects back to the client how he or she is behaving. This next exercise allows participants to judge whether providing a 'mirror' for a client is useful in active listening.

*Exercise 5i:   Mirror Listening*

Ask participants to form into pairs and decide who is A and who B.

For a change, ask B to start off a conversation but to pause after each sentence giving A a chance to mirror/reflect back *exactly* what B has said. Let this run for just a minute and without debriefing, then reverse roles.

In the whole group spend a brief time, about 5 minutes, discussing the pros and cons of *total mirroring*.

## TUTORIAL INPUT

Some participants may express difficulty in reflective responding and so findings may include comments that if clients want mirrors they should use video or tape recorders; parrots belong in the wild or the zoo; reflecting back in this way does not allow clarification, or help either helper or client advance the helping process;

clients cannot find out whether they have been understood or not; there is no *emotional* content in this form of mirroring, and so on.

This can arise because the habit of assessing what is being said, or thinking about the reply as someone is talking, can mean that certain social skills need to be unlearnt. Reflective responding appears simple and its sheer simplicity may invite some participants to look for the difficulty—or disregard its importance.

It will have become apparent also that reflecting back only facts or content will not advance the helping process as much as if the emotional aspects are included. The recognition and acceptance of the client's emotions will enable the problem or difficulty to be explored more thoroughly, since those feelings will determine how and what the client chooses to say. We know this for ourselves in terms of how differently we react to the same event according to how, simplistically speaking, good or bad we feel at the time.

Paraphrasing is more than repeating what one person has said to another. The word itself probably will have echoes from school days for some of the group; 'write down in your own words what is being said in this paragraph'. This is precisely what paraphrasing means here, except that it is a verbal skill which has to be acquired.

At this stage you may be aware of shifts of unease in the group. You may sense that some participants are panicking about being able to remember what they are listening to. Assure them that this skill, like any other, is a learned one, and that in any case there is no need to paraphrase the whole of an interview with a client.

Paraphrasing is most useful when there are 'natural' pauses, when you sense that the client needs help in expressing him or herself, or you want to make sure that you have heard what has been said.

Essentially the use of paraphrase makes clear to the client that he or she is being heard and understood *because the helper is able to use her own words to reflect exactly another person's verbal and body speak.* Just saying 'I understand' is no guarantee that you, in fact, do. You need to demonstrate your understanding in order to connect with the client.

Let the group find this out again for themselves.

*Exercise 5j:*  *Paraphrasing*

Ask participants to work in pairs, preferably with someone who is not well known to them, sit facing one another and decide who will be A and who B.

A then makes a statement; it could be personal, or about the course or about anything which can be briefly expanded upon. B paraphrases what A has said; A responds as to whether this is an accurate reflection. If it is not, A repeats the original statement and allows B to paraphrase again and so on until accurate reflection is taking place.

Allow A to make two further statements which require paraphrasing and go through the process as above until B has made six statements in all. By this time B will be paraphrasing the equivalent of a short paragraph or possibly a 'natural' pause in the conversation.

Allow 5 minutes for the partners to debrief and explore the experience identifying how it felt, what was hard and what came easily.

Then reverse the process.

Allow 30 minutes for both partners to have had a turn and then debrief for a further 5 minutes within the group. It is likely that most participants will feel encouraged by this exercise and recognize they do have these skills, although they may need polishing and tuning up.

## TUTORIAL INPUT

All the preceding exercises lead towards those which bring the various elements of active listening together. The length and subject of the training course will indicate how much time can be spent on the component parts and how long participants can practise the end product.

Often groups are surprised by the exhaustion they feel practising this fundamental skill. Again, it may be useful to point out that this contrast between *active listening* and the way we listen in everyday life without being as conscious of what it involves, indicates how much can be missed in primary communciation. Being aware of what is involved in active listening is likely to enhance communication in all spheres of life, and is one important way of giving and demonstrating respect for ourselves and other people.

*Exercise 5k:  Putting it Together*

Ask participants to form themselves into triads and decide who will be helper, client and observer. Make sure each small group has sufficiently distinct territory not to be overheard or crowded by others.

Emphasize that 'clients' have the right to choose subject matter which they feel comfortable about sharing with other people. We all have taboo areas, and although it seems obvious to state this elementary right, some participants may find it helpful to have this privacy acknowledged.

As usual it is helpful for the tutor to have a few ideas for discussion on hand; these could include:

an issue I feel strongly about;
a powerful memory of childhood;
neighbours;
a pet hate.

Allow 15 minutes for the client and helper to work together with the observer sitting just outside the pair as unobtrusively as possible.

Debriefing in the triad should include contributions from each of its members always with the proviso that *constructive criticism* is more effective as a learning agent, and ensures as far as possible that participants feel intact rather than destroyed. Allow 10 minutes for this part of the process.

Reverse roles so that each member of the triad has experienced each of the three positions.

Debrief in the whole group noticing which areas seem to require further work.

*Variations*   These can include working in pairs—more particularly when there is less time, *or* using video as the third partner in the triad.

An alternative open to groups which are small (six to eight), and members have established a strong basis of trust and honesty within them, is to invite one person to be client and the rest of the group to act as a group helper. The tutor in this instance may choose to be observer and facilitator of the debriefing session which follows. Only groups which have a strong sense of identity, and have experience of working together, are likely to work in this way.

At the end of this session participants will have begun to confront some of the issues involved in active listening, and will also recognize how comprehensive a skill it is.

# SESSION 6: EMPATHY

## Issues for the trainer

This session is based on the work of Carl Rogers, considered to be the father of humanistic psychology. His practice was based on the belief that empathy, coupled with genuineness and total acceptance of the client, created the right climate in which therapeutic changes could take place. He emphasized above all that it was the relationship between helper and client which brought about growth and creativity in the client.

In this training manual, however, we are not exclusively concerned with training counsellors—though arguably all of us who provide a help to those in need are in some sense therapists. The concern of this session is to emphasize the importance of a skill which is most often seen in a therapeutic context as one which is basic to all who have clients in a huge range of settings.

TUTORIAL INPUT

We have already considered how clients may present themselves for help (Chapter 3, Session 3; and again in Chapter 4, Session 4) and have begun to look at what is involved in the helping process. The concern of this session is one which underlines all other interpersonal skills.

Probably the most fundamental of these is that of accurate empathetic understanding. It is this skill above all others which generates a climate of psychological freedom in which the client can explore problems. Empathy involves more than listening to the client. Understanding has to be conveyed through the helper's responses. Freedom to explore can involve a high degree of risk for the client who will require support to enable change to be negotiated.

Empathy and *sympathy* are sometimes confused, and occasionally used interchangeably. Both words involve feelings and one way to distingush them is to see them lying along a spectrum. *Sympathy* is a responsive and therefore reactive feeling one person inspires in another, which may create a harmony between the two but is generally evoked by a particular circumstance. We have for instance a sympathy for, with, to, in, another's state of mind. Sympathy can sometimes be seen as patronizing and even false.

*Empathy*, on the other hand, is an ability to project oneself into another person's experience while remaining unconditionally oneself. Empathy, unlike sympathy, is a state of being; I am/you are empathetic.

Carl Rogers asks a series of questions about empathetic understanding in his book *On Becoming a Person* (Constable, 1982):

(a) Can I let myself enter fully into the world of (the client's) feelings and personal meanings and see these as he does?

(b)  Can I step into his private world so completely that I lose all desire to evaluate or judge it?

(c)  Can I enter so sensitively that I can move about in it freely, without trampling on meanings which are precious to him?

(d)  Can I sense it so accurately that I can catch not only the meanings of this experience which are obvious to him, but those meanings which are only implicit, which he sees only dimly or as confusion?

(e)  Can I extend this understanding without limit?

In brief, empathy is the ability to enter another's frame of reference and feel what it is like to be that person.

*Exercise 6a:   Empathetic understanding*

Ask the group to form pairs and give each person a few minutes to think about someone who knows them well, either at home or work. Persons in turn will then talk to their partner about themselves, but from the position of the person who knows them (5 minutes). The listener should then reflect and summarize (5 minutes).

When each partner has had his or her turn, give the pairs time to debrief, suggesting these questions for them to consider: 'Did the listener accurately reflect how you think another person sees you?' 'How did you feel while you were putting yourself "in someone else's shoes"?' 'Were there interventions which particularly helped or hindered you?' 'What other discoveries did you make in this exercise?'

Allow time for the whole group to share thoughts and feelings generated by this exercise.

## TUTORIAL INPUT

Arising out of the previous exercise, move on to a buzz session (see Section 4: Chapter 13, page 176) with the whole group about unhelpful ways of responding which demonstrate a lack of empathy. Follow this with:

*Exercise 6b:   Barriers to Self-exploration*

Ask the group to think about what could either inhibit or put a stop altogether to exploring a problem or difficulty. Encourage them to work from their own experience rather than putting foward theories. Collect a list of their suggestions on the flip chart without categorizing or analyzing them.

The list may include direct statements like 'I know what you mean . . .'; 'You shouldn't have done that'; 'That was a silly thing to do'; or more general statements such as 'taking direction away from the client'; 'grilling or interrogating'; 'the helper inappropriately self-disclosing', and so on.

When you think the list has been exhausted, point out to the group that these and other unhelpful responses invariably arise from the client's *external* rather than *internal* frame of reference. These kind of responses tend to lead the client away from the responsibility for creating a collaborative relationship, and are not conducive to generating the safety or trust which the client must feel before taking the risks in disclosure.

## TUTORIAL INPUT

Before pursuing further vocal responses, it is important once again to remember the importance of body language. Words are either congruent or incongruent with what the body is saying. Apparently undemonstrative people will be communicating through their bodies a great deal about the emotional context from which their words are arising. They may convey calm, control, being laid back, anger, don't care and so on—all without a word.

*Exercise 6c:    Body Language*

In pairs and standing up, ask one partner (A) to stand as if waiting in a queue and imagine what it feels like to be there—waiting at a supermarket checkout, to get into the cinema, or for a bus. Ask the other partner to observe in detail how the other is standing—are feet together or apart? Is the back straight or slumped? Is the head held up or down? and so on.

Ask B to mirror this and discover what it feels like to stand in A's shoes.

Change over. Then allow the pairs to discuss briefly the differences or similarities they discovered in one another's body posture. This should not take more than about 5 minutes.

## TUTORIAL INPUT

This leads into a discussion about possible pitfalls which a helper may discover when a client is describing a situation. What might they be?

Is the reverse situation problematic? Why not?

It is important to realize that empathic ability is not dependent on either great learning or vast experience. It is a skill which enables the helper to sense the private world of the client while retaining a complete sense of self that can enable the helper to perceive what Carl Rogers calls 'meanings . . . which [the client] sees only dimly or as confusion'.

In an everday sense we know this is possible from our own experience when in some difficulty we cannot see 'the wood for the trees' but in talking it over with a friend or colleague they can perceive, as we cannot, the confusions that have arisen.

The next exercise aims to sharpen up participants' perception of their clients' emotional state.

*Exercise 6d:    Empathy Formula (1)*

Participants work in pairs taking on the role of client and helper. Ask all participants to think of a situation which has happened to them, which carries some emotional charge and which they are prepared to share. Topics may include situations like:

talking with my child's teacher on a parents' evening;
feeling powerless when I visit a doctor;
not knowing what to say to someone who is depressed;
feeling angry about the lack of job opportunities where I live;
feeling put upon by my family who do not share domestic tasks.

Allow about 3 minutes for participants to think about their own topic and to work out a small paragraph (in their heads) which they will talk about as clients. The helper is instructed to listen and then to summarize using the formula: 'You feel . . . because . . .'. The client is then asked to respond as to its accuracy. The helper should keep trying until the client is satisfied that the summary is correct. Allow 5 minutes for this and then debrief for a further 2 minutes. Then change over.

## TUTORIAL INPUT

The discussion may indicate that the formula seems stilted and sits uneasily within the helpers' usual forms of expression. Reassure those who feel this that any new learning creates a degree of self-consciousness for a while. In time this kind of response will seem quite natural, and each person will discover his or her own particular way of expressing it. Emphasize if necessary that the exercise is designed to enable clients to feel both understood and willing to continue to explore their problem because of this understanding.

Empathic understanding should enable the client to make a statement (CS); the helper to respond (HR); and the client to continue the train of thought as a result of that response (CS). So the process looks like Figure 4.

The second part of the exercise allows participants to move away from the formula and use their own words.

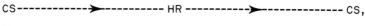

Figure 4.

### Exercise 6e:    Empathy Formula (2)

In the same pairs, and either continuing the same topic or using another, participants are invited to listen to another small 'paragraph' but this time respond using their own words instead of the formula, 'You feel . . . because . . .'.

Allow 5 minutes as before, with 2 minutes debriefing before changing over. After both partners have had a turn discuss briefly in the whole group what differences they felt between the two exercises.

## TUTORIAL INPUT

Participants often feel at a loss when there is no right or wrong way to demonstrate a skill. As tutor you may sense a discomfort in the group. It may be helpful to suggest that participants can practise empathetic responses on their own, in their own time. It is after all a skill which is not confined to the work place and, in fact, will suffer and become false if it is.

Suggest that participants think about situations as they have done in the two previous exercises, perhaps write them down, and then make or write empathetic responses either using the formula or their own words. Point out that many of us carry on internal dialogues with ourselves when we have a difficult problem to manage. Practising empathetic responses is merely a continuation of the same activity.

Suggest also that participants begin to observe how often they use empathetic responses in everyday life—what are their usual responses? What effect does the use of empathetic response have on others and, in turn, on you? It may help to keep a record so that there is a way of evaluating change as it takes place.

If there is time, the tutor can expand on the exercises used above by looking at for instance:
(a)  What are painful feelings for me to express?
(b)  What feelings do I find it difficult to work with in others?
(c)  Are there topics or problems I think I cannot handle and would have difficulty in empathizing with? What would I do if this situation arose?
(d)  How comfortable do I feel about silence?
This session can be rounded off with a final and longer practice.

*Exercise 6f:    Practising Empathy*

In triads of client, helper and observer, participants are invited to talk about any topic of their choice. The only proviso that it is a *personal* issue. The state of the nation or the problems of coming up with interesting menus week after week are not personal enough for this exercise.

Allow 15 minutes each, giving a further 10 for debriefing in each role.

The exercise will take a minimum of 30 minutes. Unlike the practice in previous exercises, give the responsibility for time-keeping to the helper. This is a reality in the world outside the training room. This emphasizes the discipline involved in the helping process; there is a beginning, middle and an end, and should there be a need to negotiate another session, time has to be allowed for this.

As tutor you may like to move around the groups and be a silent observer or offer help if this seems appropriate.

*Variations*   Using video with all these exercises is undoubtedly the most effective way for participants to see how they perform, but it is also time-consuming and more costly. While it is helpful for all types of groups at all stages of expertise, video has particular value for those of us who are accustomed and experienced in working with clients—from the point of view of pinpointing habit. We acquire mannerisms and ways of working about which we are unaware, and which may inhibit good working practice. Video offers the unvarnished truth to the participant in the most direct way.

# SESSION 7: GETTING THE INFORMATION

## Training objectives

(a)  To clarify the difference between open, closed and leading questions.
(b)  To practise using open questions.
(c)  To clarify the difference between effective questioning and obstructive inter-rogation.

## Issues for the trainer

We have already confirmed that communication involves both *receiver* and *sender* skills. The ability to elicit information in order to both clarify the nature of the problem and identify helping strategies is linked to the listening and empathy skills already explored. It cannot be emphasized too strongly that the helper's main

function is to assist the client to discover ways forward—rather than take on the
role of an all-powerful provider.

Unless the situation is one of crisis, or the client is too weak or inexperienced
to take any responsibility, it is fundamentally unhelpful for the helper to provide
solutions without involving the client in the process. In the short-term it may
appear helpful to let clients off the agonizing hook of making decisions, but in the
long run they will not have learned how to help themselves when the next
difficulty arises. They will have learned that someone else can provide the answers,
and that there is someone else who can be blamed when the solutions prove to be
the wrong ones.

The problem for the trainer is that there will probably be some participants on
the course who hold a strong belief that the best way to help someone is to tell
them exactly what to do, and to look after them while they do it. The idea that
clients should be encouraged to take responsibility for themselves may be resisted
by participants who are used to thinking of clients as inadequate or incompetent.

## TUTORIAL INPUT

People with problems can be vague and disoriented. The original difficulty may
have become exacerbated by confused thinking, and be expressed in vague or
generalized statements. The helper's task is to encourage the client to be concrete
and specific, and to identify the factors which have created the problem. One
obvious way of doing this is through the use of questions.

Right at the beginning of this session it is useful to remind the group that asking
questions is for the benefit of the client rather than to satisfy the helper's curiosity.
If you are about to ask a question, it is a useful exercise to ask yourself first whether
the question will enable the situation to be understood more clearly, or whether
you just fancy having that bit of the jigsaw filled in.

To begin to identify the problematic nature of asking questions, ask the group
to form quickly into pairs for the first exercise.

*Exercise 7a:    The Effect of 'Why?'*

Participants should decide who is A and who B. Ask A to talk for just 2
minutes on any topic at all. B is instructed to interrupt and ask 'Why?'
questions. Without debriefing, ask the pairs to change roles.

When both partners have had a turn, allow 2–3 minutes debriefing time
in the pairs. Ask participants how it feels to be asked 'Why?' questions; how
does it help or hinder the helping process; are there other ways that can be
identified which will fulfil the same function?

In the whole group, share the findings of the pairs. It may be useful to jot
down these comments on a flip chart as they will probably identify other
pitfalls contained in questioning. These may include factors like:
(a)   the client feeling grilled and interrogated;
(b)   the client feeling that the helper is intruding—possibly wanting in-
        formation for her sake and not the client's sake;
(c)   causing the client to lose her own track and being distracted;
(d)   being led by the helper down paths the client does not choose;
(e)   the client feeling that the helper asks questions without necessarily
        hearing the answers;
(f)   causing the client to give up and let the helper take over.

*Exercise 7b:    More Unhelpful Questions*

Moving on from the previous and more specific form of questioning, ask the whole group for other unhelpful questioning interventions. List them on the flip chart. They should include:

(a)  asking *leading* questions: elicit examples from the group like: 'So you think your partner is wrong to take that decision on his own, don't you?' *or* 'What you really want to do is to leave home and live on your own, isn't that right?'

(b)  asking questions at the wrong time, possibly not allowing the client room for thought;

(c)  asking questions that may be too probing before the client is ready to share or trust the helper with that level of personal information;

(d)  asking *closed* questions;

(e)  asking questions to fill up silence.


*Exercise 7c: Closed Questions*

Ask participants to think of a time when they were having a conversation which was stilted and apparently not going anywhere. Ask them to make a list of the factors present which inhibited free-flowing conversation? The list is bound to include questions which can only allow a 'Yes', 'No' or a variation on 'Don't know'. These are known as closed questions: for example, 'Do you come here often?' *or* 'Do you like films?' This is the kind of conversation that can feel like an interrogation. Each question actually closes down the chance to develop a thought or respond creatively.

The next stage in the exercise is to convert closed questions into open ones. Ask participants to write down about six closed questions (or you could have a selection prepared on a flip chart). Then, in pairs, participants work out ways of getting that information by asking an open question. They will find that the open questions usually begin with the words How? What? Where? When? and Who? For example: 'I don't know many people here, how about you?' *or* 'What do you think of the latest Woody Allen film?' Point out in the later examples how many invitations to develop conversation are included in the open questions. This leads on to the next input.

## TUTORIAL INPUT

It becomes clear that open invitations to talk are useful in numbers of different ways:

(a)  The first contact with the client most usefully starts off with a question: 'How can I help you?' *or* 'How have things been since you were last here?'

(b)  They enable clients to elaborate points: 'Could you tell me some more about that?'

(c)  They encourage clients to be specific about how they feel, and allow the helper to become clearer about the nature of the difficulty: 'I'm not clear about what you mean by feeling low. Could you give me an example?'

(d)  They help clients to focus on what they are feeling: 'What do you feel now as you're describing this to me?'

When effective questioning is used, whether at work or on social occasions, we find that people invariably offer more information than is actually asked. For example, 'Could you tell me about the sort of difficulties you are having with your neighbours?' allows the client to recognize that the helper has heard the general nature of the problem and is encouraged to be more specific and concrete about the particulars. The facts will be contained in the emotional climate of the words used and will indicate how the client is feeling and why. 'They make me mad, keeping me awake all hours of the day and night and I suffer from my nerves too. I've had to go to the doctor's for more pills on top of the ones I'm taking for my depression.'

When clients are upset, and feel that their lives are out of control, they often indicate this by placing responsibility for their thoughts and feelings on other people. It is also a colloquial way of speaking, and many people effectively exclude themselves as being responsible for what they say.

In the example above the client has said that 'they' have made her mad. While her neighbours have contributed to her 'madness', apparently through keeping her awake—though as yet, we don't known how—this client has failed to take responsibility for her action. Had the client said 'I feel so mad/angry/upset,' she would be indicating that she has some amount of responsibility for how she is feeling. As it stands, this client suggests that she feels helpless and the situation is out of her control.

Helpers can encourage their clients to take responsibility for their feelings by suggesting they used statements starting with 'I'. Even when clients do, or begin to, make statements beginning with 'I', they may still escape into generalized accounts of their feelings. Move into the next exercise to explore this.

### Exercise 7d:  Open Questions

Participants work in pairs taking on roles of client and helper. Ask the client to make a generalized feeling statement, starting with 'I'. For example: 'I feel so upset . . . depressed . . . dreadful . . . confused . . '. Ask the helper to ask open questions which will explore further what these statements might mean. For example: 'Upset?' 'What's making you feel like that?' 'Would you tell me some more about your confusion?'

Allow 5 minutes each so that both partners practise open questioning and then 2–3 minutes to debrief in the pairs. In the whole group discuss the benefits of this form of questioning and encourage discussion of other forms of open questioning which encourage the client to go on talking.

## TUTORIAL INPUT

A client who feels accustomed and comfortable with an open invitation to talk probably needs minimal interventions on this kind. All the helper need do is to provide the client with encouragement to continue. This process can be facilitated as much through body language as verbal:

(a)  Continuing words like 'Oh?, and then?, Mm Mm, So?'
(b)  The repetition of one or two key words as we noticed in the previous exercise, like, 'Angry? Upset? Happy? . . .'.
(c)  Tell me more.

### Exercise 7e:  Practising Questions

Participants set up groups of three; each person taking on client, helper and observer role.

Allow 10 minutes for the client to talk about a problem or difficulty. The helper uses appropriate questioning and the observer looks at both. Often when an inappropriate line of questioning is pursued, a client registers this first through body language, however imperceptible. It may be a flicker of an eye, a slightly longer pause before answering, a shift in the chair.

Allow each member of the group to take turns in being the client and allow 5 minutes for debriefing within the group between changes. Encourage each participant to give honest and constructive feedback (there is more about this technique in Section 4) so that there is an opportunity to learn from the process.

Check out in the whole group whether there are any comments or questions arising from this exercise.

*Variations*   If there is time and/or you think it is important for a particular group to explore the use of questions further, form the groups into pairs to work on other, only briefly mentioned aspects of this skill. For example:
(a)   using and experiencing *leading* questions;
(b)   asking too many questions, too soon;
(c)   using questions to fill up silence and exploring why a helper may have this tendency.

### Exercise 7f:   *Distinguishing between Open, Leading and Closed Questions*

Provide the group with definitions of open questions (which encourage the client to express what he or she is thinking and feeling); closed questions (those which are useful for obtaining information and facts) and leading questions (where the action suggested by the helper is contained in the question, or where the question demands a particular answer).

Have the participants arrange themselves in small groups (four or five people in each group), and provide each group with a written client statement; examples are:
(a)   'Up till now religion has been very important to me. I don't just mean just births, marriages and deaths, but I went to church regularly and prayed and meditated very day. Now, though, life seems meaningless and my religion doesn't seem to help at all.'
(b)   'I have been feeling really upset lately. So much has been happening at work and in my private life that I just feel out of control of everything. If I don't pull myself together soon, I don't know what will happen!'
The instructions for each group are as follows:
(1)   Read the statement and imagine that a client has just said this to you. In your group work out one open, one closed and one leading question you could ask this person.
(2)   When you have worked out the questions, each question should be asked to someone in the group. Each one should be taken by a different person, and the 'client' should be played by different group members each time, so that as many people as possible are involved in actually asking questions and responding.
The exercise is then followed by a general discussion as to the merits of each kind of question.

### Exercise 7g:   *Exploration and Focusing Questions*

This exercise is a good one for practising the use of open questions and also leads into the focusing phase of the helping process.

Ask participants to work in pairs taking the role of helper and client, and provide each person with a handout on which are printed the following series of questions. Explain that during the exercise the time should be split in half so that each partner gets equal time. The helper should limit interventions to asking only the questions on the handout, and encouraging the client to explore the situation. The aim is to demonstrate understanding and interest. Invite participants to talk about some issue or problem which concerns them, when they are playing the client role, so as to make the exercise as 'real' as possible.

*Exploration querstions:*What is actually happening now?
What is not happening?
How does it affect you?
How does it affect others?
What would you prefer to be happening?
What would you have to do to ensure success?
What are you willing to do?
How is that different from what you are actually doing?
What stands in the way of your changing?
What is the worst that could happen?
How might you sabotage yourself?
Is there some way in which others could help you?
What has been done before?
What are the expectations of others on you?

*Focusing questions*
Is there a time limit?
Is there a crisis?
Is there any aspect of the situation about which you (or others) have very strong feelings?
Is there some aspect it would be easier to start with?
What do you want to do?

The feedback to this exercise will explore the effect of being limited to open questions—and their advantages and disadvantages. The focusing questions demonstrate how it is possible to begin to order the information which the exploration questions elicited.

# SESSION 8: FOCUSING

## Training objectives

(a)  To define focusing skills.
(b)  To clarify focusing objectives.
(c)  To practise focusing using case studies.

## Issues for the trainer

Once again, it is important to emphasize that the urge to help those in distress is full of pitfalls for the helper. Many people find it personally uncomfortable to be with others who are 'going through a bad patch' and who seem unable to do very much about it. Quickly finding solutions for other people's problems and running their lives for them allows us to feel less uneasy and powerless in the short term. However, if one of your aims is to help clients manage their situations better, then we need a process which offers a longer-term result.

That is why the emphasis in this training is on encouraging the client to take as much responsibility as possible during the process.

There are many pressures on professional helpers; for instance, time limits, keeping client numbers up, invitations from clients to play all-powerful problem solver, needing to get results, all contribute to the possibility of leaving out a vital stage in the helping process: that which enables the client to focus on the issues which are central to the problem.

## TUTORIAL INPUT

We have reached the stage when the client has explored the presenting problem. There is a mass of information embedded in a range of feeling and emotion. The clients is probably feeling somewhat relieved now that the problem has been aired; there is some truth in the saying, 'A troubled shared is a trouble halved'! The task now is to order the information which the client has given so that decisions can be made as to where to begin taking action.

There are two issues the helper needs to be aware of at this stage: when to start encouraging the client to start focusing—*timing*; and when the client appears prepared to move on to this stage—*readiness*.

### Exercise 8a:   Readiness for Focusing

Ask the group as a whole to suggest how they might assess client readiness for focusing. This can be done as a brainstorm, or participants can divide into small groups to prepare their own lists (5–10 minutes). Suggestions could include:
(a)   When the client seems to have reached a point when the problem has been shared and explored;
(b)   a level of emotional equilibrium has been achieved through exploration of the problem;
(c)   a good working relationship has been achieved between client and helper in which it is safe for the client to move into the hazards of what seems unknown.

## TUTORIAL INPUT

Participants wanting some more exact formula for the right time to move on will be dissatisfied with this subjective assessment. Practice through experience is one way of getting this affirmation; empathy with the client's needs is another. A third alternative lies in looking at the objectives of focused thinking, what is it for and why?

### Exercise 8b:   Objectives for Focusing

In the whole group, encourage participants to offer practical reasons for focused thinking. The list will probably include:
(a)   enabling the client to take control of thinking, to regulate the chaos

which we could see as the *trees*, to begin to see order as represented by the *wood*;

(b)   clear thinking is the first step towards clarifying feelings and action;

(c)   exploring personal belief systems which may get in the way of taking effective action;

(d)   moving the process on distinguishes this from informal chat or discussion.

## TUTORIAL INPUT

Another way of describing focusing is to enable clients to take a grip on the problems which are temporarily weighing them down rather than feeling that circumstances are controlling their lives. A major factor contributing to a client feeling overwhelmed and unable to see the wood for the trees is an unrealistic belief system.

In Chapter 7, Session 16, we look at beliefs which decrease confidence, and this is usefully applicable within this session also. If clients have unrealistic expectations of themselves—for example, 'Everything I do must be perfect' *or* 'That's the way I am and I can't change'—the options of effective actions are severely limited.

To clarify with the group how distorted thinking will get in the way of effective action, move into the next exercise which looks briefly at one belief or code of practice.

> *Exercise 8c:   Clarifying a Code*
>
> Give the instruction, 'On your own, write down quickly and without great thought, up to five things you think you should be or do—e.g. be a better mother, do more in the local community . . .' (3 minutes). Discuss briefly any feelings or thoughts raised by this exercise, and then lead the discussion into an exploration of what *should* or *ought* implies. These are some of the thoughts which will probably be shared:
>
> (a)   an external rather than an internal frame of reference;
>
> (b)   someone else is 'pulling your strings' rather than you;
>
> (c)   shifting responsibility on to someone or something else rather than assuming it yourself;
>
> (d)   finding someone or something to blame when things go wrong.
>
> When the discussion has run its course, ask the participants to rewrite their original thoughts, but this time preceding each one with the words 'I choose to . . .'. and again share thoughts and feelings that this raises.

## TUTORIAL INPUT

This exercise gives an opportunity for participants to recognize anew the overwhelming importance of *listening* to clients—not just the words and how they are said but the underlying message which conveys both state of mind and emotions.

Focusing is a discipline which encourages clients to think for themselves about where to start with their problem solving.

It is helpful for the client to have a summary of all the issues raised in the initial exploratory stage of the interview. In some cases actually writing down the points, perhaps on a flip chart, can be very helpful. To confront the problem in writing may be the beginning of recognizing the size and complexity of the problem itself.

Focusing is also about prioritizing and working out which course of action to embark on. Whatever the concerns which have been raised, they will all contain some blueprint for action. The problem may lie in knowing where to start.

### Exercise 8d: Focusing Case Study

The criteria listed below may have arisen from the previous exercises; if not it would be useful to present them to participants—either as a short input or a handout.

*Eight Factors for Focusing:*
(1) How urgent is the concern, either through its frequency or the degree of stress it is causing?
(2) Is this concern more or less important than the others?
(3) Can this concern be broken into more manageable or specific parts. If so, what are they?
(4) Can the problem be resolved in the time available, or does the concern need to be re-evaluated in the light of the time available?
(5) Is there any particular concern in which you feel more confident of success? If so, would this be a good place to start?
(6) What spin-off effect would starting with this concern have in other areas?
(7) Can you manage this concern on your own? Is it under your control? Do you neeed the help and resources of other people to help you act?
(8) How valuable is this concern? Is it worth the time, effort and resources needed?

They can then be used to consider a case study. The case studies should be prepared in advance (see below for examples and also Section 4, Chapter 11; Preparing a case study). They can be given on handouts, or presented as a tape.

Divide participants into groups and ask them firstly to list all the problems they think the client is facing, and secondly to put them into an order of priority (10–15 minutes).

When the list is prepared, ask participants to work out how they would involve the client in the decision about where to start. This part of the exercise can be developed into a role-play.

### Exercise 8e: Negotiating the Focus

Divide the group into two halves (or if the group is a very large one, make up an equal number of small groups). Provide each group with a written or taped case study. Ask one group to prioritize the problems from the helper's point of view, and the other to consider it from the client's. Ask each group to draw up a list of items numbered in order of priority, (10–15minutes).

The groups then meet and present their lists to each other. The discussion will be around any differences of perception between the client and helper priorities, leading on to how those differences can be negotiated.

Some examples of cases which could be used follow. It is useful to think of these as fall-back proposals; cases which participants have experienced in their own working lives are probably more useful.

*Young woman seeking help at a CAB*

'I've just dopped Gary at the nursery and I've got the other one with me because I can't get anyone to mind him. I can't leave him at home because he's there and I don't trust him alone with the little one. I don't know what time he came in last night; I slept with the kids. I heard him crashing around but we've got no electricity. I don't know what to do. I'm at the end of my tether.'

*Boy, 16, talking to a youth worker*

'I sit in my room mostly, looking out the window and I watch this girl going past the gate. She was at the same school as me but I didn't talk to her much then. I wait for her to come home; I think she's got work at the Bank. Sometimes I wait behind the front door when I think she'll be going by. Once she saw me and smiled. I really want to ask her to go out but how can I do that?'

*Woman, 30, with young baby talking with her health visitor*

I've got lots of "if onlys . . ." in my life at the moment. I want to talk about my feelings. The baby and me are fine. I'm very lonely. I want to meet professional people but it's not easy in this country; life's not like that here. A friend of mine was very good to me when I was pregnant but since I had the baby she hasn't 'phoned or got in touch. I've got my pride, I can't go on making the running. The other day I spent most of it crying and then the baby spewed up everything I'd just given her. And I want to go home at Christmas; it'll be warm there.'

*Girl, 17, talking to her social worker*

'I don't want to leave the Home. I like it there, I've been there five years and I know everybody. I don't want to live on my own and I don't want to have my own place. Everyone thinks I'm mad because I like what I've got. Do you think I'm nuts?'

> *Exercise 8f:  Case Discussion*
>
> This exercise is useful for groups sharing the same kind of work. Have one person present a case he or she is at present dealing with, or has just finished, to the rest of the group. The group then discuss the factors in this case which affect the focusing. If there is a willingness in the group to role-play, seek volunteers to act out a scenario.
>
> However the case is presented, instruct the group to take on the role of helper by making suggestions as to how to enable the client to decide where to act first. It is always useful to pursue each suggestion to its logical end, so that if one participant suggests one way forward, the group as a whole checks out its feasibility, using the eight factors for focusing.

# SESSION 9: NEW VIEWS

## Training objectives

(a)  To consider how the helper can provide clients with new perspectives.
(b)  To clarify the difference between paraphrase and summary.
(c)  To explore how complex information may be fed back accurately.
(d)  To demonstrate strategies that may lead to a new view.

# Issues for the trainer

This first stage in the helping process is now moving to its close. The helper and client have talked about the problem and should be clearer now about the various aspects of the situation. For some clients this is actually enough help for them to manage things for themselves; others will need more assistance and support.

However, it is wise for a helper who senses that the client is satisfied at this stage to check whether the problem is actually resolved or just dumped. Dumping unwanted baggage doesn't make it go away; it has an unerring habit of accumulating. Watch how one plastic bag of rubbish attracts others. In order for unwanted baggage to be disposed of entirely, action has to be taken to enable this to happen. And so it is with problem solving; exploring the nature of the problem is the first stage; what to resolve and how to resolve it are the other two.

This final session looks at how the threads of the first phase of the interview are brought together.

## TUTORIAL INPUT

We will soon be ready to move into the next phase of the helping process; the *decision* stage. What will help the client most now is for the helper to provide some new view of the situation. Although talking about the problem to a helper often has the effect of providing relief, it rarely in itself provides any resolution. The problem is that the client may well be drained of energy because, if the problem is a difficult one, the client will have already spent many hours thinking and worrying about it. Maybe different strategies have already been tried and failed.

New perspectives generate energy. Think of a time when you have been in the depths of a problem, and maybe someone had just said or done something that has suddenly given you a completely new way of thinking about it; like viewing the world through a different pair of spectacles. It is as if you experience a surge of energy and feel once more like getting to grips with the problem.

During this session we will explore some different ways of generating new perspectives.

Giving the client feedback is one way of doing this. It is a way of defining the boundaries within which helper and client are working. Feedback helps us to become more aware of what we are doing and how we are doing it. This can be frightening: ignorance isn't blissful and neither is the process of growing self-awareness. One of the reasons that feedback may feel daunting for client and helper alike is that it is sometimes confused with giving negative criticism.

The aim of feedback is to enable the client to see more clearly in order to recognize what choices are available.

*Exercise 9a:  Giving Feedback*

In the whole group, have a quick brainstorm about giving helpful feedback —what should it focus on? Write the suggestions down on the flip as they arise. From their own experience, participants have knowledge about the sort of feedback they find helpful and the sort which can seem destructive.

Here are some suggestions for aiding accurate feedback which can be added to the suggestions of the group, or can be given as a handout:
(a)  Clearly 'own' your messages by using personal pronouns. Terms like 'most people' or 'some members' make it difficult to know whether you

really believe what you are saying or whether you are repeating the
thoughts and feelings of others.

(b)   Make your messages clear and specific. The other person needs to
understand your frame of reference, your intentions or the leaps in your
thinking if he or she is to make use of your feedback.

(c)   Verbal and non-verbal messages should be congruent. If you say 'Here
is some information which will help you' with a sneer on your face and
in a mocking tone of voice you will be sending two conflicting messages
and the result will probably be confusion.

(a)   Check that your feedback is accurately received. Check often
whether the person you are with is understanding what you mean.

(b)   Feedback should be descriptive rather than evaluative or interpretive. 'You keep interrupting me' is more helpful than 'You are a
self-centred egotist who won't listen to anyone else's feelings'!

(c)   Feedback is more effective if it is directed to behaviour that can be
changed, and if it is about specific rather than general things.

Suggest that participants work in pairs. If the group know each other
well, ask them to give some feedback to each other based on their
knowledge of each other. If they have only met as a result of the course,
suggest that they give some feedback based on that.

*Exercise 9b:   Feedback Circle*

Have participants sit round in a circle (or several circles if it is a large group)
and number off '1', '2', '3' and so on until each person has a number. No 1
begins, and talks for just 1 minute or so about some aspect of his or her work.
Then each person in turn offers one piece of feedback, based on the handout
suggestions. Before moving on, the group as a whole check that the feedback
has been within the 'rules'. When the exercise ends, the group discuss their
thoughts and feelings about the experience.

## TUTORIAL INPUT

Briefly point out that feedback is not just a matter of being kind: omitting the bad
and the ugly renders the good valueless. It is, however, more likely to be
acknowledged if negative feedback is sandwiched between positive. It is also clear
that feedback involves reflection on what the client is saying and how it is said,
as well as possible comment about these reflections from the helper's frame of
reference. This latter aspect of summary may bring to the forefront issues which
the client may have been avoiding or have been unaware of.

Summaries may involve reflection only, but are possibly more effective if they
involve feedback which includes the helper's 'hunches' and comments which arise
out of the reflection. These would be phrased like—'It seems to me that in addition
to . . .' or 'Arising out of what you have said . . .'.

Summaries also enable the helper to point out links between what the client may
have offered early in the session with what she has offered later. In this sense alone,
summary is more than the ability to paraphrase or reflect back the essence of what
the client has explored.

Paraphrasing is a little like 'in other words'—but they are those of the helper
and not the client. It has four clear functions:

(1)   to convey to the client that she is being understood, heard and that you are
within her frame of reference;

(2)  to crystalize clients' comments by reflecting what has been said but in a more concise manner—being neither a parrot nor a mirror;

(3)  to provide a check for both client and helper that there is shared and accurate understanding between them;

(4)  to adjust and correct either misunderstandings or misapprehensions on the part of the helper.

We have seen in previous sessions that reflection has greater emphasis on the emotional and feeling component of the client's exploration. Inevitably it contains some amount of reflecting on the content of what has been said by the client, but we have noted that the helping process is more likely to make progess if feelings rather than content are explored.

Nevertheless, the client may have offered complex and what may often seem confused information which carries the emotional message. This in itself will indicate much about the client's general mental and emotional state at the time of the interview. It is crucial that the client is clear about content so the use of paraphrase is highly functional; it gets to the nub of what is being said.

*Exercise 9c:   Paraphrasing*

In pairs, one helper and one client: ask the client to talk for 2 minutes about something which is important to her. Allow a little time for pairs to reflect on what this might be. The helper is asked to paraphrase in a sentence or two the essence of what the client has offered. Ask the pairs to check out the accuracy of the paraphrase and then change roles.

In the whole group briefly check out how this feels as client and as helper. As tutor tease out and re-cap the function of paraphrase and emphasize when necessary that the helpers are paraphrasing the clients' exploration and not their own interpretation of what they think is going on (10 minutes).

## TUTORIAL INPUT

So what are the differences between paraphrase and summary? They appear to share similarities: the differences are a matter of degree and totality. While paraphrase is a means of drawing together information at 'natural' breaks; looking at it in relation to summary it is like a comma stands in relation to a full stop. Summary is quite literally the sum of the parts.

Functionally, summary can further clients' self-exploration and enable them to gain greater understanding of their problems. It also enables the helper to encourage the client to take action. This is achieved by recapitulating, by condensing and crystalizing form, content and feeling of the client's exploration and by presenting the summary in such a way that the implications of the problem can be seen. Out of this, possible goals for action can begin to emerge.

Summary can be used at various points throughout the interview, particularly when the client's problem is complex or when it is presented with some confusion. At this stage its purpose is to provide the client with a fresh view of the situation. It can provide a valuable direction and coherence for the client and enable the identification of salient issues. It provides a bridge between the initial exploratory stage and the next stage of setting action goals. One way that the helper could encourage the client to take what may seem to be a major step would be to invite her to summarize using a flip chart.

Clearly this will be most effective if this method is an integral part of the helper's own process. Flip chart or even newspaper and large felt-tip pens should not only be available, but should form part of the background furniture and fittings, so that the client can see them. Using large sheets of paper in this way demonstrates, as nothing else can, that the helping process is also a *training* process. This method avoids 'going round in circles' and allows client and helper to face and confront what is going on. It also provides a checklist valuable for both partners in the helping process.

*Exercise 9d:    Practising Summarizing*

In triads of helper, client and observer, the helper spends 15 minutes helping the client with a problem—ideally one that is of real concern. The helper may use summary throughout this process if appropriate, but the main thing to keep in mind is that a final summary, before time is up, is required. The session therefore has to be structured. The final summary should include all aspects that have been discussed in this session.

After the helper's summary the client is invited to take the next step —draw conclusions in preparation for taking the next step of clarifying and determining goals.

The observer is then invited to make constructive comments about the helper's summary, but in relation to the client's conclusions or implications. A hint from the tutor about the function of feedback as it has been discussed in this session may be useful before the triads start.

Each triad will take approximately 20 minutes for one person to be helped, and should be responsible for its own timing.

Change over so that each person has an opportunity to practise in each role (1 hour, including general feedback in whole group).

*Variations*    These include using video instead of an observer. Some participants may like to have flip chart paper available to use during their session as helper. Both these options are time-consuming and the tutor will have to tread the fine line between encouraging initiative while recognizing realities of time.

## Issues for the trainer

The aim of this session is to provide participants with ideas about providing new perspectives for their clients. So far we have worked on feedback, summarizing and paraphrasing.

A very great skill contributing to this particular phase of the process is the ability to think creatively. Here are a selection of exercises which demonstrate how lateral thinking can be practised.

*Exercise 9e:    Writing a Soap Opera*

This is a lighthearted exercise, which often surprises people with regard to their creative ability. Ask a volunteer to select one word at random from any book available. This can be done by one person running a finger down a page and someone else calling out 'stop'—and taking the nearest word the finger is pointing to. Write this word on a flip chart, and allow the group to freely associate words related to it. The subject-matter is entirely unimportant. When the paper is full of words—or suggestions have dried up, ask participants to make up small groups of about four or five people. Their task is to concoct a plot for a soap opera using at least six of the words on the board (10 minutes).

These are then shared.

It really is amazing how given these entirely random words, people can turn their minds around the problem. The exercise can demonstrate how sometimes, by giving people random criteria, they can come up with a creative solution, since it is fairly likely that if the only instruction was to 'write the plot of a new soap opera' the groups would have found it much more difficult.

### Exercise 9f: *Graffiti*

Give all participants a large sheet of flip chart paper. Ask them to write a sentence at the top which would be sufficient to briefly describe a particular problem they have been trying to solve. (If they cannot think of one, then a made-up one will do.) Then ask them to write down all the things they have thought of doing, or have actually done, to try to manage the problem. When they have finished, put all the sheets up on the wall around the room, and invite everyone to read them—marking them with any other suggestions or comments they can think of as they do so (20–30 minutes).

This is an interesting way of collecting a lot of reactions in a fairly short time, and very often there are some contributions which provide a different way of approaching the problem.

### Exercise 9g: *Generating New Perspectives*

This could be useful as a concluding exercise to this session on new views. It can be conducted as a brainstorm or a small group discussion reported back to the large group. Ask participants to think of as many ways as they can of providing a new view of the problem to the client. Suggestions could include:
(a)  Providing information.
(b)  Demonstrating skills.
(c)  Teaching theories.
(d)  Asking questions like. 'What is the worst thing that could happen?'.
(e)  Suggesting reading, and so on.

# Chapter 5
## Helping the Client: Phase 2: Decisions

### SESSION 10: SETTING GOALS

### Training objectives

(a) To emphasize the importance of setting small achievable goals.
(b) To demonstrate how goals can be measured.
(c) To practise the decision-making process.

### Issues for the trainer

Perhaps at this stage more than at any other, the helper may be seduced into making decisions for, rather than with, the client. The group may need to be reminded that the helping process is concerned with helping the client bring about change. 'You can take a horse to water but you cannot make him drink' is as true for people as it is for four-legged friends. Sheer longing for clients to find some peace from their problems may cause the helper to direct them down paths which they have not chosen for themselves. Pressures of time and urgency can also impel helpers to assume that solutions they have found for themselves will provide the answers for their clients' problems as well.

TUTORIAL INPUT

Problems belong to clients; it therefore follows that solutions must belong to them as well. The goal is to work with the client to find the solution. One way of demonstrating the complexity of this is the analytic tool known as force field analysis (Figure 5) (Lewin, 1969; Spier, 1973).

Figure 5 represents the various forces which may help or hinder the achievement of goals. The nature of these forces is an important element in decision making, and we shall come back to this idea in the next session. Before that let us consider

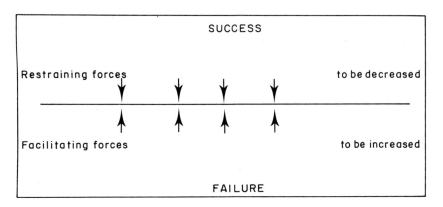

Figure 5. Forcefield analysis.

exactly what goals are. The idea is simple. The essence of the helping process we are working on is that it is systematic and logical. So far we have been steadily preparing the way for making decisions about what action to take. This next stage of goal setting is about what can be accomplished, and not about how it will come about. By confusing two parts of the process the client may become overburdened and muddled, and the logic of the procedure may get lost. For example, there is a crucial difference in deciding to be slimmer (the goal)—and deciding how this might be accomplished (the programme or action plan).

*Exercise 10a:    Turning Aims into Goals*

Ask participants to jot down a list of up to six general aims they can identify for themselves at the present time. Examples could include topics like:

(a)  'I want to be a better mother.'
(b)  'I wish I could allow myself more time to do what I want to do.'
(c)  'I want to give myself permission to make mistakes and be wrong.'

Suggest that participants write their list quickly 'off the top of their heads'. When everyone has a few examples to work on, in collaboration with partners, turn the general aim into a specific goal:

(a)  'I want to allow my children to be untidy in their territory and tolerate the differences between my obsessive tidiness and what I see as their sloppiness', *or*
(b)  'When I am criticized by my children I want to accept that criticism as their opinion of me and not a world view', *or*
(c)  'I want to stop nagging the children and be more constructive in my criticisms of them' (15 minutes).

When this has been done, hold discussion on any points which participants raise as a result of the exercise.

## TUTORIAL INPUT

Goals differ from resolutions—pacts we make with ourselves at various significant times of the year. Resolutions are invariably about converting ourselves, being our

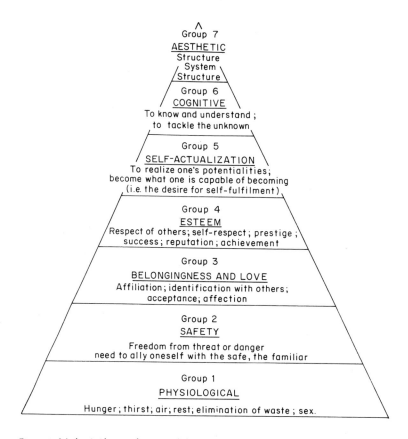

Figure 6. Maslow's 'theory of sequential development' (satisfaction of needs) (Maslow, 1954).

own missionaries: 'I shall be a better person'; 'I shall not be so bad-tempered in the mornings.' Resolutions have a high failure rate; we feel temporarily better because we appear to have made decisions but they are usually vague enough to let us off the hook of carrying them out.

Goal setting may be placed in another particular context.

From our earliest childhood we seek to survive by creating a secure and meaningful life for ourselves. This sense of security depends to a large extent on our ability to predict the outcomes of our own and others' behaviour. The meaning in our life is dependent on how well we perceive the world fits in with what actually happens to us. Each one of us is motivated by a set of needs which must be fulfilled in order for us to develop and grow.

Abraham Maslow, an American psychologist, has drawn up what he calls a 'hierarchy of needs' (see Figure 6). He argues that in order to reach our full potential, or what he calls self-actualization, we must first attend to our primary or lower-order needs. It may be useful to share this with the group, particularly if participants are working with clients who suffer from what Maslow would call basic deprivations. For example, a young woman who is seeking help about the violent relationship she has with her partner may find it even harder to reach a decision if she is dependent on him for her basic physical needs like food and shelter. This may well form part or even the whole of her problem.

It may have become apparent that a client lacks self-esteem (level 4) and as a consequence does not attract either respect or appreciation. Although this may not be the presenting problem, it will inevitably contribute to it.

### Exercise 10b:   Maslow's Model

Ask the group to work in pairs to share examples of, and their reaction to, a client who is so needy, in terms of Maslow's model, that the presenting problem pales into insignificance. Suggest that they try and think of clients they have worked with and how they managed. Is Maslow's model helpful or could it inhibit the goal-setting process? (15 minutes). Debrief in the whole group.

### Exercise 10c:   Blank Pyramid

Provide the group with a blank pyramid (see Figure 7) and give them time to fill in the levels with examples of how they, or their organization, provides for that particular level of need for their clients (15 minutes). This can be followed by a discussion which could focus on gaps they might have identified, sharing examples of how the needs are met by different people or organizations, and thoughts as to how the gaps might be filled.

## TUTORIAL INPUT

Maslow's hierarchy of needs is a useful reminder that all client problems take place within the context of that individual's life. This point may seem obvious, but it is

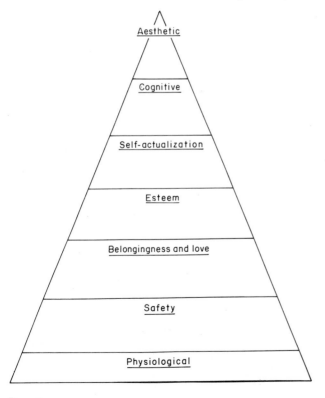

Figure 7.

valuable to be reminded that our ability to effect change is limited by very specific boundaries. For example, a young woman who has children but no home, and finds herself living in bed-and-breakfast accommodation will be severely limited by her material circumstances. They necessarily affect the extent to which she feels able to make choices which will probably enhance her feeling of self-worth.

It is important to recognize that every one of us can find justifications or excuses for not changing. Because these tend to come from the heart rather than the head, we need to measure our goals with objective criteria.

## Six signposts towards goal setting

### 1.   Be specific, concrete and clear about the problem

Is the problem stated in such a way that it appears solvable?

Clients may find it easier to allow others to take responsibility for what is not going well in their lives and in this sense would not be owning their problem. Stated in these terms, the problem would not be solvable; for example:

> I had a terrible childhood; my parents were cold and distant and I was never able to talk to them about my problems. I guess that's why I'm in such a mess now . . .

This problem is neither specific nor concrete, and it is certainly not clear. It brings us to the next signpost;

### 2.   The specific problem will be related to a general one

Problems very often have many facets. Nothing is more defeating than trying to solve everything at once. The exploratory stage will probably have revealed different aspects of the whole problem. It cannot be stressed too strongly that this is the time to prioritise the specific goal; to choose the one which is small and achievable. Nothing breeds success like success; clients need all the encouragement they can get to choose the goal which they estimate will bring them most reward.

Going back to the previous example, having worked on the specificity of the problem, for example:

> I realize I still blame my parents for turning me into the sort of helpless slob I think I am. I don't ask for help even when I know I can get is so I sit around and feel helpless.

it becomes apparent that the client is now owning the problem. One goal might be to ask for help when it is needed, another might be to become involved in voluntary activities or to get training to have a better-equipped chance of finding paid work. All these possibilities are related to the general whole. The important question is to enable the client to find the alternative which will bring success without an enormous amount of defeating labour – which brings us to the next signpost:

### 3.   The goal should be a realistic one for you, under your control and within your scope of achievement

Still pursuing the client with the terrible parents, this client may well recognize and accept that one thing that cannot be done is to change personal history—for instance you cannot magic up different parents! However, it also needs to be understood that it is also probably not realistic for this client to pursue a long course of training as well as becoming a volunteer in a local community project while being a good neighbour to the old lady who lives upstairs.

For someone who has lived a life of inactivity and a great deal of inertia, this goal is wildly unrealistic. For someone who has never pursued a long-term project of any sort, three years of study and training may be too great an undertaking at this stage. A short refresher course in getting back to study may be far more appropriate as a first step, since it is more likely to be structured so that it is within the client's control.

## 4.The goal should be of value to you

Most of us perform better when we have a personal investment in what we do; so by choosing the goal which carries positive values for us we have a far greater chance of being successful. However, our yardsticks for what is valuable may not be shared by others.

Supposing our client selects the goal of being a good neighbour. The helper's responsibility is to clarify whether this goal is chosen because the client considers it socially worthwhile, or because it will please the helper (a not inconsiderable element in many clients' choice of goals), rather than through a genuine desire to do it because it 'feels right'. It is the latter which will result in a substantial gain in self-esteem. This clarification by the helper with the client will be an important part of the process of goal setting as many people find it difficult to come to terms with making decisions which could be labelled as 'selfish'. A more positive approach is to talk with the client about 'self-concern', introducing the idea that the ability to care for oneself is the first step to being able to care for others.

## 5.The goal should be measurable

Having a sense of how things were before a change took place, and how they are after it has been achieved, is a very specific and often tangible reward for undertaking the goal at all. It gives us proof that the 'light was worth the candle' because there is something to show for it. Although tangible proof is not always possible, especially if the desired change is one of attitude or belief, a record of changing thoughts and feelings can serve as a very positive reminder. It may be helpful to suggest that the client keep a diary or journal of the pursuit of the goal, so that in time it will be possible to look back and see what changes have taken place.

Helpers can search for ways of marking achievements, for example by identifying and validating all successes, however small. As our client begins to assume a degree of self-responsibility, a certificate for the course of study, for example, would be enormously rewarding. The helper could also point out that seeking help with the problems in the first place, and finding out that it is possible and permissible to ask for it at all, is an example of the rewards of taking a risk.

## 6.The goal should be achievable within a reasonable time frame

The final signpost is also very practical. Although most people like to feel free of time pressure when they are carrying out a task, actually having all the time in the world is generally unhelpful. Probably one of the reasons that resolutions so often fail is because they are future-orientated; 'jam tomorrow' is not the same thing as 'jam today'!

Working out the time boundaries for the achievement of the goal is a further way of recognizing the client's reality. Some people are tortoises and others hares. Some work better under pressure and others like to feel there is an expanse of time.

By going through this logical and systematic process of goal setting, the client is setting up signposts which lead to the road of action, for inherent within the goal is the germ of how the goal will be achieved.

*Exercise 10d:    Goal-setting Scenarios*

Have ready a number of scenarios printed on individual cards that can be worked on by small groups. The objective is for each group to come up with a set of goals for each problem that have been tested using the above criteria (30 minutes for exercise and 15 minutes debriefing). The discussion should focus on the difficulties or advantages of the process, rather than the content of the problems.

*Examples*

Susan, 31, has a young baby of 3 months. She decided not to marry the father and broke off the relationship before the birth. She worked as a theatrical designer right to the end of her pregnancy, and has lived abroad for much of her working life. Now she feels isolated and wants the father of her child to resume his relationship with her. She wants to get back to work but has problems in making ends meet.

Miriam, 45, has recently had a serious operation which has left her feeling weak and lacking in energy. She tried to go back to work but was told to go home as whe was not well. She feels her husband cannot go on much longer tolerating her sickness and lethargy. One of her children has taken drugs since he left school six years ago, and she feels responsible for him while he lives at home.

Simon, 25, is lonely and finds it very difficult to make relationships with the opposite sex. He thinks he is unattractive to women and he is ashamed that he is still a virgin. He has recently had his first love affair with a girl he knew at school, but she told him that she was getting married shortly. He feels devastated and even more confirmed in his opinion that he's unlovable.

Richard, 50, has been married for 25 years to the same woman. They have two grown-up children who have moved away from home. His wife has a high-powered job; he has not progressed within his firm since his last promotion, 10 years ago. He feels depressed, without hope, and sees little point in going on. His wife appears to manage without him and he never had much contact with his children because he was too busy building up his reputation in the firm when they were young. He feels like giving up.

*Exercise 10e:    Personal Goal-setting*

Suggest that participants select one area of their own lives where they would like to initiate some change, and ask them to work on their own for about

15 minutes devising at least one goal which would move them on towards their ambition. Then ask them to find a partner and share the goals with each other. The main task of the partner is to check whether the goals fit the criteria. A worksheet can be useful for this exercise. (see goal-setting worksheet).

An interesting addition to this exercise is to ask participants to make an arrangement to contact their partner in, say, a month's time when they can check how the goals are progressing. Make sure that people actually take out their diaries and arrange a specific time when they will make contact.

# SESSION 11: THE ACTION PLAN

## Training objectives

(a) To create an action plan.
(b) To explore the importance of generating options.
(c) To practice using criteria for developing and monitoring options and action plans.

## Issues for the trainer

This session builds on goal setting with the focus becoming increasing focused on action, thus moving from the decision to the action phase of the helping process. To avoid needless repetition, it would be useful to continue on the examples from the previous session.

### TUTORIAL INPUT

The last session explored the *what* phase of deciding what action to take, this one looks at the *how*. Figure 7 shows the helping process as a pyramid; we are now on the line between decision and action —more than halfway towards the peak.

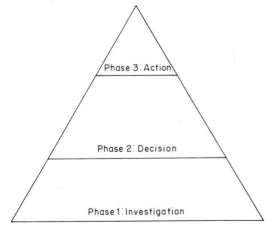

Phase 3: Action

Phase 2: Decision

Phase 1: Investigation

Figure 8.

When clients have the kind of problem which impels them to seek help, their vision is often restricted and hampered by a feeling of impotence. Their thoughts become polarized; they can see either/or solutions and often fail to explore the range of alternatives which usually lie between those extremes.

The following exercise encourages action options:

*Exercise 11a:    Brainstorming Options*

Use one of the problem examples which the group has produced goals which have been tested against the six signposts for goal setting. For example:

Simon who finds difficulties in making relationships with women.

Goals could include:

meeting more women:
becoming more self-confident:
leaving home and finding own accommodation:
trusting his own judgement rather than his mother's about women.

Take one goal and ask the group to *brainstorm* (see page 177) all the possible courses of action would encourage Simon to achieve his goal. Write them down as they are called out on the flip chart and remember they are not being evaluated at this point. For example:

join a singles club,
go to discos,
pick up a girl you fancy,
have a party,
organize an office outing,
ask your mates to bring along a blind date for you,
join a computer dating outfit,
place an ad in the local paper,
join a lonely hearts club,
give up,
answer ads in *Time Out*,
join the local church,
take evening classes at night school,
become a political activist,
take an 18–30's singles holiday (5 minutes).

## TUTORIAL INPUT

Once started, the list of possibilities appears endless. So what stops our client taking action? Simply thinking of ways of achieving his goal may well be an initial block. Clients may need a great deal of encouragement to consider alternatives, however wild and improbable. Believing that a problem is insoluble is a trap in itself. The brainstorming process often releases a great deal of creativity—and it is surprising how often a suggestion which would have been discounted immediately as impossible, leads to some action when it is considered.

This next exercise gives an idea about how to evaluate the brainstorm result.

*Exercise 11b:    Yes, No, Per*

Ask someone in the group to share a goal which they wish to achieve, and do a brainstorm exercise with it. Then explain that usually when we are trying to make a decision about something we tell ourselves that either it *is* or it *is not* possible. This time we will give ourselves an extra option—that of *perhaps*. This means that as it stands it probably isn't possible or practical, but with a little thought and modification, perhaps . . .

Go down the list, asking each volunteer to say 'yes' if it is something definitely to be considered; 'no' if it is not and 'per' if it is something which could bear thinking about (5 minutes).

The next exercise uses the idea of force field analysis, referred to at the beginning of this phase, and begins to hone in on realistic alternatives for Simon, those which we considered possible within his frame of reference.

*Exercise 11c:    Force field analysis (restraining forces)*

The object of this exercise is to explore possible restraining or hindering forces in any of the options listed.

In the whole group, again using the brainstorm technique, work through some of the options in terms of restraints on possible action. For example:

Possible option—joining a singles club.

Possible restraints:

lack of money,
fear,
don't know where to find one,
think everyone will know I can't make it on my own,
heard they have a bad reputation,
never done it before,
shy.

Check out in the whole group which possible restraints do not seem to relate to Simon's case. Are they all applicable and justifiable, given the sort of person he seems to be? Restraining forces are likely to be a mixture of reasons (like lack of money), and excuses and justifications (like the risk of trying something new). Here the danger of pushing the client towards a course of action which he feels incapable of pursuing, at this time, can be very great: hence the importance of starting with a small, attainable goal which will be encouraging and inspiring as a basis for taking slightly bigger steps.

*Exercise 11d    Forcefield Analysis (Helping Forces)*

Having looked at the possibilities which may decrease action, in the whole group, using the same options, *brainstorm* possible forces which will increase and facilitate action. For example:

Possible option—joining a singles club.

Possible facilitating forces:

strong desire to meet women,
know where I can start finding a singles club,

think that someone at work joined one,
feeling of hope that I can do something about my loneliness,
willing to try something if it'll work,
at least it's a start,
most clubs have dimmed lighting don't they? they can't see I'm shy,
there'll be other people like me there,
it's better than sitting at home with Mum in front of the telly,
it's quite exciting when you think about it.

Having worked through a couple of options with the group, ask them to form pairs and work through the remaining options for action using the restraining/facilitating criteria to evaluate feasibility.

## TUTORIAL INPUT

By now our client has probably more feasible options for action than he can handle. However, although brainstorming can inspire hope and creativity it does not in itself provide an action plan. Each of the action options could lead to an action plan, although the process of examining restraints and facilitative possibilities will have probably eliminated some. It is likely, too, that in going through this exercise our client will have begun to favour one or more courses of action.

Prioritizing options becomes the next step. How does the client begin to assess which option would be the best one upon which to take action? Which option is the most useful in terms of being able to achieve success. The latter point is most important; there is probably no reason why all the options could not be achieved at some point. However, the first step is the most crucial as it provides the baseline for all future action.

The five yardsticks against which action options can be tested are known as

### C.A.A.S.E.

Control: do I have full control over this action option or am I dependent on others for its achievement?
Applicability: is this action option applicable to the achievement of my goal?
Appeal: do I like this action option? There's no point at all in taking the medicinal approach—doing something unappealing or downright nasty because it'll do you good in the long run.
Standards: does this action option agree with my own code of practice, the ethics and morals by which I live my life?
External factors: are there any obstacles in the rest of my life that could prevent achievement of my action option?

*Exercise 11e:  C.A.A.S.E.*

Ask the participants to work in pairs, and go through the options previously generated using the C.A.A.S.E. criteria. Suggest that one of the partners makes a list of the options down one side of the paper, marking them 1 to 10. Between them explore the criteria in order to produce a list of action options that are prioritized.

Check these out in the whole group and explore what differences may have occurred in the separate groups.

Negotiate within the whole group which action option seems to be the most feasible one upon which to draw up an action plan.

# Chapter 6
## Helping the Client: Phase 3: Action

### SESSION 12: TURNING THE PLAN INTO ACTION

### Training objectives

(a)  To clarify the action options.
(b)  To practise devising action plans.

TUTORIAL INPUT

It will already have become clear that, for many helpers, their main function is to work with the client through the explorative investigation and decision phases —for many clients this is enough for them to go ahead with action necessary. In other situations it is the helper who, once the information is gathered, has to take whatever action is necessary. However, on some occasions helpers can provide support for the client while they are taking the action, and so this is the point at which all the talking and planning will turn into action and we move into Phase 3 of the process. This next session is designed to pinpoint exactly what the client will need to *do* in order to make some change in the situation which is causing the problem.

So, returning once again to the example we used in the last session, and having chosen the action option which meets our client's needs more effectively than any other, an action plan needs to be drawn up. As we all know, the wish is not father to the deed. While there is relief in deciding upon a course of action, unless there is a plan attached to carrying it out, the option may remain just that!

*Exercise 12a:  Action Plan (1)*

Write the action option on the top of the flip chart. For example: 'Joining a computer dating outfit'. Then invite suggestions from the group about where our client can start and explore them as they arise so that a plan forms on the flip chart. For example:

(1)  Look up computer dating outfits in the Yellow Pages, press or magazines.
(2)  When? I'll buy the paper tomorrow, and look up Yellow Pages after work.
(3)  I'll write to all of them as soon as I've got the information.
(4)  Then I'll fill our the forms they send me or go and see them.
(5)  When I get my first date I'll go along and meet the person.

*Exercise 12b:   Action Plan (2)*

Invite participants in pairs to choose any of the other options tht have been evaluated as feasible ones, and ask them to draw up an action plan for one of them.

*Exercise 12c:   Personal Action Plans*

In a group which has developed a high level of trust it can be enlightening and rewarding for participants to do these exercises on their own real-life examples.

*Exercise 12d:   Action Plan Case Studies*

Ask participants for examples of case studies where action plans would be relevant, and hold a group discussion exploring as many possibilities as possible.

# SESSION 13: CLIENT SUPPORT

## Training objectives

(a)  To consider ways of supporting the client through action.
(b)  To demonstrate how support can be given.

## TUTORIAL INPUT

To experience how it may feel to move from the position of being isolated by a problem or difficulty into one of being supported through action, plunge straight into the next exercise. By now the group will have worked together sufficiently long to have built up a degree of trust.

*Exercise 13a:   Trust Circle*

Ask participants to stand in a large circle at arm's length away from one another so that everyone is isolated from everyone else. Ask them to close their eyes for just a minute and reflect on being alone.

Ask 'How do you feel?' 'Is it a pleasant or a scary sensation?' 'Do you feel unbalanced?'

After a minute, ask everyone to open their eyes and raise their right arms to shoulder level and as they do so to move forward in the group so that each person makes contact with the next in the circle. Then ask them to close their eyes again for another minute and check out the differences between standing alone and standing with others.

Check out with the group how this physical enactment of support may relate to that which a helper can offer a client.

## TUTORIAL INPUT

The core of the helping process is client's action towards bringing about change. Talking about change is not at all the same thing as implementing it. At this point it could be useful to enlarge a little on why change is so often resisted—even when the change will be an improvement. Peter Marris (in *Loss and Change*) has identified as the conservative impulse, people's tendency to accept only those things which can be taken into their existing perceptual structure, and avoid, reject or redefine anything that cannot be assimilated. In a very basic sense our survival depends on our ability to predict events. The consequences of events are only predictable if they fit into the perception of the person who is interpreting them. The interpretations we make can only be understood in terms of our own purposes, preferences, antipathies and our learned experience of the world – our 'life script'. Each one of us handles the uncertainties in our lives by trying to conserve the fundamental structure of meaning we have developed for ourselves.

Any change causes some level of uncertainty because change involves loss. What is lost is the completeness of the structure we have created to ensure we understand and can predict our world. It may be the loss of something immediately observable, for instance a salary, a job, funding, a piece of equipment, a dearly loved person, a treasured object. Or the loss may be more difficult to measure – loss of status, reputation, peace of mind, and so on.

Each loss requires a period of adaptation, of reorientation of thinking and feeling so that we can integrate the new situation into our structure of perceiving our world. This process is often known as mourning.

Most of us establish habits of behaviour and action which generally serve us well until we discover that they no longer work. Even so, changing them for what we perceive to be a better course of action is both fearful and challenging.

If the action plan has been effectively constructed, clients may sail through it. They may, however, not be able to anticipate possible pitfalls that arise. If this is the case, what type of support can a helper offer?

*Exercise 13b:   Support Options*

Brainstorm in the whole group various possibilities of support. Write them down on the flip chart. These could include:

(1)   Contracting to see the helper at certain times in the early stages of action implementation—what might this involve?

(a)   encouragement to slow down/speed up,
(b)   challenging,
(c)   empathetic responding
(d)   appropriate questioning,
(e)   exploration of feelings about,
(f)   bringing about change,
(g)   relevant helper self-disclosure,
(h)   confrontation,

(i)     immediacy,

(j)     reinforcement of facilitative factors

(k)     check out the adequacy of the rewards in changing.

(2)     Involving the resources which friends, family and workmates can offer.

(3)     Keeping a journal of progress which records steps forward as well as backward as a way of measuring change.

## TUTORIAL INPUT

The aim of the support is to plan for preventive action, if necessary, or to help the client stay the course. The aims are *not* about encouraging dependence on the helper and allowing the client to avoid being self-reliant.

The most effective way of exploring what support means in the helping process is to work on some case studies. Ideally, if participants have their own action plans, so much the better. If not, have ready some prepared action plans.

*Exercise 13c:    Client Support*

You may choose first to work through one client's action plan with the whole group with one person electing to be the client and the group offering suggestions about the type of support needed. In this case the tutor acts as a type of filter through whom the suggestions are made and the 'client' acts on them.

Alternatively, it may seem more appropriate to form into helper/client pairs to work on action plan support. Give time for the chosen scenario to be absorbed by the client partner. Reverse roles after 15 minutes. Debrief in the whole group.

Examples of action plans requiring support:

(1)     Charlotte wants to cut down on her work. She has produced an action plan which gives her permission not to work. It worked well in the early days but she is finding that she is slowly becoming seduced into saying 'yes' whenever she is offered something she finds challenging.

(2)     Edward wants to cut down on his eating. He knows he is in danger of getting a heart attack. He is beginning to recognize that his action plan was geared to his work, and weekends are a real minefield.

(3)     Erica wants to be able to manage her anger towards her mother more effectively. She has got in the habit of bottling it up and sulking when things go wrong between them. Her action plan included confronting herself when she became angry and then checking this out with her mother. She is now feeling under pressure, and thinks she is avoiding any contentious topic which could cause a confrontation. She feels she is behaving unnaturally.

(4)     Chris wants to be able to save some of his earnings. He never seemed to have money for anything. His action plan involved some concrete proposals about saving which he has managed very successfully (he has brought his building society paying-in book to show the helper). He is troubled now that he is being too successful and his mates at work are passing snide remarks that he is getting mean.

## Issues for the trainer

The basic training which will prepare people for taking on their role as a helper is nearing its end. We have focused on each part of the process and participants will have had opportunities to discuss and practise the various skills which they need. There are two concerns left for consideration.

The first is the question of referral. It is inevitable that some clients will present problems which fall outside the brief or the skills of the helper, and so need to be guided towards the most appropriate assistance. There will also be times when helpers themselves require referral and this issue, too, needs to be explored before the training ends.

The second topic is evaluation—that is, how success or otherwise can be measured. These two issues are the content of the last two sessions of this basic training.

## SESSION 14: WHEN, HOW, WHERE, AND WHY REFER?

## Training objectives

(a)  To establish when referrals are appropriate.
(b)  To practise referring without appearing to reject the client.
(c)  To explore reasons and options for a helper's need for referral.

### TUTORIAL INPUT

In this session we are going to consider the issue of referral both from the point of view of the client and the helper. We tend to assume that it is always the client who needs referral, but the helper too may need to consult with someone else when the going gets rough, or when an impasse has been reached. Helper referrals are usually in the form of supervision and we shall explore this topic at the end of the session. First, though, let us look at how referral affects the client.

### Why referral?

During the exploratory stages of the initial interview it may become apparent that the helper cannot meet the needs of a particular client. This may arise through the lack of particular experience or skill, like marriage guidance or bereavement.

Perhaps the organization in which the helper works is not able to offer enough sessions to meet the client's needs, or the problem presented may be so deep-seated or of such duration that the helper feels that another agency could meet the client's needs more appropriately. Very occasionally a personality clash occurs between client and helper. Being labelled 'a helper' does not mean that you can help all who ask for it. Far better to refer at an early stage than struggle with additional problems which seem to be based on a conflict of personalities rather than professional criteria.

The question of referral may also arise at the action planning stage. It may become apparent that the client then needs specialist advice which can be obtained elsewhere – careers advice, or psychotherapeutic counselling, for example.

Referral may occur as a result of one party leaving the locality. The client, for example, may move house or the helper progress onwards or outwards from the organisation.

*Exercise 14a:   Why Refer?*

Divide participants into small groups and give each group a blank sheet of flip chart paper. Ask them to write down a list of all the reasons they can think of for referring a client (5 minutes). Display charts and discuss generally with the group.

*Variations*   This can be done in pairs, or in the whole group as a brainstorm exercise.

## When to refer

Referrals in the early stages of the helper/client relationship are likely to be less emotionally fraught for both parties. As the relationship develops, separation may become an issue and the client may experience feelings of rejection or abandonment.

If both parties know that referral is going to arise through moving locality, it is best to work on this in anticipation of the event rather than leave it to the last moment. It may be more appropriate not to take on a client if there are possibilities that the work is more long-term than can be guaranteed by that particular helper.

Any referral can seem disruptive and disappointing. Clients who have to pluck up courage to seek help in the first place are going to feel more confirmed in the idea that help is impossible to find if they are referred on. Neverthless it may be the most effective of action and needs to be taken.

*Exercise 14b:   When to Refer*

Display on a flip chart, or give participants as a handout, the pyramid picture of the helping process (see Figure 8, page 85). Going through each stage, discuss with the group the implications of referring at each phase both from their and the clients' point of view.

## Where to refer?

*Exercise 14c:   Where to Refer?*

(1)    Ask participants to make a list on their own of categories of organizations or individuals to which they might want to refer clients; for example:
legal aid advice,
DHHS claims,
parent and toddler clubs.

(2)    Check out whether these referrals can be made within the existing organization. Are there gaps in information about what can be supplied within the workplace?

(3)    Are there instances in which you could begin to offer help but later need more specialist advice, information or counselling? for example, working with a battered wife. Make a list of these more uncertain areas.

(4)     Can you pick up the phone and make an appointment with all or any of your referral agencies? Do you have a name(s) of workers there?

In the whole group, discuss how effective the referral system appears to be with the participants. Does an efficient referral system encourage a greater number of clients to be referred, perhaps when the case could be dealt with on the spot? Whose responsibility is an inefficient referral system? What are the possible consequences of this for helpers?

If there are deficiencies in the system, how can they be remedied?

## How to refer

Good referral is a combination of the elements we have considered so far: timing (when), reasons for doing so (why) and knowing of other, more appropriate options (where) together with an awareness of and sensitivity to clients' feelings.

*Exercise 14d:   Feelings about Referral*

In the whole group brainstorm first how the client might feel about being referred:

> hurt
> abandoned
> rejected
> insecure
> not again!
> resigned
> relieved
> hope yet!

Next brainstorm how the helper might feel about referring a client:

> failure
> not good enough
> inadequate
> deskilled
> relief
> confident
> fine
> appropriate

Discuss these findings in the whole group; some participants may wish to share experiences of referring clients with others. Focus on the feelings rather than the content and action involved.

## TUTORIAL INPUT

Whatever and whenever the need for referral arises, it demands skilful handling. It is always appropriate that the referral is a joint decision, although the initial suggestion may come from the helper. The helper should ensure as far as possible that clients are not made to feel that their case is hopeless or that they are beyond help. However reluctant a client may be about making decisions, being told what is good for you can instil feelings of powerlessness and rage.

### Exercise 14e:   *Referral Skills*

In the whole group discuss what skills are likely to be needed when referring a client. These will include:

(a)     empathetic responding;
(b)     understanding of the existing relationship, however brief;
(c)     appropriate questioning;
(d)     immediacy;
(e)     tact;
(f)     listening;
(g)     clarifying;
(h)     giving information;
(i)     summarising;
(j)     ending the relationship.

Explore any thoughts and feelings arising from the discussion. Then move on to practise giving a referral.

### Exercise 14f:   *Practising Referral Skills*

Preferably use examples provided by the participants themselves and form helper/client pairs. Allow 15 minutes for the work to be carried out and a further 5 minutes for debriefing. Reverse the roles.

The following possibilities could be offered if participants cannot find their own examples:

Rhona, 15, turns up at a girls' project one evening. She tells one of the youth workers that she has been turned out of her home after a row with her mother. She has been squatting and has not eaten for a couple of days, is tired and fed up.

A young woman with a newly born baby appears at the baby clinic for the first time. She talks with the health visitor about her loneliness and isolation. She wants to go back to her parents' home but they live abroad and she has no passport.

During an appraisal session, Frank tells his manager that he has recently discovered that his teenage son was taking drugs. He cannot handle the situation and is desperately afraid that his other two children will be influenced by their older brother. His wife seems to have retreated into ill health since this discovery.

Maxine's on a youth work project, studying car mechanics. She's being harassed by the boys and is finding the going tough. She's spoken to the manager of the garage and to the workers on the project but things haven't improved. She burst into tears and blurted it all out when she saw the counsellor at the family planning clinic.

After everyone has had an opportunity to practise referring, discuss any points which have arisen in the whole group. What was most difficult as helper? How did you feel as client? Are there particular areas which you could improve on?

*Variation*    Play a tape (or provide a tapescript) of a client presenting a case such as the examples above. Ask participants to write down the way they would approach the possibility of referral to the client. Then go round the group with each person putting his or her approach into words. The members of the group can give each other feedback about their approach and also increase their own repertoire as they hear each others' suggestions.

This exercise can be further extended by developing the examples into role-plays.


## TUTORIAL INPUT

As we mentioned at the beginning of this session, it may be appropriate for helpers themselves to seek referral. Most agencies who provide a caring/helping service for clients recognize the need for the same service to be applied to its helpers. Supervision should be an integral part of any helper's work.

Even though supervision is available, there may be occasions when a helper feels it imperative to seek help in addition to the existing provision. Causes may range from a heavy and complex case-load, stress and pressure from overwork or underwork, personal problems, a confrontation with a personally distressing issue, an awareness of a tendency to find solutions for clients' problems because there is not time to let them find their own, lack of sleep, inability to relax, etc.

Referring oneself for help is not a sign of weakness but a recognition that there is a need to pause and reflect on what is going on.

As a final ending to this session it may be useful to have a brief and general discussion in the group about participants' ability to seek referral themselves. Sometimes it becomes evident that helpers are very good at their job but are far less able at helping themselves.


*Exercise 14g:    Referral for Helpers*

Ask the group to brainstorm a list of reasons why they might need referral for themselves, and then discuss each item with a view to clarifying the 'When, How, Where and Why' questions.


*Exercise 14h:    Barriers to Referral*

Ask the group to work in pairs, and discuss with each other what kind of things would prevent them from seeking or finding referrals for themselves. When these are shared in the whole group it might be useful to separate the various suggestions into categories—for example, internal (thought, feelings, fears, etc.) and external (lack of resources, time, etc.) thought, feelings, fears, etc.) and external (lack of resources, time, etc.) barriers.

This exercise can be extended into a problem solving one—with the group creating action plans to deal with the barriers they have identified.

## SESSION 15: EVALUATION

## Training objectives

(a)  To explore and differentiate between the concepts of evaluation, assessment and monitoring.
(b)  To develop criteria for assessment baselines.
(c)  To explore a structure within which to identify strengths and weaknesses.
(d)  To practise evaluation skills.

## Issues for the trainer

Evaluation is related to assessment and measurement. Any change in our lives is measured, consciously or unconsciously, by a *'before and after'*. True-life stories in magazines often hold an enduring fascination precisely because our hero/heroine has undergone some massive, gruelling or otherwise radical change in his or her life.

Conversions which clients bring about are not usually as blatantly spectacular as this. The most profound changes which individuals achieve are often related to attitudes or beliefs, and noticeable only to the client concerned, at least to begin with. These in turn bring about behavioural changes which are more likely to be noticed by others. Whatever the nature of the change, be it with a primarily internal or external focus, it can be monitored and evaluated.

TUTORIAL INPUT

Evaluation necessarily relates to the specificity and the concreteness of the client's goals. This in turn relates to the helper's role in this process. It is a two-way process. One way of looking at it is to see a stark and different parallel between teaching children in school and exam results. Good results can suggest, among many other things, that the teaching input was satisfactory or at least adequate, and that the pupils were motivated, coerced or impelled to succeed. Before the 'big public exam' pupils are continuously assessed or marked, they have mock or trial exams and they are monitored to check whether they are up to the mark.

There are some similarities between this and the helping process in terms of evaluating and monitoring progress. Most of us are encouraged by a form of payment by results; we can see where we are going and have a sense of achievement which encourages us to continue. Here, the 'payment' is based entirely on the individual client's reward system and is obtained through feedback to and from the helper.

Evaluation does not only refer to the end product or change which the client has brought about; to do so would severely limit the possibilties of changing the action programme if appropriate and would deny the importance of continuous assessment which is so fundamental to carrying out the action plan. Nevertheless, as the word 'evaluation' tends to refer colloquially to this final assessment of change, we shall use the terms monitoring and/or assessment to refer to that aspect of evaluation which refers to the continuous process. Evaluation therefore is the method by which we assess the whole rather than the parts of the helping process which takes account of the monitoring and assessment as it is built into the action plan.

All this begs an obvious question; how do the client and helper establish a *baseline* upon which to monitor and assess and later evaluate change?

### Exercise 15a:   Establishing Evaluation Baselines

Participants may wish to use examples already worked on, or their own personal examples. In either case it is necessary to have a set of goals clearly formulated so that it is possible to establish a baseline for measurement of progress.

Let us say, for example, that John's aim is to lead a more healthy lifestyle. His goal is to eat more health food than junk foods, to take regular exercise and to take off at least one day from work. One of his plans of action involves eating regularly, not buying junk foods, not eating late at night just before he goes to bed and reducing his alchol intake.

In this case, John's baseline for this part of his plan of action might be:

(a)   making a note of his eating patterns before he sought help;
(b)   making a list of the sort of foods he considers junk foods;
(c)   making a list of what he considers to be health foods;
(d)   noting how often and why he ate late at night;
(e)   the pattern of his alcohol intake.

This type of practical action plan lends itself more easily to an assessment of a baseline.A more problematic alternative would lie with Jenny, who feels inhibited socially. She wants to cope with her shyness which she considers is crippling her social and personal life. Her goal is to be more socially assertive, which is not easy to measure. Her action plan involves going to assertiveness training classes.

In this case the baseline would have to be established on the basis of existing, shy behaviour. For example:

(a)   not going out to parties when she does not know anybody there;
(b)   waiting until someone approaches her rather than making the first approach;
(c)   getting tongue-tied with strangers;
(d)   not making contributions at meetings in case she is noticed;
(e)   never saying 'no' because of possible, difficult repercussions;
(f)    staying at home most evenings with her family and a couple of friends she has known since school;
(g)   not going to evening classes because she is afraid of what might happen to her.

On the basis of these and/or other examples ask participants to form into a couple, discuss a mutually agreed goal with action plan and formulate a baseline for it. Allow 10 minutes and then debrief the whole group. Clarify any of the less specific action plans as they relate to establishing the baseline for monitoring and measurement. Move on the next exercise and explore what monitoring and assessment involves.

### Exercise 15b:   Monitoring and Assessment

Invite suggestions from the whole group around the practical implications of monitoring and assessment. What are the implications for the helper and for the client? Note them down on the flip chart. These could include:

(1) Providing regular sessions for the client to feedback progress—what skills are involved here? (see session on feedback in Training Techniques (Page 180)
    (a)  responding,
    (b)  challenging and/or encouragement,
    (c)  confronting progress or its lack,
    (d)  appropriate questioning,
    (e)  exploration of feelings involved.

(2) Are there other ways of monitoring which could be built into the action plan?
    (a)  keeping a journal of progress,
    (b)  involving friends, family workmates.

(3) What evidence has the client for change as it takes place?

(4) Is the goal on the way to achievement? Does the action plan need modification?

(5) Is the helper helping effectively, or are her interventions hindering? How would you as helper know this either way?
    (a)  client does not return for planned sessions;
    (b)  motivations of client decreasing;
    (c)  no demonstrable change towards goal achievement;
    (d)  client remains enthusiastic and motivated;
    (e)  progress is palpable;
    (f)  client indicates that she wishes to work with helper;
    (g)  client able to see that other change is possible on the basis of existing changes achieved.

(6) Does the helper require some/more supervision about a particular case?

This will raise further questions, particularly if helper intervention appears to have been less effective; questions like:

(7) Was enough time spent on the explorative stage?
(8) Were the goals specific enough?
(9) Has the client 'bitten off more than she can chew'?
(10) Has the helper 'imposed' goals? action plan?
(11) Should this client have been referred?
(12) What feelings around client achievement or its lack are being aroused in the helper?
(13) Is the helper too personally involved in the client? Thereby taking success/failure of the client personally?
(14) Did the helper go over a particular stage(s) in the helping process when she felt it was necessary?
(15) What external pressures (time, organization, etc.) contributed to the outcome for the client?

## TUTORIAL INPUT

Looking at 'successes' and 'failures' is always an effective way of assessing both helper and client participation in the process. This exercise concentrates on the helper.

*Exercise 15c:*   *Successful Cases*

In groups of about four participants, each spend a little time thinking about case which went well and which you feel able to share within the small group. Suggest that as each person talks about their case, someone else in the group takes notes. The task of the group is to pinpoint why the case can be judged as successful. For instance, how was the action plan monitored and continuously assessed? Allow 10 minutes for each participant to share a 'success' and 5 minutes between the change-over for brief discussion within the small group.

Debrief in the whole group. Clarify which transferrable skills and methods can be applied to other cases?

This next exercise leads to an exploration of what participants might gauge as 'failures'.

### Exercise 15d:    What Went Wrong?

Using the same small group and format, explore why and how the helper felt, thought and believed a particular case did not go well. Encourage specificity and again invite a scribe for each group to make notes. It may be useful to go over the helping process and investigate where and at what stage(s) helper intervention was hindering. Allow the same amount of time—this exercise is not designed for participants to wallow in self-punitive feelings but a means of identifying what might have gone wrong.

Debrief in the whole group.

## TUTORIAL INPUT

As a result of these two exercises participants have the opportunity to assess themselves, to confront their strong and weak points and recognize which part of the helping process needs further attention.

It becomes clear that monitoring and assessment are an integral part of the helping process if it is to enable change. By encouraging feedback from the client the helper enables reinforcement of the action plan. The more the client achieves, the smaller the gap between original intention and successful completion of the action plan.

In this sense achievement itself is a form of monitoring and assessment for the client – as well as, in an indirect way, for the helper. Pursuing this way of looking at monitoring, it follows that non-achievement, however this has been established in relation to the action plan, can contribute constructively to the continuous assessment of progress.

## Issues for the trainer

This session focuses on the way that evaluation can be used as an important element in the completion of the work between client and helper. Relevant also to this stage are Chapter 1, Evaluation of training (pp. 18–20) and Chapter 11, Endings (pp. 158–161).

## TUTORIAL INPUT

We have made the point that evaluation takes place at the end of the process. Where there have been a number of sessions the number will probably have been negotiated during the contract-making stage, and time for evaluation can be planned. Where there is only one session it may be more difficult to provide the time necessary, and the evaluation will probably need to be fairly speedy. However, ending well is as important as beginning well if clients are to feel that they have achieved anything substantial by coming.

Endings can be difficult and sometimes emotional, especially if the client has come to expect, and wishes to continue with, the help and support being offered. It is considerate for both parties to anticipate the ending before it actually occurs. The onus more usually falls on the helper to acknowledge that, for instance, the next two sessions will complete the contract, and to invite the client to begin thinking about evaluation. This is an appropriate time to evaluate what has taken place throughout the entire helping process.

At this point it becomes evident that to have a record of the presenting problem, and how this was worked through, provides a helpful yardstick. The helper can invite the client to chart progress from the point at which they first met and the problem as it was presented, to what goals were worked out and the progress on the action plan.

Allowing the client to complete the process provides evidence that change has been achieved. Helpers can of course encourage clients to acknowledge areas of change that may otherwise be ignored, perhaps because they happened indirectly or early on in the action plan.

Self-assessment and evaluation is often a good deal more harsh than that meted out by others. The helper may feel it is appropriate to intervene and clarify the client's judgement if it appears either too sweeping or even inaccurate.

Sometimes, for example, clients say that it has taken so long to get where they've got. 'I've only moved inches!' It seems entirely appropriate to remind clients who are in danger of belittling their progress that they have achieved a change in attitude and/or behaviour in a matter of weeks against the years they have behaved in their old style. Such ways of measuring, by providing a perspective on the whole of the client's life, can often only be provided by the helper who can more easily see the wood and the trees on the client's patch.

Clients may defer to helpers to tell them how they have done, rather like a school report, but the principle of self-responsibility should continue until the client has left the room. For the helper to be flattered or seduced into this form of collusive action may undo much that has been achieved beforehand. The question can be turned back to the client: 'How do *you* think you have changed?'

*Exercise 15e:   Evaluation Practice*

In the whole group, discuss existing evaluation practices. Explore what is most effective and why; is it client-orientated or does the helper evaluate the client? How do helpers evaluate their helping? Are there deficiencies and if so, how are they to be rectified? As a result of this basic training on the helping process, do participants envisage changing their practice, and if so, how?

*Exercise 15f:   Self-progress Evaluation*

Invite participants, working in pairs, to help each other evaluate their progress on the course—from the very beginning to the present ending point (15 minutes).

In the whole group, collect lists of which of their partner's strategies they found most helpful in assisting their evaluation, and any that they found hindered the process.

# SECTION 3
## Continuing Training

# Chapter 7
## Increasing Confidence

The main aim of this section is to provide a programme which will support the basic training described in the previous section. Training is not like the magic potions so often found in fairy tales, where all someone had to do was to take a sip and be changed for ever. However well designed and skilfully tutored, a training course will not effect change on its own. A good course will increase participants' awareness and motivate them to want to develop their skills. However, when trainees finish their basic training and get involved in the job it is sometimes difficult for them to maintain the enthusiasm that good training engenders.

Helping other people is a difficult job. We have already seen just how many skills it requires to do well. Working with people who are troubled and confused can in itself be troubling and confusing for the helper. Even though as a society we have more knowledge and technical skills than ever, there are still many problems which people experience and cannot solve. In fact, the nature of the problems which people bring are ever more complex and difficult to manage.

Support for those who are involved in helping is very important, and most organizations offer some form of supervision framework, in which the worker can discuss his or her work with someone who can guide them in their development. Continuing training provides another kind of support with a programme linked to the needs identified as a result of training needs analyses (see Chapter 2).

For this section we have selected the areas which come up most often in a wide variety of organizations.

## SESSION 16: WHAT IS CONFIDENCE?

### Training objectives

(a)  To explore the concept of confidence.
(b)  To identify seven personal resources.
(c)  To provide a framework for participants to identify their strengths and areas for growth.

# Issues for the trainer

Many people believe that confidence is something that comes and goes – completely outside their control. This session is designed to show people that it is possible to work consciously to increase their confidence and that they do not have to accept the incapacity that a severe lack of confidence can bring.

Some parts of this session are based on the ideas in Claude Steiner's *The Other Side of Power* (Grove Press, 1981), a good source of new ways of understanding the concept of personal power.

## TUTORIAL INPUT

Confidence stems from a feeling of personal power – a sense that one can deal with, whatever is happening in a competent and appropriate manner. It is like a tidal sea; at times it is there and carries one along, and at other times it drains away and leaves one feeling small and abandoned.

Power can be defined as the capacity to effect change – in oneself and one's surroundings. It is different from control – which is the ability to push people around. One problem for us is that we live in a society that muddles up those two things – and many people believe that being powerful means pushing people around. This means that as soon as we meet someone bigger than us, or someone who is better at pushing people around either physically or psychologically, we are bound to feel powerless.

Understanding that power is more than just the ability to control will help you increase your confidence.

### Exercise: 16a:   *Power*

Ask participants to remember a time when they have felt, or generally feel, at their most powerless. Ask them to write down a word or phrase that will remind them of that. Then ask them to remember a time when they have felt, or generally feel, at their most powerful—and again to write down a work or phrase that will remind them.

Explain that each person has seven sources from which their potential power stems.
(1)   *Self-esteem* (a sense of one's right to exist and be valued)
(2)   *Knowledge* (understanding the facts of the situation).
(3)   *Communication* (the ability to understand and be understood).
(4)   *Affection* (the willingness to care for and accept others).
(5)   *Passion* (enthusiastic commitment).
(6)   *Control* (being able to influence others and/or the environment).
(7)   *Transcendance* (knowing when to rise above what cannot be changed.

As you talk about each element, ask participants to give themselves a score on a scale from zero (none at all) to 10 (as much as possible) for each one, in both of the situations they previously selected.

Thus when you have finished, they will have two sets of scores. They will be able to see the resources in which they are high and low.

Then suggest they work individually, in pairs, or in small groups to work out in practical terms how they could increase the low scores.

Allow 30 minutes for this exercise.

*Variation*    If this is a group who have worked together for some time they might like to draw up a 'team graph' by adding together the various scores. This is an interesting way of encouraging a work team to share their strengths and weaknesses—and often results in people finding very practical ways of supporting each other.

# SESSION 17: BELIEFS WHICH DECREASE CONFIDENCE

## Training objective

To identify common personal and organizational beliefs which decrease confidence.

TUTORIAL INPUT

From our earliest childhood we develop a set of beliefs about ourselves and the world based on our attempts to understand what is going on around us. Most of these beliefs are formulated very early in our lives, and they are rarely reviewed or edited. It is possible that some of those values are outdated, inappropriate or mistaken. This session is an opportunity to explore some of them in order to decide whether they are accurate and useful. If they are not, you may decide to replace them with something more appropriate.

*Exercise 17a:    Personal Beliefs*

Ask the group to make a list of all the roles they can think of that they play in life. Collect them on a flip chart; they will probably include examples like: wife, mother, woman, father, son, nurse, lawyer, helper. It does not matter if there is a mixture of personal and professional roles (3 minutes).

Then ask participants to complete the sentence, 'A good . . . (name of role) must . . .'. They can do this individually, or working in pairs or small groups. Tell them to only to complete the ones which come easily to mind —those will be the ones about which they have strong beliefs (5 minutes).

Allow participants time to share their thoughts and feelings about the result of this exercise—either in pairs or small groups (10 minutes).

Back in the large group, each person reads out one of the beliefs they have identified. Some examples are:

(a) 'A good nurse must never show her true feelings.'
(b) 'A good advice worker must have knowledge of every important law at his finger tips.'
(c) 'A good social worker must always be accepting of clients whatever their behaviour.'
(d) 'A good wife must consider her husbands needs above her own.'

The group then consider how each belief might decrease the person's confidence. The tutor can point out how much of our belief system is based on the notion that acceptable means perfect. The problem with perfection in human behaviour is that it is not really attainable. For instance, nurses will have feelings towards their patients, colleagues, doctors, relatives. Obviously there will be feelings which are not appropriate to express to some people—and some feelings which are. The belief that it is *never* right will activate a loss of confidence on any occasion that the nurse has strong feelings which she wants to share with someone. These strong beliefs rob us of the power to choose how we will behave.

*Variations*   Brief groups only to suggest professional roles, or to list organizational beliefs.

### Exercise 17b:   *Self-criticism*

Ask participants to write down privately up to five things for which they frequently criticize themselves (2 minutes).
   Tutor then asks a series of questions:

(a)   'What is the evidence for the beliefs underlying your criticism? Are these beliefs rational? What would you have to do to accept it?'
(b)   'When was the first time you were told this about yourself?' 'Who told you?'
(c)   'What is the advantage to you of not changing? What would you lose if you gave this up?'

Give participants time to think of their answers and to note them down beside the criticisms they have listed (10 minutes). This can be followed by a general discussion.
   To end the exercise, ask participant to rewrite the original list, preceding each criticism with one of these phrases: 'From today I will no longer be . . .' or 'I choose to . . .' or 'I used to be . . .'.

### Exercise 17c:   *Feeling Positive*

This is a good exercise for a group who know each other fairly well. Each person is asked to write his or her name on the top of a blank piece of paper, and then pass it to the person on their right. This person then writes something positive about the person whose name is on the paper, e.g. 'John is very kind'; 'Jenny is always willing to help'; 'Simon has a lovely smile'. Then the papers are passed on again, with the next person also writing a message—and so on until each person receives her own back again.

*Variation*   Each person folds over the page after writing the message, so that no-one sees what other people have written.
   At the end of the exercise, each person can read out the list, prefacing each statement with the words, 'I am . . .'.

### Exercise 17d:   *Life Story*

Give everyone a large sheet of blank paper and ask them to draw a representation of their life story so far, using whatever image or symbols they choose. Ask them to mark the important milestones in their life in some way. For example, someone might use a railway track as the image, and mark each milestone as a station; someone else might draw a snakes-and-ladders game, and so on. Emphasize that they should include all the things they consider important to themselves—not only those milestones which would be validated by the outside world (10 minutes).
   When they have done this, ask them to work in pairs, or small groups, sharing their life story with each other.

The next stage is for them to help each other identify the skills and knowledge they have gained as a result of all the milestones, and make a list (20 minutes).

This is an excellent confidence-raising exercise, since everyone realizes that, regardless of what official recognition they may have of their abilities, they have gathered an enormous resource of skills and knowledge through their life experiences.

# Chapter 8
## Assertiveness Training

### SESSION 18: WHAT IS ASSERTIVENESS?

### Training objectives

(a) To define the differences between assertive, passive and aggressive behaviour.
(b) To apply these definitions to practical situations.

### Issues for the trainer

There are very strong connections between this session and the previous work on confidence building. The self-awareness which the exercises in the last chapter can begin to develop is enough to encourage some people to go ahead and become much more confident. However, for many others understanding the possible source of their loss of confidence does not actually help them to become more effective. Assertiveness training has developed in response to the need many people have to know what to do in situations where they feel ineffectual or out of control.

People often come to courses with unrealistically high expectations which can cause problems for the trainer. The contract setting exercises described in Section 2, Chapter 3, Exercises 1g and 1h, provide a good opportunity to negotiate realistic objectives.

It is important to communicate that assertiveness training does not guarantee happiness, increased popularity, or a problem-free existence. What it can offer is an increased sense power, of being more in control of one's life and not so much at the mercy of other people or circumstances.

Another point to make is that although changing one's behaviour is sometimes surprisingly easy, very often it requires a great deal of practice. Participants will realize during the training that the passive or aggressive responses they may wish to change arise from learned behaviour. It was probably learned a long time ago, and by now has become so habitual that it feels 'right and natural' even though it may not be pleasant or comfortable.

So the process of change is, in fact, reconditioning. There are useful parallels which can be drawn; some participants may have had experience of dieting, giving up smoking, or learning a musical instrument. Each of these activities requires reconditioning of minds and bodies into different behaviour. Participants will probably be able to remember the difficulties they encountered such as boredom, cravings, failures, irresistible temptations and so on. None of those problems need stand in the way of eventual success, if the person is determined. The trainer can include a session on personal action plans, applying the principles of setting goals as described in Section 2, Chapter 5. Session 10 as a way of helping participants to proceed in a practical way.

## TUTORIAL INPUT

There have been many attempts to order our understanding of human behaviour by identifying common patterns and labelling them as categories. There are obvious dangers in doing this because human beings will not fit neatly into sets of descriptions. During this session we are going to use four categories to help us analyse different responses to different situations. Because we do not all fit neatly into these groups, everyone will probably recognize a bit of themselves in each one, since there are times when we are all assertive, passive, directly aggressive or indirectly aggressive. These are the four labels we are going to use, and Table 1 gives the main indications for the different types.

These types can be described as if they were four actual people although, of course, they do not really exist – no-one sticks in one type of behaviour all the time. The useful thing is to identify which one reminds you of yourself in different situations.

People make very early decisions related to their experience of the world as to whether they will best survive by reacting passively or aggressively, and that these decisions tend to stay with us and influence our behaviour. One way of doing this is to ask participants to imagine that they have suddenly been spirited away from where they are now and popped out into another world. They did not expect to go and do not know where they are. They look around them and see that everyone is very busy; they do not understand the language, nor what people are doing. They know they want to survive and notice that a couple of people are quite interested in them, so they realize that they have to keep them close enough to look after them until they can survive on their own. Everyone else is six times as big as them! Some participants will be quite puzzled; others will see the connection between this description and birth and infancy. One person looking around the world will decide that the only way to survive is to fight harder than anyone else! Both decisions are wise, because they make sense of the situation. However, a wise decision taken when you are too tiny and too inexperienced to understand what is really going on may not be so wise 20 years later!

*Exercise 18a:    Four Responses*

Ask participants to work in small groups—four or five people in each group. hand out the worksheet (Table 2). Each group has 20 minutes to choose one situation and work out how each of the four people (passive, assertive, aggressive and indirectly aggressive) would respond.

Table 1. Four styles of behaviour

| | Assertive | Passive | Aggressive | Passive/aggressive |
|---|---|---|---|---|
| Point of view | I will stand up for my personal rights and say what I think and feel without violating others' rights to do the same. | I will not express my thoughts and feelings at all, or with such diffidence that they can be easily ignored. | I will stand up for my rights at the expense of others. | I will express my thoughts and feelings in such a way that others will not realize I am competing with them. |
| Basic message | I respect you and expect you to respect me. This is what I think, this is how I feel and this is how I see the situation. | I don't count. You can take advantage of me. I don't matter as much you. | This is what I think If you think differently, you are stupid. What I want is more important than what you want. | I won't tell you exactly what I think and feel, but I expect you to guess what's in my mind and behave as if I am more important than you. |
| Crisis behaviour | Evaluates situation and takes action. | Flees or gives in. | Rebels or attacks. | Rebels or attacks covertly. Finds someone to blame. |
| Feedback | We respect each other. | Guilt, anger, frustration, disrespect | Hurt, defensive humiliation. | Confused, feels manipulated, frustration. |
| Goal | Communication (to understand and be understood; to give and receive fair play; to negotiate). | To appease others and avoid conflict. | To win, if necessary by humiliating or overpowering others so that they are less able to stand up for themselves. | To win, but to be seen as non-competitive. |

Table 2. Four responses worksheet
_____

Choose one of the following situations and work out four responses to it corresponding to the four behaviour types: Passive (a), aggressive (b), Indirectly aggressive (c) and Assertive (d). Write out the responses in the spaces below:

Confronting someone who is making an unreasonable demand on you (for example, a manager giving excessive or inappropriate work)
A:
B:
C:
D:

Responding to someone who has just made a sexist or racist remark
A:
B:
C:
D:

Asking someone who has outstayed their welcome to go (for example, a colleague who 'just dropped in for a chat' when you are very busy; or a friend who stays on till the 'wee small hours')
A:
B:
C:
D:

Refusing an invitation
A:
B:
C:
D:
_____

When the 20 minutes is up, the groups come together and share the responses they ahve thought of.

There will probably be some discussion about the various answers; check that the 'assertive' answers are actually assertive and not polite passiveness or covered aggression.

Suggest that people go back 'into the small groups and check out with each other whether they demonstrated any of the behaviour types while they were working on the exercise (10 minutes).

*Variations*   Brief participants in the small groups to share situations in which they find it difficult to be assertive, and then to work out how the four types would respond to those situations.

## SESSION 19: TAKING RESPONSIBILITY FOR YOURSELF

## Training objectives

(a)   To demonstrate how language can be used to emphasize the responsibility each person has for what happens to him or her.

(b)   To work on a practical example.

## Issues for the trainer

Self-responsibility is a difficult concept to present to people because we are brought up to believe that other people can make us feel, think or do things. This exercise provides an intriguing opportunity to demonstrate the implications of the fact that assertiveness rests on the principle that each person is responsible for him or herself.

> *Exercise 19a:   Responsibility Language*
>
> Ask participants to write down privately a description of a relationship in which they are presently involved, which is not as satisfactory as they would like it to be. They should write it as if they were speaking to the other person involved. Then briefly explain as follows.

### TUTORIAL INPUT

The English language makes it very difficult to accept the fact that each one of us is responsible for what we do, think or feel. In this exercise by changing some of the words or phrases we commonly use to describe our experience of the word we will demonstrate how important this is.

An American psychologist called John Weir became so dissatisfied with English as a language for expressing accurately what goes on in people's inner world that he devised a 'new' language.

The first rule is that 'I am always the subject of my living'. Instead, for example, of saying 'My anger prevented me enjoying yesterday evening' I would say 'I made me angry, I stopped me enjoying myself'. There are 101 ways of not saying 'I . . .' when we are speaking about ourselves. 'We all feel angry when we are critized'; 'Anybody would feel depressed'; 'One doesn't want to make a fuss'; 'That's upsetting', and so on. In this new 'responsibility language' you will always state the reality that 'I cause me to . . .', or 'I make me . . .' or 'I choose to . . .'.

*Some examples:*

| | |
|---|---|
| A thought just came to me | I made me think |
| I'm delighted/sad/angry/ . . . | I delight/sadden/anger me |
| You're confusing me | I confuse me with your words |
| I don't know what to say | I don't know how to say me |
| It doesn't matter | I don't matter |
| That's depressing | I make me depressed. |

The other rules are:

| Instead of:   'You'   say | 'The you-in-me' (when you are describing your subjective experience of someone). 'I love you' thus becomes 'I make myself love the you-in-me'. |
|---|---|
| Can't | Won't |
| But | And |
| Should, would | Shall, will |
| Ought | Choose |

Then, after any discussion arising from these ideas, ask participants to rewrite their description – substituting the 'new' language wherever necessary. Participants may prefer to work on their own, or with a partner. The tutor then can direct a general discussion on the implications of absolute self responsibility.

*Exercise 19b:    Changing Language*

Ask participants to sit in pairs; starting with the words 'I have to . . .' everyone will give a list of all the things they can think of that come into the category of what they have to do. When everyone has exhausted their ideas, instruct them to repeat the list, but this time prefacing each item with 'I choose to . . .'. Give the pairs time to share thoughts and feelings which arise as a result of this exercies.

The next part of the exercise starts with people completing the sentence: 'I can't . . .', again repeating it until they have no more ideas left. This is then converted into 'I won't . . ', again time for feedback.

## SESSION 20: THE FIVE R'S: HOW TO DEAL WITH INTERPERSONAL CONFLICTS

## Training objectives

(a)  To introduce an assertive approach to communicating in conflict situations.
(b)  To identify a real-life situation and practise the approach.

TUTORIAL INPUT

This approach is intended to help analyse conflicts, determine needs and rights, propose a resolution and, if necessary, negotiate a contract for change.

The approach requires preparation and planning. The advantages are that this kind of preparation forces people to clarify the situation they are in and identify their needs. People gain in confidence by knowing what they are going to say, and they can avoid outbursts that they may regret later. It is often a good idea to write down the 'new script' in advance, and having a writtten record of what was intended means that it is possible to review its effectiveness without having to rely on memory. Situations in which the approach can be useful include:

asking for help or information;
clarifying instructions;
asking for improved working conditions;
pointing out irritating habits;
protesting about unjust criticism;
establishing independence;
dealing with sulking;
asking for something that is wanted.

## Stage 1: Reflecting

Before you launch into actually talking to the person with whom you are in conflict, take some time to consider what your motives are, particularly if you intend to criticize them. Criticism can either be used to coerce or punish someone; or to educate, protect or help them. If you just want the other person to feel bad because of the way they have treated you, or you want to force them to change their behaviour, it is likely that all you will achieve, at the best, is an uneasy truce, and at the worst a deepening conflict. You will certainly lose the cooperation of the other person.

You are much more likely to succeed if you have a genuine desire to help the other, or to give them information they may not have, or to protect them from being hurt by continuing their behaviour.

## Stage 2: Reporting

Reporting means saying exactly what is happening. Be as specific and objective as possible. Avoid generalizations – 'You *always* . . .'; 'You are thoughtless . . .'. Avoid guessing at the other's motives or accusing them of bad faith. Talk about specific actions or events, 'I notice that you have been late three times this week'; or 'When you interrupt me . . .'. The point of this is that if you criticize people's personalities or behaviour in a general way, they are much more likely to be defensive. If you talk only about specific behaviour in an objective way, there is less need for these people to protect themselves from what may seem to them to be an unfair or untrue attack.

## Stage 3: Relating

Relate the effects of the behaviour describing its emotional impact on you ('I feel . . .') and any personal beliefs or values about it ('I think . . .' or 'I believe that . . .'). Concentrate on the effects of the actions rather than your negative feelings. 'I think that your behaviour and my reaction to it are preventing us from having a good working relationship' or 'I feel insignificant when you criticize me so often' rather than 'I hate it when . . .'.

## Stage 4: Requesting

Request in concrete terms whatever you need to be different. Make sure the request is reasonable and within the power of the other person to meet. You may be able to negotiate; 'If you do this for me, I'll do that for you.'

## Stage 5: Results

Spell out the positive consequences of the change being made. People are much more likely to cooperate with you if they realize that there is a reason for what you want, and that you are not just trying to manipulate them. You should also have worked out the negative results, so that you can tell this to the person – but use this as a last resort. An example might be: 'I'll work more happily and efficiently if I feel everyone has a chance to contribute ideas as to how we run' (positive result); 'I will make a report on how unfairly I believe I'm being treated if I am not included in the decision making' (negative result).

*Exercise 20a:    Five R Script*

Before the input, ask participants to think of a relationship in which they want the other person to change in some way, and to write down exactly what they want to say to the other person as if they were talking to them (3 minutes).

After the input, ask participants to rewrite what they have previously written, making sure it follows the formula of the Five R's, (10 minutes).

After any general discussion, ask participants to move into pairs. Each one will say his or her new sentence to the partner, repeating it at least four times. Participants do not need to give any information about the actual situation which has led up to the problem. The listening partners will not ask any questions or discuss the problem, but may want to comment on how the content of the new message sounds to them. Then the roles are exchanged, so that the listeners have a chance to repeat their sentences.

As each partner repeats the message, he or she will gradually begin to adapt the rather stilted-sounding formula to something he or she is more comfortable with (5 minutes).

This exercise can then be followed by a general discussion.

*Exercise 20b:    Five R Samples*

Participants work in small groups. Ask each person to share with the small group an example of a situation in which this formula would be useful. The group will then choose one of the situations, and work out a Five R's script together (20 minutes).

Participants then come together in the whole group, and share the scripts they have created.

*Variation*    The tutor can provide each group with examples of situations.

# SESSION 21: DEALING WITH CRITICISM

## Training objectives:

(a)   To determine the differences between manipulative and justified criticism.
(b)   To define assertive responses: 'fogging' and 'constructive questioning'.
(c)   To provide structure for practising both approaches.

TUTORIAL INPUT

The criticism we receive can be of two kinds. We can be censured by someone whose main purpose is to control us, or make us feel guilty. This kind of fault-finding is usually about our appearance, our lifestyle or our personality. The other type of criticism is directed towards us because we have made a mistake of some kind. In this instance the main purpose of the critic is to solve whatever we have caused.

The most effective kind of response to the first kind of criticism is one which will give a clear message to the critic that you will remain the judge of your own behaviour and character. It is most applicable when someone is criticizing you for not being the way they want you to be, or when someone will continue criticizing you after you have taken responsibility for a mistake. These are the four steps:

(1) Listen to the criticism.
(2) Acknowledge whatever truth there is in it:'It's true that I am sometimes late.' 'You're right, my room could be a bit tidier.'
(3) If there is no truth, acknowledge that this is the other person's perception of you: 'I can see that's how it must come over.' 'I can understand that you see me that way.'
(4) Acknowledge the feeling that the other person has: 'I can see you're upset/ angry/irritated . . .'.

The second type of criticism can also be responded to assertively by constructive enquiry. This response is applicable when you have made a mistake, lost or forgotten something, unwittingly broken a contract, or when you have misjudged a situation. Ther are also four steps:

(1) Accept responsibility for what you have done: 'Oh, you're right, I did forget to do that.'
(2) Criticise yourself for it: 'I'm really getting very forgetful.' 'That was very silly of me.'
(3) Express your regrets for the result: 'I'm sorry; you must have been waiting for ages.'
(4) Ask questions to help in problem solving: 'Tell me, what specifically is wrong' (where the criticism is general, e.g. 'Your work just is not up to scratch'). 'What do you think we should do now?' 'Have you any ideas as to how I could avoid that happening again?'

The questions will prevent the other person from continuing to criticise and engage them in a problem solving conversation instead.


*Exercise 21a:  Responding to Criticism*

Working in pairs, participants take it in turns to 'criticize' each other and practise assertive responses (10 minutes).

*Variation*   Before asking participants to move into pairs, the tutor invites criticisms from participants, and then role-plays assertive responses.


*Exercise 21b:  Criticism on Tape*

Tutor plays tape recording of various types of criticisms, and participants are asked to write down the most assertive response to each one.

*Exercise 21c:  Dealing with Difficult Criticism*

Working in small groups, participants share examples of criticism they find most difficult to deal with. The group chooses one, and works out a role-play showing an assertive response (15 minutes).
    When the whole group reconvenes, each group gives its role play, and the various approaches are discussed.

*Variation*   Groups role-play an unassertive as well as an assertive response to each situation.

# SESSION 22: MAKING SURE YOU ARE HEARD

## Training objectives

(a)   To introduce 'broken record' technique,
(b)   To identify situations when it is useful
(c)   To provide structure and opportunity to practise.

TUTORIAL INPUT

The technique called 'broken record' is very useful when you want to make sure your views are heard in conflict situations, when refusing unreasonable requests, when saying no, when asking questions for clarification, when correcting someone who is in a position of authority, when expressing feelings or opinions to someone who is not listening.

You will speak like a broken record, being persistent and sticking to the point of what you want to say and repeating it over and over again, ignoring all side issues.

Don't be deterred by, or respond to, anything which is off the point you are making, just keep saying in a calm voice what you want to say until the other person hears you. Start by identifying your goal and making a clear statement:

'I want to return this defective radio.'
'I can't work this evening.'
'I don't want another drink.'

Repeat the message without picking up on any counter-statement which will cloud the issue.

'But the point is . . .'
'I don't think you heard me. I'm not able to work this evening.'
'I guess I'm not being clear.'
'Let me say it again . . .'
'That's really irrelevant to the main issue . . .'

If you have a certain point to make, and you also know that you have difficulty staying on the point, write it down and memorize it before you meet the person involved.

If an important side issue comes up, you can say something like, 'I'd like to talk about that as soon as we have settled this . . .'. If you say that you are going to address a side-issue later, it's important to do what you have promised.

If the other person does not seem to be hearing or understanding what you are saying, you can try asking him or her to repeat back, using phrases as, 'what do you think I am saying?' or 'What do you understand my position to be?'

*Exercise 22a:   Broken Record*

The tutor asks the group to identify situations where 'broken record' would be useful, and lists them on a flip chart as people call them out (3 minutes).

The group then work in trios, each pair choosing an example to work on. One person plays the assertive role and the other is instructed to be as devious and manipulative as possible in trying to move them off their 'broken record'. The third person in the trio acts as a helper for the assertive role-player, interrupting if she notices that it is becoming difficult to maintain the 'broken record' reminding the person that it is not necessary to explain or justify or answer questions.

Each person takes it in turn to play each role (15 minutes).

# Chapter 9
## Coping With Difficult Clients

### SESSION 23: WHO ARE THE DIFFICULT CLIENTS?

### Training objectives

(a)  To identify the types of clients who are difficult to work with.
(b)  To explore the fears which arise from the difficulties.

### Issues for the trainer

Even very experienced helpers discover there are some people with whom they find it difficult to relate enough to help effectively. Clients may be extremely angry and hostile, or withdrawn and passive; perhaps affected by a physical disability which inhibits their ability to communicate clearly, or suffering from a mental or emotional disorder. They can leave the helper feeling frightened or frustrated and trainers are often asked to provide courses on how to deal with 'difficult clients'.

The trainer is faced with several problems. Firstly, it is important for people to understand what reasons may lie behind clients' 'difficult' behaviour. It is tempting, once people are labelled as 'difficult', to see them as 'different' and then believe that it is not possible or even necessary to understand what may lie behind the behaviour.

Secondly the trainer needs to help people understand their own responsibility for their reactions. In any group of people discussing difficult clients, it rapidly becomes apparent that what to one is a 'person who is impossible to help', to someone else this is an exciting challenge; or to a third person 'no problem at all'. A client described as 'frightening and menacing' by one person can be seen as 'interesting and amusing' by another. One helper finds it easy to calm down and work with an angry client; another feels powerless and intimidated. Each helper's reaction is highly influenced by her own particular personality and perception.

These training sessions will help participants explore their own fears and responses, and develop constructive ways of helping themselves as well as their clients.

Thirdly, the trainer may have to destroy the myth that it is possible to help every single client to solve their problems, and that not to do this is a sign of failure onthe part of the helper. Although much of the work on the basic course is intended to dispel this idea, many people hang on to it, hoping that they will become the 'perfect helper'. So participants need reminding that, although their responsibility is to do the best job possible, there may be times when they just do not have enough skill, or when the client chooses not to use the help available.

Because reactions to these difficulties are so personal, training in these areas is most effective when it is backed up by regular and sensitive supervision.

*Exercise 23a:*    *'Who's Who?'*

Ask each participant to draw a picture of the most difficult client they can remember, or if they cannot think of a specific person, of the kind of client which they think would provide them with most difficulty. A cartoon sketch is all this is needed—emphasize that this is not an exercise designed to test people's artistic skill (3 minutes).

Working in pairs, each person than shows the sketch to her partner and defines just what it is that the client does which creates the problem (5 minutes).

Then invite each person in turn to say two or three words which they would use to describe their choice. At this stage it will become apparent that there are certain categories which clients fall into; e.g. passive demanding, talkative, confused, incoherent, and so on.

Then ask each person to jot down or think about what is the worst thing that could happen to them when they are with this particular client. Then breaking into small groups (three or four people in each one) the participants share their fears (10 minutes).

When the group reassembles, there can follow a discussion on the nature of the fears which have been revealed; exploring which are rational and irrational.

*Variation*    If people are very resistant to drawing, participants are asked to write down a series of words to describe the difficult client.

The sections which follow each focus on a particular category of clients who can be difficult to work with. The selection is not exhaustive, but our suggestions can be modified if any particular aspect you wish to stress is not mentioned.

## SESSION 24: THE ANGRY CLIENT

## Training objectives

(a)   To explore physical and emotional responses to anger.
(b)   To relate these responses to possible underlying motivation for anger.
(c)   To work out helpful strategies for dealing with anger.

*Exercise 24a:   The Anger Process*

Ask participants to make up small groups of four or five people. Give participants time to think about an angry client who they have found it difficult to deal with, and to remember what the client did. They can jot down their thoughts if they wish. When they have done this, ask them to put the notes aside for a moment (3 minutes).

Then ask participants to remember a recent situation in which they became very angry. Emphasize that this need not be a very significant event, but could be something which was actually relatively unimportant—for example, waiting in for a repair person who does not arrive; someone nipping into your parking space while you reverse. It should just be some occasion on which they felt extremely angry—if only for a short while.

Each person tells her story briefly to the small group. The sheets are headed, 'thoughts', 'feelings' and 'behaviour', one sheet for each heading. Give each group a set of three, and ask them to firstly write down all the things they could remember thinking while they were angry (i.e. the words that went through their heads), then what they remember feeling (their physical and emotional response) and finally what they remember doing (15 minutes).

The various flip charts are displayed and compared, followed by a general discussion based around such questions as 'Is there any similarity between what you do when you are angry and what clients do?' 'If there are differences are they of kind or degree?' 'Is there anything that anyone could have done for you which would have dispelled your anger at the time?'

## TUTORIAL INPUT

At this point give the group a brief description of the physiological reasons for and effects of anger. The physical sensations which are labelled 'anger' are very familiar – increased breathing and heart rate, tenseness of muscles, rush of blood to the face, increased adrenalin are the automatic response of the nervous system to some perception of threat. It is useful for people who want to control their anger (or the anger of others) to understand how it is triggered. Sometimes, of course, it is all too obvious, but there are times when motivation for the anger which is being expressed is less clear. For instance, someone may have been bottling up emotions for some time, and then there is just the 'last straw' which acts as a catalyst for the expression of all the stored-up anger. Fear usually lies underneath anger; for many people anger is easier to express than fear. In our culture, for instance, men are most acceptable when they are 'being brave' and to show fear is not very acceptable. Men therefore are much likely to express anger when they are afraid.

*Exercise 24b:   Why Get Angry?*

Ask the group for as many reasons they can think of for clients being angry, and collect the ideas on a flip chart as people call them out (5 minutes). Examples:

Having to wait a long time to be seen.
Being referred to different people.
No immediate solutions to problems.

Fear of the future.
Being treated without respect.

When the list is complete, go through the list asking people to indicate
whether it would be in their power to reduce the amount of stress which may
be leading to clients' anger. (For example, is there a better system for the
waiting room? How are referrals actually carried out? How can clients be
treated with more respect? Is there actually anything a helper can do if the
client is very afraid of the future?) (5 minutes).
Participants then work in pairs, and select two of the items which they have
indicated they have some control over and identify what they would have to
change if they wanted to reduce the anger caused (10 minutes).
The whole group can then come together and share ideas.

### Exercise 24c:    *Factors which Increase Anger in the Workplace*

Write on a flip chart, 'Are there any factors inherent in your job which you
feel could contribute to the likelihood of a client getting angry?' Ask the
group to consider the question and to break up into small groups to make
a list of any factors they can identify (10 minutes).

When the results have been discussed, write up on another flip chart
'What needs to exist or be changed or introduced into your workplace to
alleviate the increase of client's anger?' If the list of factors is very long they
can be divided up between small groups, so that a wide range of problems
can be considered (20 minutes).

### Exercise 24d:    *Anger Scenario*

Give participants a brief to set the scene for an event which might take place
in the workplace which ends with a client becoming very angry and hostile.
Depending on the size of the group, participants can work in pairs or small
groups (10–15 minutes).

The groups come together and share the results, either by presenting a
role-play or describing the scene they have developed. The exercise should
point up elements in the workplace which can increase clients' hostility, as
well as possible events in the client's life leading up to the show of
aggression.

## TUTORIAL INPUT

In an angry situation your main goal is to try to reduce the feelings of anger so
that you can communicate with the other person in a constructive way. Here is a
four-step approach which will help you do that. It is useful when someone is
expressing anger and you want to deal with the problem rather than just escape.
(1) Recognize and acknowledge the anger: e.g. 'I can see you are very angry.'
(2) Express your wish to solve the problem: e.g. 'I want to hear what you have
    to say. Let's try to work this out together.'
(3) Get the other person to lower his or her voice and sit down. you keep calm.
    e.g. 'Why don't we sit down and see if we can talk about this.'
(4) Use active listening to hear all the complaints before moving on to problem
    solving, e.g. 'It sounds like this has been bothering you for some time'; 'This
    must have seemed like the last straw.'

It often helps to admit the possibility that you might have been part of the problem.
e.g. 'Maybe I could have arrived a bit earlier'; 'I did make a mistake.'

This way of approaching anger assumes you are willing to handle the problem and move beyond active listening to try to resolve the conflict. It is more than simply placating the other person. It can be a good preparation for the assertive constructive questioning described in Session 21.

*Exercise 24e:   Anger Role-play*

Split the group in two halves. Give each member of one group a short written brief which describes a reason why they are feeling angry (e.g. 'Your doctor does not have an appointment system, and you have been waiting for at least 45 minutes, and the receptionist has just told you that the doctor has been called away to an emergency and won't be able to see you until he gets back.'

Each member of the other group is given a matching brief (e.g. 'You are the receptionist in a busy doctor's practice where there is no appointment system. The person who is last to be seen has been waiting for at least 45 minutes. The doctor has suddenly been called away to an emergency, and you have just explained this to the patient who has been waiting').

Each member of one group then pairs off with a member of the other group, and each pair role-plays the scene for a few minutes.

The discussion which follows should focus on how easy people found it to use the 'formula'; what got in the way'; is there anything that the person dealing with the anger would do differently on reflection, etc.

The roles can be switched, with a different situation given in the briefs.

*Variation*   The group can work in triads, with two people role-playing and the third acting as an observer who can provide useful feedback when the role-play has finished.

*Exercise 24f:   Angry Clients*

Ask participants to bring an example of a situation involving an angry client, if possible from personal experience. Ask a volunteer to describe the situation and to assign roles of the people involved to other participants in order to role-play the situation. At key points it is useful to stop the role-play and ask the various role-players how they are feeling.

After the role-play, ask the participants to identify the factors which contributed to the aggression.

This can be followed by a discussion of the options available to the helper in that, or similar, situations.

*Variation*   Replay the scene with different players using different responses. Replay the scene in slow motion. Replay without words.

# SESSION 25: COPING WITH CLIENTS WHO ARE MENTALLY OR EMOTIONALLY DISTURBED

## Training objectives

(a)   To describe different kinds of mental or emotional disturbance.

(b)   To provide simulations which help participants empathize more easily.

(c)   To help participants to determine helpful and unhelpful helping strategies.

## Issues for the trainer

It is probably because helpers themselves are so often disturbed by 'disturbed clients' that this topic is often requested in post-basic training. Participants often come to this kind of session believing that if they are given a lecture detailing the symptoms of different kinds of mental illness, and how to deal with them, then their problems will disappear. There are two problems here. One is that the idea of mental illness is something which often causes strong reactions of discomfort or fear in many helpers – and so the temptation is to dismiss any possibility of providing advice or help to clients who are identified as mentally ill.

The other is that many people are labelled as 'mentally ill' because their behaviour does not make sense to the helper. Some kinds of mental illness do cause people to behave in strange ways. However, people who are experiencing emotional distress can also be difficult to understand, even though they are physically quite healthy. Some physical problems affect behaviour, even though the person is perfectly sane. So an important element in the training session is a structure for understanding the range of possible reasons for the client's behaviour.

It also needs to be emphasized that it is not the intention of this session to prepare people to clinically diagnose and treat clients. The information is given in order to assist helpers to give their clients as much of the help they are asking for as possible.

### TUTORIAL INPUT

Because there are so many physical and mental problems which can affect a client's ability to communicate and understand clearly, it is useful to identify some categories so that we can begin to think about the most helpful responses.

There are three different sorts of clients who may come into the category of difficult because of some mental or emotional problem.

### 1. The client who has learning difficulties

These clients may appear simple or slow. They experience the full range of emotions, but lack some intellectual abilities. The main problem for them is that they have difficulty in explaining and understanding complex information. As a result of the constant efforts they have to make to communicate, they often feel frustrated, tired or embarrassed.

*Exercise 25a:   Simulating Learning Difficulties*

This exercise is designed to help people understand a little of the experience and feelings of someone who has learning difficulties. Prepare a handout which is based on some familiar piece of writing. Choose something which is familiar to the particular group of people on the course if possible. Type or print it, missing out every other letter. Table 3 is an example which has been used for a group of Citizens Advice Bureau workers. It is an extract from an application for an Attendance Allowance.

Give a copy of the printed form to everyone in the group, and without any explanation ask them to fill it in. After a few minutes, hurry them along by indicating that time is nearly up.

After about 5 minutes ask people to reflect on their experience. Ask them to remember what they thought and felt, and then go around the group with each person using one or two words to describe his or her feelings. The usual kind of response includes: 'Frustrated' 'I thought everyone else was doing it'; 'I knew it was familiar, but I just couldn't work it out'; 'Bored'; 'Irritated' and so on.

The discussion which follows should focus on connections between this simulated experience and how things might really feel for someone who has the kind of learning difficulties reflected in the exercise.

*Exercise 25b: Helping People with Learning Difficulties*

After the above simulation it is useful to give the group an opportunity for exploring the ways in which they can best help clients with learning difficulties.

Ask participants to split up into small groups, four or five people in each group. Ask them firstly to share the thoughts and feelings they experienced in the simulation, and then to discuss what could have helped them most (5–10 minutes).

Table 3
***

### C A M  F R:  A T N A C  A L W N C

Fl i al ditis i CPTL LTES, Ak smoe es o fin ti fo i yu cn d i yusl Ali fo a iald hl udr l sol b md b te mo te, o fste mte, o mi pye for cid bnft, bcri scin l l rfr t te dsbe pro, Tc oe bx we akd YS N.

#### D S B E  P R O

| | | |
|---|---|---|
| a | S rae M / r / is M. . . . . . . . . . . . . . . . . . . . . . . . . . | |
| | O hr am s . . . . . . . . . . . . . . . . . . . . . . . . . . | |
| b | A d e s. . . . . . . . . . . . . . . P s c d . . . . . . . . . . . | |
| c | T l p on  n m e . . . . . . . . . . . . . . . . . . . . . . . . . | |
| d | D t o br . . . . . . . . . . . . . . . . . . . . . . . . . . . | |
| e | N t oa  I srne o  R t rmn  P n in  N me (i a y) . . . . . . . . . . | |
| 2 | W a ar yo mi nes fr ate to o spriin fo ohr P op I? . . . . | |
| 3 | W ti te nm ad drs o yu dco? . . . . . . . . . . . . . . . | |

#### L V N  A A  F O  H M

| | |
|---|---|
| 4 | D yu lv i a eieta hm nrig hm badn shol otl r smilr acmoai? O |
| | D yu ted a eieta clee o rsdni tann cus? YS O |
| I | Ys o ite o te o te bv qeton: |
| | We dd yu trt t lv i te comoai? |
| | De (prxmt l). . . . . . . . . . . . . . . . . . . . . . . . . . . |
| | Dd h lcl uhrt r Dsrc Hat A toiy arne te c omoain? YS O |
| | Dd hy rag t py n o te ot? YS O |
| | Gv te ae ad drs o ay atoiy novd ih ragn o pyn fr or acmoai . . . . . . . . . . . . . . . . . . . . . . . . . . . . |
| 5 | Aeo a optl nptet t rsn? YS O |
***

Groups then come together and make a list of strategies which are most helpful to people with learning difficulties. The tutor can add in suggestions which don't come from the group. The list should include:

Clients with learning difficulties are most helped by:
(a)  being reassured they can take their time;
(b)  the use of paper and pen in complicated explanations—it is often easier to explain something with a drawing or a chart than in words;
(c)  dealing with a problem step by step, with the helper explaining what is being done.


TUTORIAL INPUT


2: The client who is over burdened

These clients may be emotionally or socially ill-equipped to deal with the pressures of their life. Their intellectual capacity is not lacking, but their emotional strength may be insuffiecient for them to manage. For some clients this will be a temporary state; for instance they may have experienced some shock or loss in the recent or distant past.

Or they may have experienced a bereavement and be suffering from grief reactions which could include physical feelings of distress (short breath, tight chest, choking sensation); an inability to maintain warmth in relationships; aloofness or irritability; restlessness and inattention; lack of capacity to initiate and keep up organized behaviour; feelings of unreality; preoccupation with image of the deceased person. Any change entails some loss, and bereavement symptoms are experienced by people who have lost their jobs, or their homes, a limb, familiar surroundings and so on.

Or they may be threatened with some impending change in which case they may be experiencing a great deal of emotional distress. In response to the realization of the impact of the threat they may become very emotional, perhaps hysterically weeping; or withdrawn and very cool and collected; they may suffer from a very restricted attention span, loss of memory; automatic, stereotyped behaviour. It is only after these first reactions are worked through that the person is more ready to face the situation and consider the options.

Very elderly clients may come into this group, for as they get older they may well experience a great deal of loss. There is the obvious fact that the people around them, their friends and relatives, may become ill or die. There is also the loss of youth, of a job and the status it brings, of faculties like sight and hearing, of mobility and so on. Old people as a rule have a very low status in society, they are not accorded the position of wise elders as in some other cultures. They often become lonely and depressed; and as time goes on they may begin to suffer from senile psychosis which is characterized by a gradual diminution of mental functioning.

People who are very depressed can also be hard to help. Depression can manifest itself as a feeling – that is the person feels a mixture of sadness, despair, guilt, shame, emptiness. It can carry with it certain behaviour, for example complaining, demanding, irritability, apathy. It can be a symptom of various conditions like a cold, a virus disease, a chronic illness which is disabling or disfiguring, some drugs (e.g. tranquillizers, barbiturates). Depression often affects the level of intellectual skill, which will drop. The person will only want to deal with immediate things.

Depressed people often discount themselves and their feelings; they sometimes wear an ironic smile which is a kind of defence. People who are depressed don't sound so much sad as flat — as if the feeling that usually colours our voices has literally been depressed.

Another state which is worth mentioning in this section is that of anxiety. Some people suffer from extreme anxiety, which is an unpleasant feeling of apprehension which sets in motion a chain of defensive processes, conscious and unconscious, which can lead to distressing symptoms. These symptoms can include dizziness, agitation, restlessness, palpitations, faintness, cold or hot flushes, hyperventilation, tenseness, accompanied by feelings of fear and worry. These feelings and symptoms can seriously impair the quality of life for that person, leading maybe to a very low tolerance for frustration, a clinging dependence, or chronic irritability.

*Exercise 25c:    Simulating Confusion*

As in the previous exercise, the purpose here is to simulate some of the real-life experience of a client who is affected by any of the above.

Give out to each person a quiz. The question should be either extremely difficult, or impossible—but on the surface the quiz should look manageable. Here is an example paper:

*Please answer each question in order in the time given.*
*Do not leave any question unanswered.*
  1.   Multiply 17524 by 71524 by 715.5 (Do not use a calculator)
  2.   What is The International View?
  3.   What is the connection between a telephone, an orange and a cup?
  4.   For what was Sir Anthony Gaunt famous?
  5.   Define Angellexemia.
  6.   Explain the supplementary benefit system in no more than 15 words?
  7.   What is the link between Freud, Lord Carbuton, and Sir Edward Penton?
  8.   What would a brandolian be use for?
  9.   What famous picture is on exhibition at the Dulwich Picture Gallery?
  10.   What is a structuralist interview?

Tension can be created by hurrying the participants along, telling them that others have found it very easy, etc.

After about 5 minutes, stop the exercise and go around the group asking each person to say one sentence which describes how they have been feeling. Many of the contributions will mirror the experience of clients who are under extreme stress. For example, 'I was afraid that I would look stupid'; 'I was angry because I thought the whole thing was a con'; 'I was confused—it looked simple but I just couldn't make sense of it'; 'I wanted to beat the others, they all looked as if they were getting on really well.'

This exercise, like the previous one, can start a useful discussion on how stress can increase the difficulties that clients may already be experiencing.

*Exercise 25d:    Emotional Pressures*

After a brief input based on the various kinds of emotional pressures clients may experience, ask the group to suggest as many reasons as possible for these pressures occuring. Write down the suggestions on a flip chart as they come (5 minutes).

Then ask participants to divide into small groups. If there is a long list, give some items to each group and ask them to consider what would help clients most. The items can be divided out so that they are all considered (15–30 minutes). The group reconvenes and participants share the various suggestions. The tutor can add in any which have been missed.

The resulting lists should include:

*For clients who are bereaved*
Allow to talk.
Be empathetic rather than sympathetic.
Consider directing client to a self-help group, if appropriate.
Consider directing client to counselling, if appropriate.
Allow to cry, and express feelings of anger and guilt.

*For clients who are threatened by a sudden change in their environment*
Provide a supportive atmosphere.
Highlight the positive resources of client.
Encourage ventilation of feelings.
Encourage new ways of coping.
Direct to a self-help group if appropriate.

*For the older client*
Take your time.
Afford respect.

*For the depressed client*
Take things one step at a time.
Give the client opportunity to return.
Give praise and encouragement where appropriate.
Provide information or 'skill training' if the person is depressed through lack of self-confidence or knowledge.

*For the anxious client*
Breathe deeply and calmly, as the client may copy you (anxiety is often maintained by shallow breathing)
Deal with the problem – if that is what is causing the anxiety.
Create an atmosphere of calm acceptance.
Direct to any stress-reducing activity (therapy groups, yoga, relaxation, sport, etc.)

The next step is to ask the group to consider if they would have to change their methods of practice to incorporate these suggestions, and if so how they could go about it. This part of the exercise can be worked through in small groups, pairs or by participants working individually and then sharing their thoughts with the whole group.


TUTORIAL INPUT

3. The client who is mentally ill

Some mental illnesses cause people to withdraw into their own private world, and order their life by a set of beliefs not shared by others. Symptoms might be:

(1)  A train of thought which does not proceed in a logical and orderly way resulting in an inability to separate relevant from irrelevant material.
(2)  Reduced range of emotional reaction or inappropriate tone relating to what is being discussed.
(3)  Preoccupation with an idiosyncratic world-view. The client does not deal with the 'real world', and only understands her own rule of logic.
(4)  Hallucinating: seeing visions: hearing voices.
(5)  A belief that all or most people are hostile and out to persecute.
(6)  An absolute feeling of superiority.
(7)  An unerring pursuit of self-interest. Behaviour will range from being pleasant, where that gets the best result, to threatening or even criminal actions on occasion.

Although the medical profession uses specific classificatiion of mental disorders, there is no satisfactory definition that specifies precise boundaries for the concept of 'mental illness'. The disturbance in behaviour which leads to the diagnosis may be due to some organic malfunction, or to psychosocial stress.

The main task of a helper faced with someone who is acting irrationally is to maintain order in the interview, and judge what the problem is and whether help can be given.

*Exercise 25e:    The Meaning of Madness*

Write 'mental illness' as a heading on a flip chart, and ask the group to call out any words or phrases they associate. Discuss the implications of the list in the context of how we think about and react to mental disorder, the kind of point that might come out of the discussion society's changing perception of what is madness'. For instance, at one time in history (and still in some cultures) hearing voices and seeing visions was a sign of saintliness, now it is seen as a symptom of illness.

*Exercise 25f:    Clients with Mental Disorder*

Ask individual members of group to share their experiences in working with clients suffering from some mental disorder. Focus the disscussion on what the client may have been thinking and feeling, and share ideas regarding most effective interventions.

## TUTORIAL INPUT

Here are some strategies that may help during sessions with clients who come into this category. They are, of course, not hard-and-fast rules but they are useful guidelines.

(1)  Develop the skills of 'kind control'. Clients are often unnerved by their own lack of control and really want someone to provide a safe structure for them.
(2)  Interrupt a long or confused flow. 'Have you got a letter about that?' or 'Let me just make sure I've got this right', etc. Make the interruptions in the atmosphere of giving respect, 'It is important that I get this right.'
(3)  Sift what you can deal with from what you cannot. As far as possible ignore what you cannot deal with and concentrate on what is possible for you.

(4)   Support the 'healthy' part of the personality; give reward for appropriate behaviour.
(5)   Stay aware of these clients' high level of sensitivity to discount and slight.
(6)   Resist being drawn into any 'games'. Do not attack delusions directly; you can say that you see things differently. The basic task with any client is to discover:
Is there anything to be done?
What is it?
How can it be done?
(7)   The underlying messages you want to give to the client are:
I respect you.
I am interested in you.
I want to understand how you are experiencing your world.
I will help you if I can.
I am clear about what is and what is not possible for me to do.

*Exercise 25g:   Trigger Tapes on Working with Difficult Clients*

Make (or hire—see Section 6: Resources) some audio or video tapes showing very brief cameos of the kind of behaviour which participants find most difficult to handle. Use these to initiate discussions about the most helpful way to deal with the situation.

## SESSION 26: LOOKING AFTER YOURSELF

## Training objectives

(a)   To identify the effects on the helper of working with a difficult client.
(b)   To consider practical ways of providing support structures within the working environment.

TUTORIAL INPUT

This session is an important one, because although up to now we have been thinking about what is best for the client, after a particularly difficult interview the helper may be left feeling stressed and may be experiencing a range of distressing feelings. These kind of sessions are often very upsetting, and so it is useful if there is some support system for the helper.

*Exercise 26a:   Helping the Helpers*

In small groups, participants share a past experience of a difficult session. They then address the following questions:

After the session, how did I feel?
What did I do?
How did that help?
Is there anything else I could have done?

When the group reassembles they share the information they have gathered. This is a useful way of encouraging people to share their expertise. Some helpers will be working in an organization with a strong system of support; others will not. Those people who are responsible for creating their own support framework may appreciate an ideas exchange so that they can consider practical ways of setting up a system for themselves.

# Chapter 10
## Coping with Stress

### SESSION 27: WHAT IS STRESS?

### Training objectives

(a)    To introduce theories about the psychological and physiological results of stress.

(b)    To help participants identify their stress points.

### Issues for the trainer

Working with people can be stressful for a variety of reasons. Clients who are upset can transmit their distress to the helper. It is clear from the work we have already done that helping others demands a high level of concentration and awareness. Many helpers work in stressful conditions, for instance a high level of noise, physical discomfort, depressing surroundings, or constant interruptions. Some do not have a clear role or status in the organization for which they work. Then, of course, there is the weight of the client load, which in some cases is impossibly high.

Whatever the reasons, many 'people-carers' ask for help with managing their own stress and so sessions based on this are an important element in any continuing training programme.

This training has two themes; therapeutic and educational. The trainer has two main tasks; the first is to reassure people that the symptoms they may be experiencing are a natural reaction of their mind and body to too much (or too little) stress, and that by raising their awareness and understanding of the process they will be more able to control their reactions. The second is to help them learn techniques which will help them to do this.

This session will enable participants to increase their self-awareness and understanding of the causes and results of stress in their lives.

*Exercise 27a:    Sources of Stress*

Ask participants to make a personal list of stressful events in their lives at the moment, under the headings: *Recent events related to working life* (e.g. major changes in policies, increased work load/*Recent events related to personal life* (e.g. marriage; illness; moving house; death of family member)/*Daily work conditions* (e.g. too much or too little time; feedback only when performance is unsatisfactory; conflict between staff)/*Away from work conditions* (e.g. pollution; noise; concern over economy, politics, etc.). Emphasize that the list

Table 4

| Event | Value |
| --- | --- |
| Death of spouse | 100 |
| Divorce | 73 |
| Marital separation | 65 |
| Prison term | 63 |
| Death of close family member | 63 |
| Personal injury or illness | 53 |
| Marriage | 50 |
| Fired from work | 47 |
| Marital reconciliation | 45 |
| Retirement | 45 |
| Change in health of family member | 44 |
| Pregnancy | 40 |
| Sexual difficulties | 39 |
| Gain of a new family member | 39 |
| Business readjustment | 39 |
| Change of financial state | 38 |
| Death of a close friend | 37 |
| Change to different line of work | 36 |
| Change in number of arguments with spouse | 35 |
| Mortgage over £10,000 | 31 |
| Foreclosure of mortgage or loan | 30 |
| Change in responsibilities at work | 29 |
| Son or daughter leaving home | 29 |
| Trouble with in-laws | 29 |
| Outstanding personal achievement | 28 |
| Wife begins or stops work | 26 |
| Children begin or end school | 26 |
| Change in living conditions | 25 |
| Revision of personal habits | 24 |
| Trouble with boss | 23 |
| Change in work hours or conditions | 20 |
| Change in residence | 20 |
| Change in schools | 20 |
| Change in church activities | 19 |
| Change in recreation | 19 |
| Change in social activities | 18 |
| Mortgate or loan less than £10,000 | 17 |
| Change in sleeping habits | 15 |
| Change in number of family get-togethers | 15 |
| Change in eating habits | 15 |
| Vacation | 13 |
| Christmas | 12 |
| Minor violations of the law | 11 |

will remain private, so that people can feel free to include any events in their personal lives which may be affecting them. The list should be as comprehensive as possible, since although many people make strenuous efforts to keep their work lives separate, one will affect the other. After all, we have to take the same body and mind to work and then home again!

Invite participants to work in pairs, sharing their thoughts and feelings about the list they have made and noticing any themes or patterns that may emerge (15 minutes).

### Exercise 27b:   *Stressful Life Events*

Give out a handout based on Table 4. (This list is derived from research in 1967 by Thomas Holmes and Richard Rahe of Washington University, who interviewed over 5000 people and found a high degree of correlation between the onset of stress-related illlness and certain life events. Each event was then given a value which indicates the amount of stress it is capable of producing.) One way of using the table is to add up all the values of the events which have happened to you in the past year.

(1)     A score of less than 150 means that there is a 37 per cent probability of your becoming ill in the next two years.

(2)     A score of between 150 and 300 means there is a 51 percent probability of becoming ill in the next two years.

(3)     A score of over 300 means that there is an 80 percent probability of becoming ill in the next two years (10 minutes).

## TUTORIAL INPUT

If you decide to suggest that people add up their score, it is better to emphasize that people with a score of, say, 320 need not panic. This research was derived from an average American population some time ago. Times have changed and events which were very stressful at that time may no longer have such an effect. Any such table has to be taken from averages, and in all averages there are extremes. For example, a new job may be very stressful for someone who is extremely anxious, but only moderately stressful for someone who sees it as an exciting challenge. Another consideration is that modern thinking on this subject emphasizes the effect of our own perceptions; i.e. that events produce harmful stress only if we regard them as negative or unpleasant.

In spite of these cautions, the table is a useful general guide to stress levels, since it does clarify the fact that any change will cause some stress—even if the change is for the better.

People do often ignore the potential stress from quite ordinary life events and try to carry on as usual, without taking into account the possible build-up which may show itself some time later in some unpleasant symptom.

### Exercise 27c:   *Signs of Stress*

Ask participants to make up small groups five or six in each group) and discuss the signs and effects of stress which they themselves have experienced under these four headings: physical effects, emotional effects, effects on logical thinking and effects on behaviour.

These are examples of what they might come up with:

*Physical effects*    Stomach pain, trembling, shivering, palpitations, rapid pulse, dry mouth, sweating, tenseness in muscles, headache, sleeplessness, restlessness, loss of appetite.

*Emotional effects*    Feelings of distress, unhappiness, depression, despair, depression, frustration, fury, resentment, impatience, boredom, guilt, panic, fear, doubt.

*Effects on logical thinking*    Inability to analyse, mind racing, obsessional thinking, thoughts about suicide or murder, forgetfulness, misjudging situations, flashes of clear thinking.

*Effects on behaviour*    Avoidance of tasks, withdrawal, easily distracted, aggressive driving, smoking, drinking, shouting, crying, stammering, losing temper, loss of interest in life, increased dependence on others.

The discussion which follows should bring out a wide range of points of which these are some examples:

(1)    The similarities between the points raised by each group; that all human beings experience stress, and react in some fundamentally similar ways. It can be a great relief for some participants to realize that othe people have similar experiences to their own.

(2)    As well as similarities, the lists will show that different types and levels of stress affect people in different ways.

(3)    Stress can bring out some unexpected strengths and abilities.

(4)    Putting on a 'brave face' is admired in our culture, although often behind that bravery is an emotional turmoil. The 'being strong' ethic makes it difficult to ask for help. This is very much part of the culture in which some groups of helpers work (e.g. medicine, nursing, police) (20 minutes).


TUTORIAL INPUT

It is important to make a distinction between thoughts, feelings, and behaviour. By doing so the process of the stress response becomes clearer and so easier to intervene in or manage.

Thinking involves words and pictures; impressions and judgements. Thoughts are the words that go through our minds like 'I should have known better'; 'I'll never be able to . . .'; 'Help!'; 'I give up'; 'I can't cope'. Feelings are emotional responses such as sadness, love, happiness, excitement, grief, fear, anger, embarrassment. Behaviour is what we actually do as a result of thoughts and feelings.

This separation helps us avoid some common traps. For instance, it is sensible to make judgements about our behaviour because that is something we can change in the future. It is, however, not appropriate to judge ourselves for the feelings which are our automatic response to the stress on that occasion. Whatever we feel emotionally is OK, although the action we carry out as a result may or may not be acceptable. So it is reasonable to decide that shouting at the boss in a moment of extreme stress was not the wisest thing to have done and to decide to apologize or handle the situation another way should it arise again. It is not reasonable to feel guilty about the anger and frustration that led to the shouting.

Stress is created by our conscious or unconscious perception of threat. As soon as our brain perceives a threatening stimulus the autonomic nervous system comes into play with a response designed to ensure our survival. Simply, we prepare to fight or run away from the threat.

A hormone named adrenalin is released, which in turn raises the level of tension in the muscles. The heart pumps faster and more deeply, thus speeding up the supply of blood and oxygen to the muscles. There are changes in the tension of the bowel and bladder sphicter muscles, diversion of blood from the skin and internal organs to the limbs, the halting of activity in the stomach and an increase in sweating to cool the body. Blood pressure increases and the pupils of the eyes dilate. All these changes account for the physical sensations people describe; flushing, shaking, 'butterflies' in the stomach, tensing up, heart palpitations, sweating, dry mouth and so on.

All these changes are to prepare the body for fight or flight, and it was the evolution of this response which allowed animals to react automatically to danger. Obviously the response was evolved to deal with an essentially simple situation: a threat to life can only be dealt with by fighting or running away. But the need for human beings to prepare for a life-or-death struggle or a rapid escape has mostly disappeared as society has become more civilized. In most of the day-to-day threatening situations we face, we cannot run away or fight—we have to subdue our natural response.

Hence the build-up of stress, as the energy which has been created to deal with the threat remains largely undischarged.

Problems arise because evolution has provided us with a thinking conscious brain which allows us to perceive threats to our emotional well-being as well as threats of physical harm.

*Exercise 27d:  Identifying the Threat*

Ask the group to give as many examples of threats which can be experienced in our day-to-day living as they can think of. The list might include:

Loss of status; being ignored; being laughed at; rejection; crossing the road; being late; losing a job; and so on.

It will become clear that it is possible to perceive many threats in everyday life (5 minutes).

*Exercise 27e:   Escape Mechanisms*

Give the group an opportunity to share some examples of times when they have been under stress, and ask them to describe what they did to deal with the stress they experienced. If the group is large, the participants can work in small groups.

The discussion will indicate that there are certain categories of 'escape mechanisms' (20 minutes).

## TUTORIAL INPUT

Because stress can produce unpleasant physical and emotional symptoms, we develop ways of coping with it. We may take some *immediate action* or find some way of *moderating* the effects of the stress. Immediate action is doing something which will provide relief from stress in the short term, although may cause stress in the long term. It tends to be dramatic and unthinking, something done automatically to remove or lessen the stress. Examples would include walking out of meetings, leaving home, smashing china, hitting someone. The problem with this kind of action is that although it does alleviate the feelings of stress in the short term, it may well provide long-term problems.

### Exercise 27f:   Examples of Immediate Action

Ask the group to form quick 'buzz groups' and share some examples of immediate action that they remember they, or other people they know, have used (5 minutes).

Our attempts to moderate the unpleasant symptoms of stress also take different forms. We attempt to change our mood by using substances like alcohol, tranquillizers, nicotine, and caffeine. We engage in relaxation techniques and mediation; we control our diet. All these interventions effect us physically.

### Exercise 27g:   Examples of Moderating Action

Form another buzz group session, this time asking people to identify different ways of moderating the level of stress experienced (5 minutes).

## TUTORIAL INPUT

We also have a number of psychological defence mechanisms, originally identified and described by Freud. They are called displacement, repression, denial, rationalization, intellectualization and reaction formation.

*Displacement* is the redirection of activity into a different form. We probably have all been in the situation of expressing our anger to someone who is not actually involved in the stressful situation, but just happens to be 'in the firing line'. Some people displace their anger or frustration by playing some sport aggressively, or by digging the vegetable garden with great energy!

*Repression* is the covering up of stressful thoughts, perceptions and emotions from consciousness. Repression can lead to depression and anxiety. In a culture where the display of deep emotion is not easily accepted, many people do repress thoughts and feelings which would be better expressed. One example is where someone has suffered the bereavement of someone close. Friends and relatives may congratulate the mourner on how well he or she has adjusted to the loss, but it may be that the person is repressing the grief while trying to behave as if nothing has happend.

*Denial* means discounting the problem altogether. After all, one way of escaping from a stressful situation is to refuse to admit its existence. Someone who is very worried about the result of a particular meeting, for instance, might not attend or might walk out in the middle of the meeting, denying the importance of the event.

*Rationalization* means reasoning out an acceptable explanation for events. Although the reasoning is logical, it will not be accurate. Take the example of someone failing an examination. The person may decide that the questions were set unfairly and focused on material which had not been studied; or that the examiners were biased; or that the exams were set at a particularly difficult time. All of these explanations allow the person to avoid the possibility that he or she did not know enough to pass.

*Intellectualization* is a process by which people 'switch off' their emotional experience, so that they are detached from their feelings in situations where the feelings are potentially very painful. An example is the lawyer, faced with a procession of clients who are very distressed, who begins to see them as a series of intricate, intellectual problem-solving exercises rather than 'real' men and women.

*Reaction formation* is sometimes the result of repressed thoughts or feelings which get replaced by exaggerated versions of their opposites. Perhaps a counsellor with feelings of guilt about their own sexuality might react strongly towards clients who brings sexual problems seeing them as 'promiscuous' or 'irresponsible'.

*Exercise 27h:  Identifying Defence Mechanisms*

Ask the group to return to exercise 27e, and discuss in pairs how their own responses to stress may fit into any of these categories (10 minutes).

## SESSION 28: COPING WITH STRESS: PERSONAL SUPPORT NETWORK

## Training objectives

(a)     To introduce framework for monitoring a personal support system.
(b)     To provide opportunity for participants to reflect on their present support system.

## Issues for the trainer

So far the emphasis has been on the causes and the physical and emotional results of stress. The process of sharing experiences of stress is often greatly appreciated, particularly by people who have never had the chance to do so. However, to be of the greatest use this sharing should be followed by some practical work on how to control the negative effects of stress. The next sessions tackle this from two angles; the first with an exploration of personal support frameworks, and the second with a series of inputs and practice sessions on physiological approaches to lessening stress.

TUTORIAL INPUT

When we are under stress, one of the greatest resources we have is the network of people who can support us. Our personal support framework refers to the relationships we have with various people who can be relied upon to provide emotional help in times of need, and with whom feelings can be shared without fear of condemnation. Ideally, we have many support groups in our lives; family members, co-workers, members of our clubs, churches, recreational groups. In order to handle our stress we need to create an adequate support framework, and this session is an opportunity to explore where the strengths and gaps are in the network which exists at the moment.

*Exercise 28a:  Identifying Support Groups*

Brainstorm a list of all the groups or individuals which provide them with support (5 minutes).

There are six main functions that a good support network will serve:

(1)     *Accepting.* This person will actively listen without advice or making judge-

ments. Someone who will empathize as you share the joys of success and frustrations of failure, and who understands the value of letting off steam without minimizing the problem.

(2)   *Work-oriented support.* This person will be someone who is an expert in your field whose honesty and integrity you trust to provide you with honest and objective feedback.

(3)   *Work-oriented challenge.* Technical challenge will keep your skills sharp and help to avoid stagnation or boredom. The person who can do this for you must (a) be good enough at the job to be able to identify what could be improved, and (b) be willing to criticize constructively. You must know that the challenge is not intended to enhance the colleague's ego at your expense.

(4)   *Personal support.* This is someone who provides unconditional support even if not in total agreement with what you are doing. If this is not available at work, then you should be able to find it among your family and friends. Technical, task-oriented support and challenge generally comes from work colleagues; personal and emotional support is usually received from personal friends and family.

(5)   *Personal challenge.* Trusted family and friends can also offer emotional challenge which helps us to stretch and grow emotionally, to re-think and revise our attitudes and behaviours. Questions such as 'Are you sure you have explored all your options in this situation?' do not need to come from experts. Emotional challenge is not the same thing as nagging! This is offered as a constructive and supportive intervention, leaving us free to choose how to respond.

(6)   *Shared perceptions.* Physical reality is readily shared by those who agree that water from the sky is rain, and that a red traffic light means stop. Social reality is more difficult to define and so needs conscious sharing. For instance, you may think you're losing your ability to judge accurately when you are listening to someone who you think is speaking nonsense, but that others are applauding. If, at that moment, you catch another person's eye and exchange looks that suggest agreement about the speaker, a social reality has been shared, validating your self-perception in the process. The person who performs this function most effectively is one who shares priorities, values and views with you.


*Exercise 28b:   Personal Support Network*

The above input can be given as a short talk, or as a printed handout. The next stage is to ask people to consider the following questions in relation to themselves. They can be written on a flip chart, or given out as a 'question-naire'. Ask people to work on their own for about 10 minutes.

The following questions are aimed at helping you to differentiate the six functions of a personal support framework, and to explore how these functions are fulfilled (or could potentially be fulfilled) for you.

*Question 1*
By the side of each function write 'not at all important' or 'somewhat important' or 'extremely important'.
Accepting
Work-oriented support
Work-oriented challenge
Personal support

Personal challenge
Shared perceptions.

*Question 2*
By the side of each function write down the name of the person who is (or people who are) fulfilling this function for you. If you cannot think of anyone who is doing so at the moment, write down the name of anyone who might potentially fill the gap.

Then by the side of each name, write down whether they fulfil that function 'minimally', 'somewhat' or 'completely'.

When people have had time to complete their answers, ask them to work with a partner sharing thoughts and feeling which have arisen as a result (30 minutes).

*Variation*   If the group is a work team, the discussion can include ways in which they might provide more of the functions for each other.

# SESSION 29: PRACTICAL WAYS OF COPING WITH STRESS

## Training objectives

(a)      To make a list of ways of dealing with stress, and to differentiate between positive and negative methods.
(b)      To share information about any methods which are unfamiliar to any participants.

Issues for the trainer

By now, the group will be well aware of what is causing them stress. The session on personal support networks will have given them some ideas as to how they could use other people to help them. There are an enormous range of positive and practical ways of dealing with stress, and it is useful to have a session which allows people to share these. One result of this kind of session is that people get a lot of reassurance from the knowledge that there is such a variety of valid ways of dealing with their stress; much of it costing very little or nothing at all.

*Exercise 29a:   Coping with Stress*

Ask the group to brainstorm methods which they themselves have used to deal with stress. The tutor accepts any suggestions from the group and may add in ones which he or she knows about or has experienced. (3–5 minutes). When the suggestions run out, the group decide whether each suggestion is a positive or a negative way of dealing with stress and the tutor marks each suggestion with a '+' or a '−'.

These are the kinds of lists which are created:

*Less helpful ways of dealing with stress*
Escaping by mental flight; giving up; walking out; dependence on drugs, cigarettes, alcohol, valium, etc.; overeating; undereating; acting out; tiredness; emotional outbursts; self-pity; martyrdom; blaming others.

*More helpful ways of dealing with stress*
Using problem-solving model; setting goals; taking a break; going for a walk; having a bath; taking up a creative hobby like painting; playing sports; becoming more assertive; changing thinking habits; lowering expectations on self and others; counselling; relaxation; meditation; talking with a friend; having a treat; learning yoga; letting off steam harmlessly; listening to music; gardening; doing something different; ask 'How will this be important in 100 years from now?'.

The discussion will show that some methods of dealing with stress can be both positive and negative. For instance, running away or giving up may be the best thing to do in certain circumstances; taking drugs may be useful for temporary alleviation. What will become clear is that it is the ability and willingness of an individual to *decide* how to deal with the stress which is important. It is this ability to choose which moves the person from the feeling of powerlessness which is so distressing.

*Variation*    If this session is part of a longer workshop, one way of continuing to work from the lists is to add some columns to the list of helpful ways of dealing with stress, so that it looks like this:

*Methods of dealing with stress:*                        *Offers*         *Interest*
   (1)    Using problem-solving model
   (2)    Becoming more assertive
   (3)    Co-counselling
   (4)    Taking up painting, etc.

Group members, including the tutors, who have any experience or knowledge in any of the methods and are willing to pass that on to others, are encouraged to make an 'offer' by putting their initials in the appropriate offer column.

Any group members who would like to know a little more about any of the suggestions should sign the interest column (probably not more than five).

The four or five methods with most interest are then proposed as the content for the rest of the day (or longer).

Of course it needs to be made clear that what is offered is a 'taster' of information about each subject—not an intense workshop. This is a good way of helping people to share their knowledge and experience.

# SESSION 30: WAYS OF CONTROLLING STRESS

## Training objectives

To introduce theory and practice of a range of relaxation and meditation procedures.

## Issues for the trainer

Several examples of relaxation and meditation procedures are presented here. In a long course, the most effective way of using these is to present them at different points in the course. If there is not time for all of them, choose one example of each for participants to experience first-hand, and explain that there is a wide range of approaches, and that individuals usually find one approach more effective than the others.

## TUTORIAL INPUT

The aim of relaxation training is to build skills of body awareness and muscle control so that people can constantly be monitoring their state of tension and relax those muscles which are not needed to maintain whatever activity they are engaged in. This results in the freeing of energy for more productive physical and mental use.

Training means attending a relaxation training group where the leader will take participants through a relaxation procedure, so that their skills are built up through practice.

It is possible to make (or buy) tapes of relaxation scripts, and during this session we will experience three different types of procedures.

*Exercise 30a: Relaxation Techniques*

*Relaxation One.* This is a short relaxation (about 5 minutes) and can be used in all sorts of situations, like in a waiting room, or on a train journey, or in a rest between clients.

'Find a comfortable position, sitting with feet flat on the floor, hands by sides. . . . I'm going to count down from 10 to 0 and you'll be as relaxed as possible when I reach 0. . . . *Ten* . . . feel your body becoming heavy . . . sinking into the floor or chair. . . . *Nine* . . . Legs relaxed. . . . *Eight* . . . trunk relaxing. . . . *Seven.* . . . chest relaxed . . . breathing relaxed . . . and regular. . . . *Six* . . . arms feeling heavy . . . hands warming. . . . *Five* . . . shoulders and neck relaxed. . . . *Four* . . . head relaxed. . . . *Three* . . . jaw relaxed. . . . *Two* . . . . more and more relaxed . . . deeper and deeper. . . . *One* . . . more and more relaxed . . . the whole body is relaxed . . . peaceful. . . . *Zero* . . . deeply relaxed . . . peaceful . . . relaxed and alert . . . relaxed. . . . I'll count up to 10 again. When I reach 10, open your eyes, move your fingers and toes, stretch and take a couple of deep breaths. 0, 1, 2, 3, 4, 5, 6, 7, 8, 9, 10. Now treat yourself gently, and maintain as much as you can of this feeling of relaxation as you move about and carry on your activities.'

*Relaxation Two.* This is a yoga relaxation, which should take place lying flat on the back of a hard surface which enable the deepest level of relaxation. If you find this uncomfortable at first, use a small cushion under your head, back, knees or feet.

'Lie on the floor flat on the back, with feet about a foot apart, hands turned palms upwards and a few inches away from the body. Roll the head slowly from side to side and return to the middle, finding a comfortable place to rest.

Take a few deep breaths, using the diaphragm, the belly rising and falling, breathing in through the nose and out through the mouth. Imagine the in-breath is bringing in energy, the out-breath is blowing out tension.

Lift the right foot about nine inches from the floor and let is fall like a stone to the ground. Lift the left foot about nine inches from the floor and let it fall like a stone to the ground. Lift the right arm and let it fall, and the left arm and let it fall.

Put your awareness into each part of the body in turn, and tell yourself three times to relax that part. Like this: Feet . . . I'm relaxing my feet, I'm relaxing my feet, I'm relaxing my feet . . . lower legs . . . upper legs . . .

buttocks . . . pelvic muscles . . . lower back . . . abdomen . . . upper back . . . chest . . . shoulders . . . arms . . . neck . . . head . . .

Now the internal organs. Visualize each in turn and tell yourself three times to relax the muscles in that area. Like this: Pelvic organs; I am relaxing my pelvic organs, I am relaxing my pelvic organs, I am relaxing my pelvic organs. Intestines . . . kidneys . . . liver . . . stomach . . . lungs. . . . Allow your breathing to become light and rhythmic . . . heart . . . allow the heart rate to slow down . . . nervous system . . . eyes . . . brain . . .

The whole body is relaxed.

Allow your mind to slow down. Think of a calm lake. Allow your mind to become like the lake, calm, no ripples, peaceful. Feel the peace . . . calm . . . peace . . . hold the word 'peace' in your mind . . . peace . . . peace . . . .'

*Relaxation three.* This routine concentrations on the muscles of the face and hands. It is based on the idea that since the major part of the motor cortex of the brain is concerned with these areas, then developing the skill of relaxing them will make total relaxation easy.

'Find a place to lie flat on the floor on your back, or in a chair with your head supported . . . have your feet about a foot apart and your hands a few inches away from your side, palms upwards . . . take a couple of deep breaths, slowly breathing and exhaling gently . . . then let your breathing become gentle and relaxed . . . notice the points where your body touches the floor or the chair . . . let those points relax and let yourself sink into the floor or chair . . . let the back of your head relax . . . let your scalp relax . . . behind your ears . . . the top of your head . . . put your attention into your forehead . . . imagine the space between your hairline and eyebrows widening . . . let your forehead relax and become smooth . . . imagine the space between your eyebrows is widening . . . let this become relaxed and smooth . . . let your eyes rest gently in their sockets, not looking in any direction . . . floating . . . relaxing . . . let the skin on your cheeks relax . . . more and more relaxed . . . allow your tongue to rest gently behind your lower teeth, so it is not touching the top of your mouth . . . let your throat relax . . . you may want to swallow or yawn . . . allow your jaw to relax and feel your temples relaxing at the same time . . . let your mouth be open with the lips slightly apart or only just touching . . . feel your neck and shoulders relaxing . . . now put your attention into your right arm . . . let the upper arm relax . . . the lower arm . . . and imagine the skin on the palm of your right hand is warming and relaxing . . . imagine the capillaries opening and the blood warming the skin . . . the back of your right hand is warming and relaxing . . . the thumb . . . index finger . . . middle finger . . . right finger . . . little finger . . . the whole of your right hand is warm and relaxed . . . now put your attention into your left arm . . . let the upper left arm relax . . . the lower arm . . . and imagine the skin on the palm of your left hand is warming and relaxing . . . the back of your left hand . . . the thumb . . . the index finger . . . middle finger, ring finger . . . the whole of your left hand is warm and relaxed . . . feel your chest and upper back relaxing . . . your breathing . . . shallow and rhythmic . . . heart rate slowing down . . . and it's quite safe . . . more and more relaxed . . . the pelvis and buttocks are relaxed . . . the right leg is relaxed . . . the left leg is relaxed . . . the whole of your body is relaxed . . . the whole of your body is as relaxed as you want it to be . . . more and more relaxed . . . deeper and deeper . . . more and more relaxed . . . peaceful . . . relaxed . . . now your whole body is totally relaxed . . . no tension, just relaxed . . . peaceful . . . and you can use this method of relaxation whenever you choose . . . to relax and unwind . . . recharge your batteries . . . regain your energy . . . and alertness . . . when you're ready . . . move your fingers and toes gently . . . sit up slowly, treating yourself gently. Stretch your limbs and take a deep breath or two.'

## TUTORIAL INPUT

Meditation is a contemplative process which focuses the conscious mind away from day-to-day activities by concentrating on one's inner experience, or on an object or sound outside oneself. The effect is to produce a state of relaxed awareness.

### Exercise 30b:   Meditation Techniques

*Meditation One.*   Ask the participants to take up any comfortable position, and direct their attention to their thoughts, feelings, body sensations as they come into awareness. They should not actively try to think, or try not to think, but just acknowledge the thoughts they have, letting them come and go through the mind. Suggest that they notice any attempts to judge the thoughts, or to control the act of meditation, and allow themselves to return to the state of acceptance of the experience of mind and body.

This form of meditation can be carried out alone, or with others; at home or in the office, or in any break, and can take from 5 minutes to an hour.

*Meditation Two.*   Again taking up a comfortable position, ask people to direct their attention outside themselves, acknowledging the data arriving via the sense, what is heard, seen, felt, smelt—again with no judgement or attempt to control.

*Meditation Three.*   Sitting in a comfortable position, focus attention inwards on a sound, an image or a repeated phrase such as 'I am', 'Peace', 'I accept myself'. You can think (or say softly) the word 'I' on the in-breath and 'am' on the out-breath. If attention wanders, gently bring it back to the focus.

Another version is to focus on some object—a vase, a flower, a picture. The meditation can last from 5 minutes to an hour.

*Meditation Four.*   Choose some very ordinary activity, like untying a shoe lace, opening a letter, putting on a watch, and do it in slow motion taking at least 5 minutes to complete the task.

*Meditation Five.*   Sit comfortably, focus eyes on an object, just above eye level. After a while, let your eyes naturally close and keep your mind focused on some inner image.

### Exercise 30c:   Quick Relaxation

Here are some quick ways of providing relaxation for the senses:
For the short-term relief of eyestrain, close eyes, rub your palms together building up a warm sensation, and place them over your eyes, the heels of palm cupping both eyes, but not pressing too hard.

Close eyes and with fingertips gently massage your eyelids and eyeballs, without pressing too hard.

Relief for the ears can be obtained by placing tips of index fingers into the ears (not too deep!) then vibrating ears slowly by short back and forth movement of fingers. Do this for about 20-second periods, resting the ears for 30-second intervals.

Self-massage of neck, head and face provides relief from tension, and can be effectively energising.

*Exercise 30d:   Chucklebelly*

Laughter is a very effective way, and one of the most enjoyable ways, of discharging the tension arising from embarrassment, frustration or anxiety. In any session about coping with stress it is a good thing to encourage people to laugh. Here is one exercise that usually ends with everyone giggling uncontrollably! It is called 'Chucklebelly'.

Ask people to lie on the floor, each with their head resting on another's abdomen. The first person starts to laugh, and the laughter just spreads infectiously down the line!

## TUTORIAL INPUT

So far, this session has focused on techniques which give relief from the main symptoms of tension and stress—however, concentrating on the symptoms will not really solve the long-term problems. To address the actual sources of the stress requires a willingness to examine what it is about our present lifestyle which may be the cause.

Here is an exercise which may help as a beginning to the exploration which is clearly important if major changes are to be made.

One of the greatest sources of stress is living a lifestyle unsuitable for your nature or goals. It is useful to consider as many aspects of your lifestyle as possible. This includes line of work, choice of intimate partnerships, where you live, what you choose to do with your free time, the image you project, the people you mix with, the places you frequent and the manner in which you do things.

One way of decreasing stress is to get your lifestyle compatible with your nature and temperament. The more you know about yourself, the more able you will be to ensure you are meeting your own particular needs and wants.

*Exercise 30e:   Changing Lifestyles*

Give out to the group this questionnaire, giving participants an opportunity to work on it privately. They can then discuss their reaction to the question-naire in pairs, or in small groups. This exercise can be a useful trigger for an exercise in which participants go on to develop specific action plans for themselves.

(1)      Am I happy with my close relationships? If not, how could I improve their quality?

(2)      Do I look and act the way I really want to, or have I conditioned myself into a mould to please other people?

(3)      Do I enjoy my line of work? If I could choose any career, would it be this one?

(4)      Who are my real friends? How do they affect my behaviour? Do I feel better when I am around them? Do they really encourage me to be true to my best self?

(5)      How do I use my free time? How many of those hours do I actually

spend watching television? How much of that entertainment really
satisfies and pleases me? How much of my time is spent in ways that
leave me feeling satisfied and happy?

(6)     What have I done to improve the world? Does my entire life centre
around 'me'?

(7)     Am I happy with my financial status? What do I actually need to
satisfy my basic needs? If I have too little, what are the options?

(8)     Is there a purpose to my life? Do I know why I'm here on this planet,
or where I'm going?

## Issues for the tutor

Obviously, these questions can lead to very personal, and possibly painful, realiz-
ations. Participants may want to share the thoughts and feelings which arise as a
result of the questionnaire, or they may prefer to keep their responses private. It
is a useful exercise in any course in which the intention is to encourage participants
to a greater self-awareness, such as a counselling course.

## SESSION 31: IDENTIFYING AND REDUCING STRESS

## Training objectives

(a)     To describe five patterns of stress behaviour, relating them to the Transactional Analysis theory of 'drivers'.

(b)     To provide exercise whereby participants can identify their drivers.

(c)     To discuss the implications of this theory.

### TUTORIAL INPUT

So far these sessions have concentrated on helping participants to identify their
stress and to work on reducing the effects. However, it is also helpful to have some
framework for identifying stress in other people and knowledge as to how to go
about reducing the stress for them.

The framework that we have chosen is taken from Transactional Analysis, and has
developed from the idea that each person creates his or her own life story. Eric
Berne, the creator of Transactional Analysis, and his co-workers, believed that the
story begins at birth, and is created out of the all the experiences that affect the
growing child. As a result of these experiences the child develops a 'script' which
becomes a life-plan. Taibi Kahler, a clinical psychologist, followed Berne's idea that
the script can be played out repetitively over very short time periods, and noticed
that there were certain distinctive sets of behaviours which people seemed to move
into just before they moved into 'script' behaviour. He studied these in depth and
listed five of these behaviour sequences which he called 'driver'.

The significance of these for reducing stress is that, because under stress it is
difficult for us to remain autonomous, those are the times when we fall into the
behaviour determined by our life script—that is repetitive patterns of thinking,
feeling and acting which were developed by us as a response to our early life
experiences.

*Exercise 31a:    The Beginnings of Stress*

Ask participants to remember a time when they were under stress and ask
them to note down, or discuss with a partner, exactly what they thought,
felt and did as a result. When they have done this, ask them to think about
how familiar that pattern of thinking, feeling and acting is for them. And then
ask when was the first time they remember being that way.

As a result of that exercise, people will identify that they tend to fall into
predictable patterns as a response to stress, and that these patterns may have
developed a long time ago.

Each driver can be detected by observing a person's behaviour and by noticing
that person's words, gestures, tone, etc. The five drivers are:

Be Perfect
Please
Try Hard
Be Strong
Hurry Up

An important aspect of the way our life script develops is that parents (and any
other important figures of authority in relationship to the child) transmit values and
standards to a growing child in a variety of ways. They may give direct instructions
('You must be kind and considerate to others'); they may model the behaviour
(Mother looks after the needs of family members); they may deprive or reward the
child for certain behaviour (the child receives more smiles and hugs for certain
types of behaviour). However, they are transmitted, children are not able to
understand the subtleties of these messages. They do not have the cognitive ability
to reflect upon, and examine in depth, the messages they are receiving. The young
child is likely to receive any 'message' as a 'rule'. The child believes that she *must*
do (or not do) whatever is being transmitted at the time. In time these rules can
become crystallized into rigid patterns of thinking, feeling and acting, which will
emerge under stress (Table 5). When we are not stressed we can decide whether
the messages we carry in our head are appropriate for the present moment. But
when we are under stress we feel as if we are driven by these rules. It seems as if
we will only survive if we can be perfect/please/be strong/try hard/hurry up.

*Exercise 31b:    Driver Questionnaire*

Give participants this quiz to complete. (Taken from a questionnaire
designed by Mary Cox M.Ed. ITAPM.)

This questionnaire is not a 'personality test'. It is intended to stimulate your
self awareness and indicate the kind of stress behaviour you may typically
or frequently get into. Answer questions 'yes', 'no' or 'to some extent'.

(1)    Do you set yourself high standards and then criticize yourself for
       failing to meet them?
(2)    Is it important to you to be *right*?
(3)    Do you feel discomforted (e.g. annoyed, irritated) by small messes or
       discrepancies such as a spot on a garment or the wallpaper, an
       ornament or a tool out of place, a disorderly presentation of work.
(4)    Do you hate to be interrupted?
(5)    Do you like to explain things in detail and precisely?
(6)    Do you do things (especially for others) that you don't really want
       to?

Table 5

| Values | Result in messages | which result in drivers |
|---|---|---|
| Achievement; autonomy success; being right | Don't make a mistake; take risks; don't be natural childlike | Be Perfect |
| Consideration; kindness; service | Don't be assertive, important different, say 'no' | Please |
| Courage; strength; reliability | Don't show your feelings; don't give in; don't ask for help | Be Strong |
| Persistance; patience; determination | Keep trying; don't be satisfied; don't relax | Try Hard |
| Speed; efficiency; responsiveness | Don't take long; don't think; don't relax; don't waste time | Hurry Up |

(7)   Is it important to you to be *liked?*
(8)   Are you fairly easily persuaded?
(9)   Do you dislike being 'different'?
(10)  Do you dislike conflict?
(11)  Do you have a tendency to do a lot of things simultaneously?
(12)  Would you describe yourself as 'quick' and find yourself getting impatient with others?
(13)  Do you tend to talk at the same time as others, or finish their sentences for them?
(14)  Do you like to 'get on with the job' rather than talk about it?
(15)  Do you set unrealistic time limits (especially too short?)
(16)  Do you hide or control your feelings?
(17)  Are you reluctant to ask for help?
(18)  Do you have a tendency to put yourself (or find yourself) in the position of being depended upon?
(19)  Do you have a tendency not to realize how tired, or hungry, or ill you are, but instead 'keep going'?
(20)  Do you prefer to do things on your own?
(21)  Do you hate 'giving up' or 'giving in', always hoping that this time it will work?
(22)  Do you have a tendency to start things and not finish them?
(23)  Do you tend to compare yourself (or your performance) with others and feel inferior or superior accordingly?
(24)  Do you find yourself going round in circles with a problem, feeling stuck but unable to let go of it?
(25)  Do you have a tendency to be 'the rebel' or 'odd one out' in a group?

When participants have completed the quiz, show them how the scoring works: 1 mark for 'yes'; ½ mark for 'to some extent'; no mark for 'no'.

Questions   1–5   = Be Perfect
            6–10  = Please
            11–15 = Hurry up
            16–20 = Be Strong
            21–25 = Try Hard

A score of 3 or more in any section indicates a tendency towards that particular driver. Most people experience all the drivers at different times, but generally people do have two or three drivers which crop up regularly.

The results of the quiz can be discussed in general terms by the whole group, or more personally in pairs. It is important to point out that there are hundreds of ways of reacting to a driver and that this is what gives us our uniqueness, even though in very general ways we can identify our similarities.

## TUTORIAL INPUT

Mavis Klein, a British psychotherapist, has developed even more detailed ideas about the effect of each driver on our behaviour, and we will use her ideas in this session. We will consider each driver in turn; identifying the behaviour which is linked to it and the kinds of interventions which will help to decrease the stress both for oneself and other people. The suggestions for reducing one's own stress imply the willingness to accept responsibility for engaging in change that may mean long-term effort.

# Stress and the five drivers

## BE PERFECT

*Language and appearance clues*: these words and phrases are often used by people when they are in the grip of a Be Perfect driver: 'as it were', 'probably', 'possibly', 'certainly', 'completely', 'one might say'. They speak in completed sentences, perhaps numbering off various points. Their dress is usually very co-ordinated and elegant. Their language and their appearance are all indications of their desire to be perfect.

*Characteristics*: each driver carries positive characteristics, as well as negative ones, and persons influenced by this driver will be purposeful, moral and have very high standards. They will be task-oriented and extremely logical, and very good at seeing the best way of achieving the success or completion of a task.

*Stress caused by*: anything which indicates the danger of loss of control: for instance other people's perceived 'low' standards or illogicality: over-emotionalism from other people; failure to achieve goals.

*Stress behaviour*: as the stress increases, the person will become more and more single-minded, seeing only their own point of view. They will become more and more controlling. They may become very arrogant and aggressive in arguments and will not be able to take account of other people's different views. They will be focused on the goal and so may discount the people around. The will communicate predominantly in 'thought' language—and be very uncomfortable at displays of extreme emotion.

*Ways of reducing of the pattern of stress in self*:
(1)    Be willing to appreciate different values held by other people, rather than just seeing your own as valuable.
(2)    List down all your personal values and givev them a rating, with a high mark for the most important and lower marks as their importance decreases. Then work out how to respond appropriately. When under stress the tendency is to treat everything as important and so energy is poured into issues that are actually in themselves not important.
(3)    Become more conscious of your tendency to be self-righteous and to respond to people in a parental manner, and make a point of communicating your feelings.
(4)    Be willing to laugh at yourself.

*Helping to reduce stress in others*: these are the kind of interventions which will help to reduce the stress in someone who is responding to their Be Perfect driver.

(1)    Reassurance that they 'are not to blame'.
(2)    Be punctual and keep agreements with them.
(3)    Never discount their worries.
(4)    If you have a difference of opinion express your own values with conviction.
(5)    If you have to confront them, do it gently, firmly and calmly.
(6)    Show appreciation of their achievements, e.g. 'That report you produced is excellent.'
(7)    Give them the facts, rather than forcing them to talk about their emotions.

## BE STRONG

*Language and appearance clues*: the Be Strong is concerned with not appearing vulnerable, so language tends to be distanced from feelings. 'That makes me sad', rather than 'I feel sad'. Words like one, you, we, it are used to replace I. Face and body tend to be immobile—another indication of the urge to hide any evidence of feelings which may mean weakness.

*Characteristics*: the Be Strong driver carries characteristics like self-sufficiency, helpfulness, reliability. People who have a dominant 'Be Strong' driver enjoy tasks which are repetitive and like working on their own. They are extremely stoical in the face of difficulties and will carry on regardless.

*Stress caused by*: the fear of rejection through being seen as vulnerable; being 'forced' to say what they feel; exposing their weaknesses.

*Stress behaviour*: when under stress the Be Strong driver leads to rather withdrawn, withholding behaviour. The person becomes quieter and quieter and reluctant to communicate. It is as if every word has to be dragged out. The conversation tends to sound this way. 'I there anything wrong?' 'No', 'Are you sure?' No answer. 'I can see something is wrong—what is it?' No answer. The questioner becomes more like an interrogator, trying to get a response.

*Ways of reducing the stress pattern in self*: learn to take as well as give. The Be Strong are generous givers—always ready to help—it is as if by being this way they will never have to reveal their own needs. Even up the balance, so that you are not covering your own needs, and be willing to express them.

*Helping to reduce stress in others*
(1)     Praise them for consideration and kindness, because they often get taken for granted.
(2)     Give them a surprise treat.
(3)     Do not be effusive.
(4)     Use irony; 'I must say—you are the *most* unreliable person!'
(5)     Don't force them into expressions of vulnerability.
(6)     Don't shout, for they will retreat even further.
(7)     If you want something done, give them clear instructions. Tell them exactly what you want done. e.g. 'I woud like this report typed on A4 sheets, with all the corrections as marked. Please let me have it on Friday morning, and if there are any problems telephone me to discuss them.'

## PLEASE

*Language and appearance clues*: a characteristic language pattern is to start off a sentence positively and end it negatively, e.g. 'It really is a wonderful day, but these kind of days often end in rain.' 'This is a really good course, but I don't know how I'm going to remember everything.' Statements are turned into questions by phrases like, 'Is that OK with you?'; . . . kind of . . . ?'; 'What do you think about . . . ?'. The tone of voice is often high, rising at the end of each sentence. The person with a strong Please driver will make a lot of effort to look attractive and dress 'prettily' rather than neatly, wearing jewellry and perfume to complete the effect.

*Characteristics*: the person with a strong Please driver loves spending time with other people, and is comfortable in social situations. They are usually skilled in dealing with others, and like to look after people. They are as pleasant as possible to everyone; are extremely law-abiding and helpful; concerned with doing the right thing.

*Distress caused by*: being ignored; being criticized; their fear is that they will be rejected by being found 'blameworthy'.

*Stress behaviour*: these persons will become more and more emotional, and will not respond to demands to 'be logical'. Their language becomes peppered with clichés, and if the stress increases they will be unable to say 'no' to anyone. One of the most destructive aspects of this stress pattern is the urge to rescue anyone and everyone. Obviously if there is an emergency then taking charge is often the wisest thing to do. If there is no emergency, then rescuing (which is defined as doing something which has not been asked for, or doing more than your share) will in the long term not really help the other person. Every time you do something for someone, that person is deprived of the opportunity to do it himself or herself and learn from that action.

*Ways of reducing stress pattern in self*:
(1)     The person with a strong Please driver does feel responsible for other people, and expects them to reciprocate by taking responsibility for their well-being. So in order to break through this it is important to be willing to accept responsibility for what happens to you and what you do to others.
(2)     Listen carefully to others, and respond to what they are actually saying, rather than to what you believe they want.
(3)     Develop autonomy.

*Helping to reduce stress in others*:
(1)     Thank them politely for their help.
(2)     Stay near the surface of communication, unless you are able and willing to cope with the amount of emotion which may be uncovered.
(3)     Never lose your temper.
(4)     If you are angry, express your feelings politely.
(5)     If you have to confront them, do it with patience.
(6)     Give no strokes for clichés; stroke abundantly for authentic communication.
(7)     Provide them with a model by letting them see your autonomous response.
(8)     Acknowledge them for being the person they are. 'I really enjoy working with you'; 'It's lovely having you in the team.' This is different from the acknowledgement for the Be Perfect, which is primarily for what they have achieved. If you say 'That report you did was really good,' the Please person will be thinking, 'But does she really *like* me?'

## TRY HARD

*Language and appearance clues*: often the person in a Try Hard driver will use the word 'try'. 'Yes, I'll try to get it finished'; 'I am trying my best . . . '. When it is used in this way it usually means 'I'll try to do it instead of actually doing it.' Other typical words and phrases are: can't, I don't understand, it's very difficult . . . . Often the person appears very tense, maybe frowning or with fists clenched.

*Characteristics*: intense and committed to righting wrongs; usually on the side of the underdog and is often a worker for political or other causes; passionate; takes on lots of tasks—often doesn't complete them; sets high goals—often not achieved; very hard worker.

*Distress caused by*: being criticized for not caring or for being irresponsible; being told 'You're not trying'; for perceived irresponsibility in others.

*Stress behaviour*: one of the main effects is that much effort goes into trying—but very little is achieved. Lots of tasks may be taken on, and promises be made—but something always seems to get in the way of a success. One of the problems for someone with a Try Hard driver is that if their belief is that they are only acceptable if they try hard, how will they be able to survive when they have succeeded! It is as if it becomes more important to go on trying than to finish. The person tends to move into reactive, rebellious behaviour.

*Ways of reducing pattern of stress in self*:
(1)     Notice how often you use the word 'Try'—say instead 'I will' or 'I won't'.
(2)     Before you take on extra work—check that it is realistic for you to do so. If your schedule is full, decide what you will give up in order to take on the new job. Check also that you want to do it as opposed to believing that you ought to.
(3)     Be willing to distinguish between things you can and cannot change.
(4)     Stop comparing yourself to others.
(5)     Create standards for yourself which are not related to others.
(6)     Start *now*—not tomorrow.

*Helping to reduce stress in others*: If the person is being very competitive, ignore it. Don't get involved in arguments which are focused on comparisons, e.g. 'You don't understand as much as I do'; 'They are not working hard enough.'
(1)     Never let them off what they committed themselves to do. If you do, the implication is that you don't expect them to succeed.
(2)     Do not stroke for trying; stroke for finishing.


## HURRY UP

*Language and appearance clues*: words and phrases like: quick, get going, hurry up, don't waste time, there's no time to . . . . The overriding impression of someone in the grip of a Hurry Up driver is that they are in a hurry! They may speak very rapidly, and will usually be doing more than one thing at a time. Gestures like finger-tapping, foot tapping, wriggling about in the chair, constant checking of watch are also indications.

*Characteristics*: this person will be lively; adventurous; excited; often described as the 'life and soul of the party'; enthusiastic; quick with a capacity for doing lots of things at once.

*Distress caused by*: time to think; silence; having 'nothing to do'.

*Stress behaviour*: as the stress increases activity will become more and more frenetic.

*Reduction of stress in self*:
(1)     Learn to love life for its own sake, so that the fear that life has no meaning is less threatening.
(2)     A greater feeling of security will arise if you develop a belief system.
(3)     Realize that you do not need to earn love by proving how much you can do.
(4)     Practise your empathy and listening skills.
(5)     Be on time by not fitting in 'just one more thing' before your appointment.
(6)     Make the time to express appreciation of other people.
(7)     Make lists; create structures and order despite how you feel about them.

*Helping to reduce pattern of stress in others:*
(1)     Praise for efficiency.
(2)     Enjoy their spontaneity.
(3)     Never be intimidated by their outbursts.
(4)     Don't stroke for speed; or for the ability to do several things at once.
(5)     Stroke for taking time. 'I really appreciate how much time you are giving to this'; 'Take as much time as you need'; 'It's good to see you slowing down.'

### Exercise 31c:    Back Seat Driving

Divide the group into trios. Ask them to decide who will be 'talker', who will be 'listener' and who 'observer'. The 'talker' should then talk to the 'listener' for 3 minutes on any light topic. The topics can be drawn out of a hat if people find it difficult to think up something. The listener listener listens and responds in any way he or she wishes. The observer, with pen and paper, notes down which drivers can be detected in the behaviour of talker and listener. When the 3 minutes is up, the observer feeds back what driver clues were noticed. Switch the roles round so that everyone has a turn.

### Exercise 31d:    Motivating Others

Ask participants to write down the names of five people with whom they are in close contact (managers should list five members of staff).

Then ask them to note beside each name the last time they gave each one some attention, what they said or did. Then note what it was that prompted the attention and what the response of the recipient was.

Then, in pairs, participants should help each other to identify possible driver behaviour, in themselves and the people they chose to write about.

### Exercise 31e:    What's the Problem?

This is a good exercise for finishing a course on stress, because it can pull together the different strands of learning. Ask participants to work in pairs, and think of a typical stressful situation. When they have chosen one they should compose a letter as if they were writing to a problem page (15 minutes). Collect the 'letters', and then distribute them so that each pair gets a different letter from the one they wrote. Their next task is to devise a reply as if they were editor (20 minutes).

The various problems and replies can be read out for the group to discuss at the end of the exercise.

### Exercise 31f:    Action Plan

Another exercise for winding up a course which encourages people to think about their own personal situations. Ask each person to spend some time listing changes he or she might make in order to lessen the amount of stress they are experiencing (10 minutes). Participants can then work in pairs, or small groups, to discuss with each other the best strategies for making the changes. Each person then will write a set of goals for the immediate future.

# Chapter 11
## Endings

### SESSION 32:   ENDING THE COURSE

## Training objectives

(a)   To enable participants to evaluate the course.
(b)   To provide a structure for participants to give feedback to each other.
(c)   To help participants to clarify any action they wish to take as a result of the course.
(d)   To end the course.

## Issues for the trainer

Endings can be difficult. Sometimes there is the temptation to finish quickly particularly if, as if often the case, everyone is tired. It is worth taking time, though, over this stage because a positive and constructive course ending provides a good model for this stage in the helping process itself. For instance, helpers often talk about the difficulty of ending interviews without appearing rude or rejecting. If they are engaged in a long-term helping relationship, then the problem may be recognizing when it should be drawing to a close and helping the client to complete the process.

There are three functions to be addressed by the finishing of a course—which can be related to past, present and future.

PAST

As the course finishes it becomes part of past experience, and it is important for the participants to have an opportunity to evaluate its effect and helpfulness in terms of their investment of time, energy and money. This means looking back over the course, perhaps referring to the hopes and fears which may have been expressed at the beginning, and assessing how far the objectives have been met.

This process is obviously important for the trainer, too, since there may be useful information in the feedback relating to future course design.

## PRESENT

Participants on the course will have made relationships, had experiences which may have been pleasant and/or painful, received insights about themselves or their practice, and as a result will be experiencing thoughts and feelings. The ending of the course should give people an opportunity to express what they are thinking and feeling, to ask any questions which have remained unanswered, to deal with any unfinished business and to say goodbye to the other participants.

## FUTURE

If the course is to be more than a holiday away from work, there must be some opportunity for people to relate what they have learnt to their everyday lives. Another function of a good ending is to help participants to develop an action plan which will allow them to put some of the new learning into practice.

It is important to plan time for an ending session into the programme design, otherwise the process will be rushed and superficial.

Here are a range of exercises from which you can select those most appropriate to the kind of course you are running.

## Evaluation structures: 'The past'

These exercises can be used in conjunction with the evaluation structures described in Chapter 1 under the heading Evaluation of Training (page 18).

*Exercise 32a:   Evaluating the Course*

Ask participants to complete in writing the answers to these two questions, which are written on a flip chart.

'What I have learned as a result of attending this course is . . .'
'What I would have preferred to have been different is . . .' (5 minutes).

Participants may prefer to write their evaluations anonymously.

*Variation*   With participants sitting in a circle, go around so that each person says one thing learnt as a result of attending the course, and then one thing he or she wishes had been different (10 minutes).

*Exercise 32b:   Evaluation Review*

Ask participants to work in small groups (three or four people in a group) and to review the programme of the course session by session. One person can then make a brief report of the salient points. This is a useful structure for participants who may feel reluctant to make their points in the larger group. (Timing depends on the length of the course, and the number of groups.)

*Exercise 32c:    Assessment Checklist*

Ask participants to imagine they have been asked to compile a checklist of good helping practice for new workers in their profession or oganization, and to work in small groups on this (15 minutes). Each group will present its ideas to the rest.

This kind of exercise is a good way of assessing how much the group have remembered, and gives the trainer an opportunity to remind them of any salient points which they may have forgotten.

*Exercise 32d:    Course Journey*

Ask participants to close their eyes, and picture themselves in a car looking through the rearview mirror which is reflecting the progress of the course they have just done. Give them time to go over that road in their imagination, identifying the landmarks.

*Exercise 32e:    Progress Picture*

Each person takes a large sheet of blank paper and some coloured thick felt pens. Ask each person to represent their progress during the course, in any way they want, but without using words. Examples of how this has been done include: the course as a game of 'snakes and ladders'; a voyage through sometimes stormy, sometimes calm seas; a mountain climb; a tree with some withered branches and some new strong roots—and so on (10 minutes)

If there is time each person could show the drawing, or there can be a general discussion on the process.

# Feedback: 'The Present'

---

*Exercise 32f:    Feedback Circle*

Go around the circle giving participants space to say what they got from the session and how they are feeling now. This will give people a chance to express any good feelings or resentments which have arisen during the course.

*Variation*    Individuals say, in turn, what or who they have resented during the course, for example: 'I resent the way you interrupted me when . . .'; 'I resent the fact that I didn't get a chance to give my opinion . . .', *followed by participants saying what or who they have appreciated*, for example, 'I appreciate the suggestions you made . . .', 'I appreciate your openness when you talked about . . .'.

*Exercise 32g:    Goodbye Messages*

This is a good exercise to help a group who have been together for a substantial amount of time to give each other feedback.

Give each person a blank piece of card (about A5 size) and a safety pin, and let each one ask someone to pin the card on to his or her back. Each person then goes around writing 'goodbye' messages on the cards.

When the exercise is ended, people can take off their cards and read the messages.

*Variation*   Participants sit in a circle and write their name on a blank sheet of paper. The paper is then passed on to the person on their left, who writes a message to them. The paper is folded over, so that only the name is visible and passed on again. In this fashion the paper gets passed round the whole group, so that eventually each person gets his or her own paper which will have messages on it from everyone.

## Action Plans:   'The Future'

*Exercise 32h:   Future Plans*

Ask all participants to write down at least two things they will do differently as a result of the course.

If time permits, and the group is not too large, each person can share one of his or her decisions. This will give the trainer a chance to check that people are setting themselves specific and realistic goals.

*Variation*   Ask participants to share their goals with each other, and when they have done that, ask them to make some arrangment to contact each other at some appropriate time in the future so that they can check on how the various tasks are proceeding.

*Exercise 32i:   Problem Solving*

Ask participants to identify one problem they are currently facing, and to consider how they might use what they have learned during the course to manage this problem better. They can either write down their thoughts, or share them with a partner. If there is time, the ideas can be shared with the whole group.

*Exercise 32j:   Ccontinued Learning*

Run a brainstorm exercise on any ways that participants can think of continuing the learning of the course. Such a list might include: reading; meeting as a group on a regular basis; booking for other training courses; through supervision; devising personal monitoring frameworks: and so on.

## And finally

Here are some fun exercises which can end the course on a note of laughter and comradeship:

### Exercise 32k:   Group Hug

The group should sit, stand or kneel in a circle and hug each other in a 'group hug'.

### Exercise 32l:   Group Squeeze

The group stands in a circle and holds hands, passing a 'squeeze' round the circle.

### Exercise 32m:   Handshake

Everyone shakes hands with everyone else, saying to each person 'What I've liked about meeting you is . . .' or 'What I've liked about this course is . . .' or some similar phrase.

### Exercise 32n:   Group Name

Ask participants to break into pairs and create a name for the group. Say that the name should catch something of the essence of the group's activity as well as being snappy and, perhaps, witty. The pairs are given only 2 minutes to do this.

Then each pair is asked to join with another pair and blend their two names together. Allow 2 minutes only again.

Each quartet joins with another quartet and so on. The final outcome of the exercise is one name which is a synthesis of all the names.

The exercise should be done quickly and the time kept rigidly.

# SECTION 4
Training Techniques

# Chapter 12
## Working With Groups: Theory

Creating a fertile environment for participative learning requires group work skills. Moving away from the lecturing approach means moving towards the group and working together with them to provide the learning they require.

By taking a group work approach, the trainer will be:

(1) Utilizing the experience, opinions and knowledge of group members. In most training groups there is a wealth of experience and knowledge which can be substantial resource to draw on.

(2) Providing a forum for sharing ideas and opinions as well as the exploration and development of options.

(3) Creating a source of mutual enjoyment and support which will enhance the experience and learning of the participants.

(4) Involving each person in the group actively in the learning process.

Working with a group requires some understanding of how individuals are affected by being in a group, and how they can be encouraged to participate and learn in that situation. The trainer has two responsibilities; one is to ensure that the objectives are met — that the *task* is done; and the other is to *maintain* the kind of atmosphere that will allow this to happen.

Different interventions contribute to the task and the *maintenance* functions we have identified. *Task-related* interventions help to get the job done and are largely concerned with the content of the training. *Maintenance-related* contributions are more concerned with the functioning of the group. They take account of the individual emotional needs of the group members which should too be considered if the group is to find some way of working together effectively.

These two functions are both contrasting and complementary. For instance, without individuals assuming responsibility for the task the group would not be able to meet its objectives. The group may have an enjoyable time and create a great feeling of comradeship, but it probably would not get the job done! On the other hand, if there is no concern for maintenance the result may be that the lack of warmth and concern will impair the group's ability to work as a cooperative unit, which will in turn impede the task being achieved.

Understanding how different interventions fit into these categories will help the trainer ensure that these functions are provided for in each training group.

## Task

### INITIATING

Initiating contributions start things off. This is obviously important at the beginning of any session, but there are various times in the life of the group in which
direction needs to be changed, or some new impetus is required to raise the energy
level. ('We'll begin by . . .', 'Maybe what we should do now is . . . '; 'There is a
new way of looking at this . . .'.)

### CLARIFYING

These are interventions which tease the precise meaning out of general statements,
and make connections between individual contributions. Clarifying encourages
people to be specific and avoid unclear generalizations. ('Are you saying that . . .';
'It seems to me that what you are saying is . . .'.)

### INFORMATION GIVING

At certain times it is necessary to provide information in order that people may
have the knowledge they need to further their learning. The information may be
of a technical nature or, by contrast, it may relate to understanding what the exact
nature of the task is. It might be superficial or profound, but it is characterized by
being relevant at the particular time to what the group is trying to achieve. (On
a group work skills course, someone might give a description of how they
structured a particular exercises.)

### QUESTIONING

Sometimes it is necessary to take a step back from what is going on and challenge
the group on any assumptions it may be making. This can be done by questions
which relate to the task itself, and may help define its exact nature, or they maybe
about some of the assumptions that group members have made as they have
worked on the task. ('Is this the only option open?'; 'What do you think the client
is feeling in this situation?').

### SUMMARIZING

Summarizing pulls various contributions together in a conclusive manner. It does
not add anything new to the group's thinking but rather provides the facility
whereby the group can check what it has achieved. A summary can provide a
breathing space, allowing the group to reflect on its progress so are and providing
a base line for the next phase of work. It is a particularly useful intervention if the
group gets stuck and lacks direction. By identifying what a group has already done,
the summary will help the group look forward to its next move. ('Up to this point,
we have considered the following . . .'; 'Let's just see where we've got to') .

# Maintenance

## SUPPORTING

There are times when individuals in a group are uncertain, afraid, or upset in some way. Support is demonstration of warmth towards them and can be shown by acknowledging and including the person or their contribution. This support or inclusion can be verbal ('Yes, I think that's a really good point' or 'That reminds me of something said earlier which I found helpful') or non-verbal, in the form of head nodding or eye contact and smiling. Body language is an important feature in group communication — some individauls can often be judged as non-contributors because they say little. However they may be contributing a great deal to the confidence of individuals by their non-verbal support.

## LIGHT RELIEF

When the tension is high in a group, humour can give people the opportunity to laugh and let off steam. It is an intervention which should be used with care since humour can be destructive if, for instance, it is used with sarcasm or as an attempt to discount the task or the individual.

## SHARING EXPERIENCE

By making a personal statement about a general issue the group is working on, the persons share something of themselves, of their lives or experience. This has the effect of encouraging the group to relate on a deeper level. There is a danger that people in a professional group can become so bound up by their own professionalism that they never disclose anything of themselves and thus function on a fairly dry, wooden level. The disclosure does not have to be of an intimate nature but is the communication of someone's direct experience. It may be a direct experience of the course which is shared, by someone talking directly about the thoughts and feelings created by whatever the group is engaged in. This kind of intervention creates an atmosphere of the 'realness' of the situation and encourages people to relate more personally to whatever is happening. ('At the moment I'm feeling . . .'; 'That happened to me once and I . . .'; 'What you've said reminds me of a time when I . . .').

## PROCESS OBSERVATIONS

These are descriptions or interpretations about what is happening in the group underneath the task level. They are most useful when the emotional needs of the members of the group begin to block the task. The process observer takes a step back from what is happening on the surface and examines how people are relating and why they might be behaving as they are. ('I wonder if we need to look at why we seem to be going round and round in circles'; 'We seem to have got into a fight about who has most power around here'; 'I notice that there are some people who haven't yet had a chance to speak').

Whoever is making the particular contribution could be seen as playing a role in the group at that time. Although the trainer has a responsibility to see that both task and maintenance needs in a group are met, the appropriate contributions will very often be made by members of the group. Group members are able to, and usually do, take on a number of roles within the life of a group. The roles are generally quite flexible and each member is likely to assume a number. For example, one person might, during the life of a group, play an 'initiator', a 'challenger', a 'process observer' and so on.

By keeping an awareness of the balance between task and maintenance functions the trainer can more easily decide which contributions will be most useful and appropriate as the group progresses. One thing to watch for is the danger that individuals may get 'stuck' in one role — for instance there may be someone in the group who is very good at providing the light relief. This is a valuable function, because it helps the group deal with tension through allowing them to laugh. However it can be very destructive for someone to always be expected to be the clown. It may mean that the group are not willing ever to take them seriously, so that they only get listened to if they are making a joke.

# DIFFICULT GROUP MEMBERS

Difficult group members have something in common with poverty: both are relative.

All of us who work with groups have at some time had fears and anxieties about non-participative or downright stroppy participants. Like many other fears, to anticipate and dwell on them is often to bring about what we dread most. The reality for most of the time is that we cope, and in coping learn how to manage then and on future occasions.

Asking a few questions about these difficult members helps to focus the fears so that they can be worked on.

(1)  Who are the difficult members? Identify them and the behaviour they are displaying.

(2)  What effect does the difficut person have on you? What feelings do you have about him or her?
     (It is possible that someone you find difficult to work with has the capacity to 'hook out' unresolved issues for you and triggers off strong feelings on issues you are still working on for yourself.)

(3)  How do you respond?
     (In kind? Do you feel personally or professionally 'got at'? Or is this difficult behaviour one of the hazards of working with groups?)

(4)  How do you think the difficult group member is affecting the others in the group and affecting the task in hand?
     (For example, someone who consistently 'hogs' the floor with inappropriate biographical details may cause mental, emotional and physical unrest in the group. There may be a sense of the task being suspended while this person relays further pieces of information about his or her life story, which is manifested by increased restlessness and shuffling about by the rest.)

(5)  What do you think the pay-off might be for the difficult group member?
     (e.g. Does the person get a lot of attention from you or the group: are they able to avoid working on a difficult issue: are they competing for leadership?)

Having identified who and what behaviours are causing you problems, there are a number of guidelines which can help you manage most situations.

(1)  When you consider you are being criticized, avoid being defensive. There are differences between providing excuses, justifications and reasons. You are not required to offer any of these alternatives.

(2)  Do you consider yourself to be a fighter? Leading groups is not the time to engage in combat. Aim for a cooperative relationship between you and the group.

(3)  If you assess that someone is making a bid for your leadership, acknowledge the contribution as you would any other. Try and see how this contribution fits in with what is going on in the group, and share your perception.

(4)  Competitiveness on your part will diminish your effectiveness. Consider the meaning of 'first among equals' in the context of leading groups.

(5)  Use the support which already exists within the group when difficulties arise from a particular person. It is more than likely that if you feel there are problems, others will be feeling the same.

(6)  Sometimes a subgroup can dominate the larger group. If you think this is happening, break the whole group into smaller ones — possibly to discuss this process or an aspect of the task in hand. The dynamic existing in the large group will be disturbed, and when it re-forms, will have changed and hopefully become more manageable.

(7)  Most of us appreciate the differences which exist amongst individuals. When we work in a group we sometimes unconsciously assume that the formation of this group eradicates some or even all of the disparities which exist outside it. Occasionally we need to remind ourselves that each participant brings his or her world-view to the group which will partially determine how that person behaves in this new context. It is the diversity that makes groups so potentially creative.

(8)  Criticisms of leadership arise out of different perceptions of its function. For these to add to the creativity of the group they need to be formulated in a precise and specific fashion. Generalized statements of discontent are unhelpful, so it is important to encourage participants in specificity. Clarify too the differences between questions and criticisms. It can happen that after the leader has explained or clarified an issue, and a participant questions it, the leader feels 'got at' because it hasn't been a good enough explanation. It is not a matter of being 'at fault', but far more likely that there is a combination of needing to use 'plain English' and recognizing some people need more time than others to grasp new ideas.

(9)  And finally, if it gets to a point when you feel the group is not working at all effectively, call a halt and spend time looking at why.

## GROUP LIFE

As well as understanding groups from the point of view of individual roles, it is useful for the trainer to have some framework for understanding the pattern of development of a group — the term often used to describe this process is group life.

A description of the life of a group takes account of the feelings, hidden agendas and unconscious needs of individuals, and how these interact to influence the development of the group. Making sense of all of this is often very difficult. It is hard enough to understand what motivates just one person to behave in a particular way. When a number of individuals are interacting, the difficulties are greatly multiplied. If you asked a number of individuals in a group what they were perceiving at any particular moment, each would have a different interpretation. In spite of the difficulties, it is important to have some way of assessing what is happening in a group because of the large number of influences, some of which are unconscious and irrational forces, which affect the extent to which a task can be successfully achieved. Some of these are:

(1)  The number of people in the group.
(2)  Whether group members already know each other, or are strangers.
(3)  Whether group members have chosen to attend or have been sent.
(4)  How long the group will be together.
(5)  The style of leadership.
(6)  The comfort (or otherwise) of the environment.
(7)  Individual hidden agendas.
(8)  How the group is made up with regard to gender, race, class, age, amount of experience, etc.

Many group workers, writers and researchers have contributed models which help in understanding the group process.

We have chosen two models to describe here, because each offers a picture of the life of a group. Neither of them needs to be thought of as providing the *right* explanation; so many models have been devised that it would be impossible to judge which was the right one. However, a different model can be used rather like different pairs of spectacles. Through one set you would have one view, and if you put another pair on you would see the world differently. Most trainers try out a number of pairs of spectacles before settling on one, or a combination of views. It is helpful to have knowledge of a number of models because some groups may be susceptible to one framework, while others may require a different one.

## TUCKMAN'S MODEL OF GROUP LIFE

B. W. Tuckman (as quoted in Micheal Argyle's *Social Interaction* (Tavistock Publications, 1969) described a group progressing through four stages. Many groups progress sequentially, while others may move backwards and forwards from one stage to another. Briefly, the four stages are:

### Forming

The group is characterized by anxiety with a dependence on the leader. The group will be attempting to discover its code of conduct, testing out what behaviours are acceptable and what the norms of the group will be; how supportive, how critical, how serious, and how humorous the group will be. The uppermost question for a group in this phase is, 'What shall we do?' and indeed much of its communication takes the form of questions many of them directed at the person in charge. There is very little open exchange of views between members at this stage.

### Storming

The group atmosphere will be one of conflict, with rebellion against the leader, polarization of opinion, conflict between subgroups and resistance to control. There is likely to be emotional resistance to the task and a sense of the task being impossible may pervade. A group at this stage will often approach the task with the feeling, 'It can't be done' or 'I won't do it'. Much of the communication takes the form of criticism or justification with some people making quite long speeches. This stage often represents a testing of the leadership which, viewed positively, may be the means by which the group starts to take the task seriously and work out its personal implications.

## Norming

At this stage some group cohesion develops and norms for the group emerge. Former resistance starts to be overcome and conflicts are patched up. The group in this stage will be capable of offering mutual support to members. Increasingly a determination to achieve the task will be accompanied by an open exchange of views and feelings, and a sense of cooperation. At this point the group is approaching the task with the feeling of, 'We can do it.'

## Performing

The group is getting on with the task which has brought it together. Roles within the group are functional and flexible, with interpersonal problems having been patched up. Individuals feel safe to express differences of opinion and trust the group to find acceptable compromises if necessary. There is lots of energy available within the group for problem solving. The feeling here is, 'We are doing it!'

## Randall & Southgate's Model of Group Life

This is described in detail in *Co-operative and Community Group Dynamics*, by Rosemary Randall and John Southgate (Barefoot Books, 1980). They also identify four stages, and develop the idea further by suggesting that each stage can manifest itself constructively or destructively. The way each stage is demonstrated will determine whether the group is Creative, Intermediate or Destructive.

*Stage 1:   Nurturing*
Creative group: people are honest and open, they talk about how they feel and are able to give and take support.
Intermediate group: people talk politely but without any real interest in each other. Business is started straight away without any time set aside for individuals to share something of themselves in order to feel part of the group. Those people who are confident and able to function well in a group get on with the task without paying attention to those who feel less confident.
Destructive group: people are either smotheringly attentive, or overtly discontented.

*Stage 2:   Energizing*
Creative group: ideas and plans flow freely with individuals feeling confident to argue for what should be done, and able to give and accept challenges.
Intermediate group: work gets bogged down with details and trivia, and there may be a retreat into impractical abstract ideas. Subgroups are formed which are concerned with their own needs and interests, regardless of other members of the group.
Destructive group: people bully, cajole, invade, dominate, engage in character assassination and feel furious, frightened, rejecting or rejected.

*Stage 3:   Peak*
Creative group: people feel fulfilled and excited. There is a sense of exhilaration as the group can see the task being achieved. They are able to congratulate themselves on successfully achieving the task.

Intermediate group: there may not be an identifiable peak. The group may simply
   exhaust itself; or some members experience the peak, while others don't.
Destructive group: the peak is replaced by over-hostility, characterized by paranoid
   attacks.

*Stage 4:    Relaxing*
Creative group: people celebrate and provide opportunities for summarizing and
   reflection.
Intermediate group: dissolves, leaving people unclear as to what has been achieved.
   Reassurances that things aren't as bad as they seem are exchanged.
Destructive group: resorts to relying on external support in the form of magic or
   illusions to help cope with its failure.

We repeat that neither of the above are presented as the *right* model. The trainer
may want to test them out by observing a number of groups, or by spending time
as a member of some groups, assessing to what extent the above models help make
sense of what is happening. The value of an accurate model to describe the life of
a group is that it frees the energy which a trainer may otherwise spend attempting
to understand what is happening in a group which seems to be behaving unpredict-
ably. The energy is then free to be used in developing effective strategies to help
the group achieve its objectives.

# GROUP MENTALITIES

Besides these two models of overall group life, W. R. Bion, one of the first people
to collect and publish observations of group behaviour, identified three common
reactions of groups which are not working well. He called them group mentalities,
and the trainer may find them a helpful diagnostic tool.

## THE DEPENDENT GROUP

This group mentality nearly always operates when a group begins. The dependent
group believes that in order to face the emotional tensions in the group it needs
a *magician* or a *god* who is fully responsible for all that takes place within the group.
A dependent group wants an identifable leader who is in charge.
   This sort of group is recognized by the value that group members give to
contributions made by the group leader, and which are always considered to be
more valid, more useful, more appropriate, more noteworthy than the contributions
of other group members. Many groups will move away from this dependency but
others, Bion suggests, get stuck there or will return there, usually because of their
own insecurity and need for protection.

## THE FIGHT/FLIGHT GROUP

The assumption in this group is that it has met to fight or run away from
something. The accepted leader is one whose demands on the group provide an
opportunity for either aggression or escape. Hostility and aggression will be
displayed to members who wish to approach the problems differently.
   Alternatively, the energy of the group will be used to avoid or escape from the
matter at hand.

This group mentality is recognizable by the ways in which a group will successfully ignore any contribution from a leader or by hostility expressed towards the leader or a group member. Contributions become anectodal, and members, consciously or unconsciously, allow and condone any contribution rather than getting on with the task.

## THE PAIRING GROUP

The group accepts long interchanges between two members, the basic assumption being that any such interchange ensures the group a future. This group has a kind of 'Messianic idea of hope' that as long as somebody is talking then the group must be getting somewhere. One of the effects of a group which gets stuck in the pairing mentality is that others who attempt to participate may find it difficult to enter the discussion, and as a result will withdraw.

# LEADERSHIP STYLES

Lastly in this section on working with a group, we will focus on leadership styles. The importance of participatory learning is a recurring theme in this book, but that should not imply a lack of structure. Rather, given the potential danger of time-wasting and side-tracking, it demands a very clear and well-organized structure, in which members know where they stand and have a clear understanding of the rules of communication in that context. The responsibility for this lies, in the first place, with the trainer/group leader.

A much-quoted experiment in search for reliable guidelines as to the most effective style of leadership is that undertaken by White and Lippitt in 1968 (see *Groups: Theory and Experience*, by Napier and Gershenfeld (Houghton Mifflin, 1973). They subjected groups to three different leadership styles and drew the following conclusions:

## DEMOCRATIC STYLE

This style is characterized by a determination to include all group members in the learning and decision-making processes. The democratic leader provides structure and momentum, but is prepared to bend and mould to the needs of the group. He or she is concerned as much with how the group is to operate as with what is the task of the group.

The strength of this style is that it gives real power to group members which, in turn, is likely to energize them to achieve the objectives. Group members are able to function, at least for a while, without depending on the leader. Its weakness is that, when mishandled, it may leave the course members unclear about who is in control, causing frustration.

## AUTHORITARIAN STYLE

The authoritarian knows very clearly where the power in the group lies. The authoritarian provides structure for the group and directs the content of what the group is to consider. Whilst acknowledging individual group members, the authoritarian is not willing to hand over the responsibility for how the group operates, or what it learns, to anyone else. This leader is firm, definite and unbending.

The strength of this style is that people know where they stand and that, in the short term, tasks may be completed quickly. The weaknesses are that all course members may not contribute, and that the group cannot function well (or in some cases, at all) without the presence of the leader. Another flaw is that because the leader takes so much responsibility for what happens, it is left for individual members to opt out of taking any of that responsibility for themselves. If things go well, group members will happily 'bathe in reflected glory', but if things go badly — it will be the leader who will be blamed.

## LAISSEZ-FAIRE STYLE

This style is concerned with allowing group members to express themselves and work out for themselves what they are there for, and what they want to learn. The leader does not seek to impose, but offers suggestions which members may or may not be willing to take up. He or she is an important part of the group, but is not the final arbiter of the most useful or relevant learning and purpose for the group.

The strength of this style is that many creative ideas can emerge and be explored. Its weakness is that the group can become aimless and frustrated.

Our preference is for the democratic style of group leadership, because that style provides a model which reflects the nature of the training we are engaged in. However, no one style is appropriate for every situation. An effective group worker will have a flexible approach, understanding the strengths as well as the weaknesses of each style. The most democratic trainer may need to be authoritarian on occasions, in order to ensure objectives are met; and in other situations may choose to take the laissez-faire approach.

We will end this brief exploration of some of the influences on groups with some suggestions about the skills and qualities which make up an effective group worker. It is, of course, not a complete list, but a guide as to the factors which can contribute to a trainer's ability to work well with groups.

An effective group worker needs:

(1)  a sound working knowledge, and practical experience, of group theory;
(2)  a competent knowledge of the content area which is the focus of study;
(3)  an ability to help participants to relate course learning to their own work settings;
(4)  an understanding of the feelings which group members may be experiencing;
(5)  the willingness to respect each individual's contribution to the course;
(6)  basic listening skills, including the ability to reflect, clarify individual contributions and draw relevant points together;
(7)  the ability to challenge individuals in a supportive and non-aggressive manner;
(8)  to be confident in the training strategies used, and clear about how different methods work;
(9)  to be relaxed and able to establish good humour in the group.

# Chapter 13:
## Working With Groups: Practice

## TRAINING TECHNIQUES

Having set the scene by focusing on some general aspects of working with a group, we shall now move on to more practical considerations related to different training techniques.

## GROUP DISCUSSIONS

A group discussion can fulfil different functions. It can:
(1) allow individuals a chance to share their views;
(2) give the trainer an opportunity to check how much is being understood by the group;
(3) allow individuals to ask questions for clarification;
(4) give people the chance to be actively involved;
(5) provide an opportunity to explore the learning which can be drawn from a group exercise.

A discussion can take place at any point in a training session. At the beginning it can provide the trainer with useful information as to the prevailing views and general level of knowledge and experience of the group. At different points during the session a discussion can break up a long lecture, or give participants some light relief from a heavy work session. At the end it will provide an opportunity for evaluation and summarizing.

### Size of group

There are different views as to the 'ideal' size for a group discussion. there is general agreement that, for anything more than a superficial discussion, a group of more than eight people creates difficulties, particularly for people who are naturally shy and find difficulty in talking in a group. The group should be able to sit in a circle and see and hear each other without difficulty.

If the training course has more participants than this, then they can be split upinto smaller groups in different ways. For example:

(1) *'Buzz groups'*. At any point during the session the trainer can ask the group to make up small groups of three or four by turning to the people nearest them. This is a very good way of getting a group's immediate reaction to something which has occurred, or to a particular point which has been made. Buzz group discussions are usually short, between 5 and 10 minutes, and may lead to a larger discussion involving the group as a whole. The advantage is that every person gets an opportunity to give his or her view to someone, even though only a few people will probably speak in the larger disussion. It is also a good method of injecting some energy into a session which is flagging — perhaps towards the end of the day.

(2) *Seminar groups*. These are larger groups (six to ten people) who meet to discuss some aspect of the course and report back to the large group. They are usually asked to elect someone to report back, and may be given some large sheets of paper so that any points they make can be written down and presented to the group as a whole. they usually meet for up to an hour.

(3) *Workshop groups*. Workshop groups are of a similar size as the seminar groups but meet to undertake a specific task. It may be some form of exercise which will contribute to the experiential learning in the course, or the task may be to answer specific questions or work on particular problems. Again, there will be a reporter who contributes to the whole group when it convenes.

(4) *Fishbowl*. A small group discussion observed by another (probably larger) group which does not participate in the substantive discussion. The process is then discussed by the whole group, and perhaps repeated with roles reversed. A variation to enable participation by members of the whole group is to have one or two empty chairs in the fishbowl circle. If any member of the larger group wishes to join the discussion, or make a point, he or she can sit in the empty chair. As soon as the point is finished the chair is vacated, allowing someone else to join.

(5) *Large group share*. It is possible, even in a very large group, for people to share their views, providing the following rule is observed. No-one is allowed to comment on a contribution made by someone else until everyone who wants to speak has done so. In this way people can say what they think without having to justify or explain. It also prevents the discussion being taken over by a small group of people.

## Membership of groups

If seminar or workshop groups are a feature of a course, the trainer may decide in advance how the groups will be made up, taking into consideration factors such as gender, age, work experience, and so on — mixing them or keeping them apart depending upon the particular objectives to be met.

If these considerations are not important, the trainer may ask people to make up random groups. Here are some ways in which the groups can be formed:

(1) Ask people to number off round the room according to the number of groups needed. If four groups are wanted, then people will number 'one', 'two', 'three' and 'four', repeating this until everyone has a number. Then, all the 'ones' form a group, all the 'two's', and so on.

(2)  Have a number of coloured beads or cards — with as many colours as the number of groups needed. Each person takes a colour, and then the groups are made up accordingly.

(3)  If there are different options for the groups to work on, put up a poster for each option with a space for people to sign themselves. If the number of the groups should be limited, put the appropriate number of spaces on the poster. When that one is full, people will choose from the options left.

## Starting off a group disussion

In order to be effective in helping participants to clarify and develop their thinking, the trainer will need to help them organize their discussion. Rather than say, 'Go into groups and discuss what you have heard so far', provide the group with some way of focusing on a specific area. For example:

(a)  Ask the group to consider differences or similarities. 'What are the differences between the behavioural and analytic approach to counselling'

(b)  Ask the group to develop lists. 'Think of as many ways as you can of demonstrating to a client that you are empathising with him or her'; 'How many evaluation structures can you think of?'.

(c)  Give the group a question 'What would you do in these circumstances?'

(d)  Brief the group to discuss criteria. 'Draw up a list of the qualities a good helper needs.'

(e)  Suggest they share personal experiences. 'Tell each other about a person you know who is a good listener, and identify the qualities you notice in them.'

### Practical points

(1)  A discussion group will work best if people are able to sit in a circle.

(2)  In a large room, small groups can be scattered around the room but they should be far enough apart to be able to talk without being distracted by the other groups.

(3)  The group should have a clear brief as to what they are meant to achieve, and instructions about timing.

(4)  It is important to reconvene the whole group even if for a short while so that the results can be shared and the course retains a cohesive feeling.

## BRAINSTORMING

A quick and participative method of producing lots of ideas as possible solutions to the question in hand. It is a creative rather than an evaluative technique. Evaluation of the practicability of the ideas should be held until after the brainstorm.

The facilitator invites the group to call out as many suggestions as possible, and write them up on paper so that everyone can see all the contributions. It is important to emphasize that all offerings are admissible and welcome. At this stage any criticism is out of place. Sifting the possible from the impossible comes at a later stage. The image of the 'storm' is useful to bear in mind — one idea will spark off another and the pace should be fast, furious and fun.

## ROLE-PLAY

This is a learning technique in which course participants are presented with a situation which they explore by acting out the roles of the people involved.

Role-play is a popular way of teaching interpersonal skills, because it resembles real life more closely than some other training methods. As participants become actively involved they are made more aware of the connections between thought, feeling and behaviour which have such an influence on the style and effectiveness of a worker.

If one of the aims of the training is to change behaviour or attitudes, role-play can be particulary helpful. We are all heavily influenced by our past experiences and by a variety of social pressures which make it difficult for us to respond to every situation in the most appropriate way. We develop patterns of thinking, feeling and behaving which are repetitive and, although they may have been appropriate at some time in our lives, are not helpful to us or others now. By providing the opportunity to practise different responses, role-play offers the possibility of increasing our options as to how we can deal with different situations. However, people are sometimes wary and anxious about this technique, and so it may need to be introduced gently, perhaps by a series of 'warm-up' exercises. The use of role-play can:

(1)   provide a dynamic way of exploring problems;
(2)   involve participants actively;
(3)   give opportunities for participants to practise newly learned skills, observe and practise different ways of responding to situations;
(4)   allow people to make mistakes in a risk-free environment, without fear of failure and embarrassment.

## TYPES OF ROLE-PLAY

### Simulated role-play

Exercises are usually set up with participants being given a printed brief describing the character they are to play, with notes about the situation or the issue they are involved in. For example, one participant is given the details about Mary, a client just arrived to see the student counsellor. Mary shares a house with four other students. They are noisy and untidy, and although she does have her own bed-sitting room in the house, the noise of their radio distracts her. This is her first year, and she has never lived away from home before. She is upset because she has just learned that she has a low mark for her latest essay. She has been trying her hardest to work, but has been distracted by the other people in her house.

The other participant is given a brief to be the counsellor.

The couple then play out the counselling session, with the person playing Mary improvising appropriately to fill out the character and the situation.

It is possible to set up more complex role-plays with more characters. An example might be a situation involving a patient, a staff nurse, a sister and a relative.

# 'Real-life' problems

Another kind of role-play is where a real-life counselling situation is used. This removes the unreality of a role-play that is often a criticism from participants, and is usually used in counselling skills training. Participants, usually working in pairs, will present their own real-life problems when they are playing the 'client' role.

# Reverse role-play

Often one of the aims of role-play is to make people more sensitive to the feelings of others. By asking people to play both sides of a conflict in turn, or to take the role of the person who is in conflict with them, the trainer can encourage the exploration of different attitudes and behaviour. If, for example, medical students are to be trained in communicating with patients, then it would be helpful to them to have the experience of playing the role of someone who is anxiously waiting for a diagnosis of their symptoms. Playing out that role will help them empathize more easily, and encourage them to develop a style that will take account of the patient's feelings.

# Exaggerated character role-play

One way of helping people over their fear of role-plays is to give briefs in which there are very clear instructions as to how to play the role. For example a brief might be 'Interview this client as if you were not at all interested in her problem'· or 'Don't listen to this client — tell him that you have too many problems of you own!' These kind of very short exercises are a good warm-up for longer more substantial role plays.

Role-plays can be structured in different ways; for example:
(1) Two or more people can play out the scene to the rest of the course who act as an 'audience', giving feedback after the role-play is finished.
(2) Pairs or threes can work together simultaneously playing out the same scenes. This is a better framework for a group which is nervous of 'public performances'. Feedback can then be taken as a whole group discussion. If working in threes the group can take on the roles of 'client', 'helper' and 'observer' — the observer not taking part in the role-play, but feeding back their observations to the couple they have watched.
(3) Small groups can work separately with an audio or video recorder. The tapes can then be used for feedback, with the whole group or with the trainer.

Practical points

When preparing a role-play:
(1) Select an experience that is appropriate for the training objectives, the learners' abilities and attitudes and the trainer's preferred teaching style.
(2) Identify the learning points which should come from the exercise and develop the exercise with those in mind.
(3) Identify the behaviours that should be demonstrated during the event and take them into account.

(4) After designing the exercise and preparing any papers, visual aids, etc prepare the briefing for participants. This should cover:
(a) a short statement of the objectives;
(b) the form the session will take;
(c) a description of what is required of the learners during and after the event;
(d) an explanation of why this particular method is being used;
(e) an acknowledgement of the contribution to learning that people are making by taking part — thank them for the efforts they are making in order to help each other learn;
(f) any short inputs of knowledge/theory which may need to be given to accelerate learning.
(5) Prepare the debriefing, listing the learning points which need to be brought out.
(6) Decide on the behaviours to watch for during the event, and select an appropriate recording system.

When briefing the course members:
(1) Unless it is a very simple exercise, written briefs are necessary. People need to know if and how much they can improvise. While people are getting familiar with the briefs, be sensitive to their reactions. Check whether they really known what to do; whether they are happy about doing the exercise; do they have an specific fears?
(2) If it seems that an individual really cannot face taking part, help that person work his or her way into this kind of learning gently, perhaps by suggesting that he or she takes an observer role to begin with.
(3) Care must be taken, especially if real-life problems are to be used, that no-one is pressed into revealing details that he or she would rather remain unknown.
(4) Bear in mind that in order for this kind of exercise to be successful, the group needs to be psychologically compatible with it. If there is a high level of discomfort the objectives may well be sabotaged by the reaction of the participants. If there is no level of agreement by the group that they are willing to try it out, then it is better to use a less threatening method until they are more confident.
(5) If feedback is to be given by the other participants, then there should be guidelines about how this is to be done. For instance, if the group are giving feedback to individual participants, the trainer needs to provide a structure in which the feedback is objective and opinion free. It is useful to give people instructions to watch for particular things, for example:

How was the client welcomed?
Given an example of a useful open question?
Give an example of a useful closed question?
Give some examples of positive body language?
Give some examples of negative body language?
How was the interview closed?

It is important that the feedback session does not become an exercise in either destructive criticism or placatory avoidance.

Probably the most effective source of feedback is from the participants themselves. The trainer can provide opportunities and structure in which people can monitor their own performance; certainly video and audio tapes can be used most successfully this way.

When observing the exercise:
(1) Don't try to watch everything. Decide beforehand what will be most useful in terms of the training objectives. If recordings are being made, don't try to

write everything down. Making notes 5–10 minutes at the beginning, in the middle and at the end will provide an adequate sample.

(2) Watch what happens during the event, to see whether there are natural leads to particular learning points, since this will shape the debriefing. It may be that some learning that happens spontaneously during an exercise is not planned for in the objectives. You will have to decide whether to change your objectives.

(3) If you note some behaviour by individuals that would be useful to highlight in the debriefing session, but may cause them to be defensive, make sure that the behaviour is noted in detail (what was said, what was done, etc.).

When debriefing the exercise:

(1) Probably the most effective source of feedback is from the participants themselves. The trainer can provide opportunities and structure in which people can monitor their own performance; certainly video and audio tapes can be used most successfully this way.

(2) Don't use role-play in a course unless there is time for adequate discussion and feedback.

(3) State the training objectives briefly at the beginning of the debrief.

(4) Test reactions to the event, people may need to discharge any strong feelings which arose, and must have a chance to do this before continuing.

(5) The object of a debriefing session is to describe and analyse the experience and draw learning from it about 'the real world'.

(6) Firstly, give participants an opportunity to air their perceptions of the event. Next, any non-participants can add their views, and lastly the trainer can put forward any perceptions.

(7) Short inputs of theory can be given, by building them on to participants' contributions.

(8) Be descriptive and not evaluative. Empathize with the group, and show readiness to solve problems with them. Be careful about controlling and manipulating the group's responses. Role-play has got a bad name from facilitators who use the opportunity to show a lack of concern for individuals, to appear superior, dogmatic, aggressive or defensive. Remember that role-play is an attempt to help people learn — not a ploy to make them appear inadequate or incompetent!

(9) Ask questions. This will stimulate the thinking of the group, and help them clarify and confront the issues.

(10) Summarize members' ideas from time to time.

(11) Don't rush people into identifying with the training objectives. Ideally they will get there on their own, through the process of the analysis. If the group do not react to changes you might suggest, explore the issue and test out the different viewpoints.

(12) It is useful to collect and record the group's contributions as they make them on a flip chart. This not only charts the group's way through a complex issue, but is a way of recognizing the importance of each person's contribution.

## SIMULATIONS

A simulation is a creation in the training room of a particular environment or situation. The simulation is used to allow participants to practise skills, try out ideas or test concepts in an experimental manner, and in as realistic a way as possible Simulations can be used to:

(1)  provide people with an opportunity to practise new skills;
(2)  give people experience as near real life as possible;
(3)  test participant ability to relate learning on course to practical situations.
Simulations are useful when the real thing is not accessible to participants, for
reasons of either distance, cost or time.

An example of a simulation is in a training course for receptionists, where the
training room is set up as a reception area, and where participants act as clients and
receptionist. A well-known simulation is the training fire tower in each fire station.

Simulations might include elements of role-play and, as in role-play, the discussion following the exercise is of great importance.

## GAMES

Sometimes a game element is introduced, with rules and rewards or scores for
certain results. There are many training games now on the market. Some are in the
form of board games in which the players are faced with decisions which influence
the outcome of the game. Some games have been devised in order to generate
certain dynamics which mirror real life. An example of this is 'Starpower' — a
game which is played with coloured counters which are exchanged through
negotiation. As the players collect certain colours their score changes, and at some
point in the game the group is split into those with the highest scores, who are
called 'Circles', those with medium scores, 'Squares', and those with least, 'Triangles'. As the game continues, the power struggles between Circles, Squares and
Triangles mirror the dynamics of similar struggles in the 'real world'.

These kind of games allow people to explore difficult or complex issues in an
exciting way. They do, however, need a good deal of control and organization.

As with role-play, thorough discussion must follow the game.

## CASE STUDIES

A case study is a written account of a situation, often in considerable details, which
poses a problem susceptible to solution by a variety of courses of action. It provides
a framework for focusing a discussion on general principles and exploring important issues. Case studies can be used to:
(1)  stimulate discussion;
(2)  give participants opportunities to relate theory to practice;
(3)  generate different problem-solving options;
(4)  provide practice in decision-making skills;
(5)  develop analytical skills.
Case studies based on the participants' working situations help to give a training
course the feeling of being grounded in practicality. This is valuable for participants
who find it difficult to transfer skills from the learning situation to their own
workplace.

Case studies usually include a description of a particular event, or series of
events, or the characteristics of a person or their life style and go on to pose a
problem for the student. For example:

'John is 17; he has been employed since he left school at 16 as an "office boy"
in the post room of a large publishing company. He lives with his widowed

mother, who suffers from arthritis. Because she cannot get around very easily, John is responsible for household chores like shopping, taking the washing to the laundrette, etc. He would like to get more qualifications, since he doesn't think that he can progress very far in his job and finds it boring and tedious. He would like to go to college, and has sufficient entry requirements but is worried about managing in terms of money and looking after his mother. How would you go about advising him?'

Case studies can be used to test specific skills — for instance in the above example, people could be asked:

    'List the problems that face John, and put them in order of priority' (to test prioritizing skills).

    'List some open questions you could ask John to help him explore the situation' (to test questioning skills).

    'To what benefits might John and his mother be entitled, and what information would you need to be able to calculate them?' (to test knowledge of benefits and calculations).

    'What feelings do you think John is experiencing?' (to test empathy skills).

    What are the options open to John' (to test creative option-generating skills)

Case study sessions can be organized in several different ways:

(a)  the whole group can work on the same case study, and then discuss their findings;

(b)  the group can be split into smaller units, working on different case studies, each illuminating a particular point;

(c)  the case study can be presented as a continuing story — the group can work on one aspect, and then be presented with another and so on — in this way several learning points can be built into the one exercise;

(d)  the case study can be given as 'homework', and discussed at the next session.

## Practical points

When preparing case studies:

(1)  Be aware that case study writing can be very time-consuming. There must be enough detail to make the study credible and realistic, as well as relevant to the training objectives.

(2)  The case study should present a realistic situation which the participant can take time to analyse, consider the evidence and make decisions regarding action.

(3)  The plot can be based on personal or second-hand experience, although it is unwise to base the whole story on first-hand experience. A close personal involvement may make it difficult to present objectively.

(4)  The case should present the situation in narrative form. Avoid stating opinions on the situation, or on the characters in the case. The situation should be reported — not assessed. If assessment of a character is necessary, present it as the view of another character — not the writer.

(5)  Having chosen a story, disguise it. This involves altering the names of characters, departments, products, biographical details, etc.

(6)  Include only those details which are necessary. The story should be interesting and credible, but not over-dramatic.

(7)  If you are not familiar with the necessary details, get a specialist in the field to check the information.

(8)  If the case study is aimed at developing analytical and diagnostic skills, the real

problem will not be stated, but clues will be provided. The aim should be to provide the minimum of concealment to achieve the objectives. Otherwise the problem may be totally obscured or the participants misled.

(9) If the participants are expected to begin by evaluating the facts, the writer must include the relevant facts. Avoid the temptation to put in too many 'red herrings', which should only be included if they make a learning point.

(10) Films, filmstrips, video and audio tapes can present a situation vividly for use as a case study. However, unless they are specifically made for a particular session, they have to be chosen with care.

(11) Make sure that sufficient detail is given for the participant to be able to work on the problem without having to make up information. Or give clear instructions about what information should be supplied by the reader.

(12) Ensure that details like money values, societal changes and legal rules are up to date. If they are not, the case study will not seem credible.

(13) Beware of creating stereotypical characters. All landlords are not mean-minded skinflints; all professors are not absent-minded!

## GIVING A LECTURE

Although the theme of this book places an emphasis on participative learning, there are times when what is most needed by a group is some information. It may be about the scientific facts or research relevant to the subject being studied. It may be about the history which has led up to a certain situation, or a comparison of different opinions held by experts in the field. Whenever there is a body of knowledge to be put over, the lecturing approach should be considered because it is as good a way as any of imparting information. What the lecture will probably not do on its own is stimulate a group into changing attitudes or developing skills, so a lecture in a skills course would always have to be supported by some practical work.

The trouble with lecturing is that it is easy to do badly! If a lecture is badly organized, given in indigestible chunks, or presented in a boring way it can be a tedious and frustrating experience.

A lecture is most likely to be helpful when:

(1)  It is relevant, both to the training objectives and to the participants' own situations. For instance, 'I am going to talk about two studies recently undertaken in organizations in order to establish the most effective ways to overcome barriers to change. The studies have a great deal to tell us about the effects of change, particularly with regard to introducing the kind of new policy that your organization is presently involved with.'

(2)  The information which is to be given can be demonstrated to be beneficial for participants. For instance, 'The conclusions which can be drawn from this information will enable us to think more clearly through the problems we have been discussing'.

(3)  The lecturer creates some active communication with the audience. This can be done by questioning them during the course of the lecture, or by inviting questions from them. For instance, 'I've been talking for some time now. Has anybody got any questions or comments they would like to put forward?'

(4)  Participants have an opportunity to talk with each other and the lecturer, sharing ideas and experience. The lecture can be broken up by ad hoc buzz groups, where the participants have a chance to talk with each other about whatever point the lecturer has made.

(5)  The lecturer is enthusiastic about the material. Enthusiasm transmits itself to the audience and the session is much more likely to be remembered.

## Organizing the lecture material

How the material for a lecture is organized is very much a personal matter, but a useful rule-of-thumb is: 'Begin by saying what you are going to say; then say it, and end by saying what you have said!' In other words, like a good essay, the lecture should have a clearly defined beginning, middle and end, starting with an introduction and ending with a summary.

The substance of the lecture can be arranged in different ways. For instance, if there is a large range of material it can be presented in a logical order of classification. Each section would have a heading, and possibly subheadings, and each point would be developed logically.

If the point is to demonstrate similarities and differences between different theories or practices, tables of comparison might form the substance of the lecture.

Yet another lecture form, where the main aim is to present research findings, is when the lecturer takes the audience through the process of describing the background and the problem, giving the information and analysing this more deeply, then describing how the data lead to certain hypotheses. This would be followed by a description of how the hypothesis was tested, and what conclusions were drawn.

Any lecture session might contain a mixture of these, or other frameworks.

Practical points:

(1)  Notes should be used as a guide rather than a prop! It is tempting to write out the whole lecture, particularly if you are nervous about drying up. It is true that reading a lecture out straight from the notes will ensure that none of the content is missed, but something just as important may well be missed. That is the communication between lecturer and audience, through eye contact and sensitive response to the audience reaction, that keeps a lecture lively and relevant. If you must take notes, have them written in headings on cards or small sheets of paper and use them only as a reference.
(2)  Use as many visual aids as possible to help participants take in the information. Remember that people remember more of what they see and do than what they hear.
(3)  If participants are taking notes, help them by giving them time, and ordering the lecture logically, signalling what you will be doing, ('Now I am going to make three points . . . the first is . . ., etc.').
(4)  Make sure you can be heard! This is an obvious point, but not everyone has a natural ability to project their voice in a large space.

# Chapter 14
## Using Audiovisual Aids

Opinions differ as to the benefits or disadvantages of different audio and visual aids. Before we briefly consider some examples, we would make some general points:

(1) Don't use any complicated audiovisual aid without rehearsing. We have raised our own (and the participants') anxiety levels too high too often by being faced in the middle of a session with a machine that we cannot turn off (or on) to ever want to do it again! If at all in doubt, make sure that you arrive early enough to have at least one run through on your own, or with someone who can take you through it.

(2) If the training session is to be held in an unfamiliar venue, check in advance that any aids you require can be supplied. It is not wise to assume that they will automatically be there.

(3) If possible, have a contingency plan in case machinery breaks down, or equipment runs out.

### (a) FLIP CHARTS, MOUNTED WHITE BOARDS AND CHALK BOARDS

Probably the most popular aids of all. Flip charts are very useful when collecting participants' ideas, or when small groups will have to report back. They can also be used for emphasizing or illustrating points being made by the trainer. They have the advantage over a chalk or white board that the sheets can be retained, and typed up later. They are also more portable.

It is useful to practise writing on a flip chart or chalk board, and checking that it is readable from whatever distance participants will be from it. The most common mistakes are to try to put too much on each page, and to write too small.

### (b) OVERHEAD PROJECTORS

These are small, sometimes portable, machines which project an image onto a white screen or wall. They are used with acetate foils which can be made in advance, or written up by the trainer during the session.

Their advantages over flip charts are that they provide a strong focus for the attention of the group; foils can be made up to a very professional standard, and can be used over and over again; by using overlays of different colours information can be presented very attractively and creatively.

Disadvantages might be that they can distract the group if they are left on too long; writing foils during the session needs a great deal of practice; the light bulb is a weak point in most models, and so it is useful to have (or known where to obtain) a replacement.

### (c) PREPARED AUDIO AND VIDEO TAPES AND FILMS

These are often used in support of a lecture, or as an introduction or summary to a skills workshop session. Their advantages are that they can present information in a creative and exciting way; one film can be seen by any number of participants; if they are shown to different groups, each group will receive exactly the same content.

The main disadvantage is that used on their own, without any support from a trainer, they can rapidly lose participants' attention. Unless a film or tape has been made specifically for a session, it is unlikely to be 100 per cent relevant or appropriate, and so can lose credibility as a training aid.

Because of this, it is important never to use any tape or film unless you have seen it at least once. Titles do not always give a good guide to the contents!

These aids are most effective when used in an interactive way. For instance, many trainers use 'trigger tapes', that is very brief cameo scenes showing individual people, or situations which are intended to start off a discussion. Some tapes are made so that every now and again there is a break programmed in for discussion before the next section of tape.

### (d) AUDIO AND VIDEO TAPES RECORDED DURING TRAINING SESSIONS

If recording and playback facilities are available, audio and video tapes can be an invaluable aid to the evaluation and integration of the learning which is taking place.

## Monitoring and evaluation

If the course involves role-play, or simulations, these can be taped. They provide excellent feedback for the participant, who will see just how he or she is performing. They can be viewed by the group as a whole, or just with the trainer. The interpersonal recall approach, pioneered in America by Norman Kagan, offers a very useful framework for this kind of supervision. The trainer or supervisor takes on the role of an 'enquirer', and through the process of asking questions helps the trainee to explore the session. One important aspect is that it is the trainees who are in control of the session, since it is they who stop the tape whenever they notice or remember something they want to discuss. The 'enquirer' does not take the initiative, and only explores those areas which are of interest to the trainee.

## Testing learning

Asking a group to make a short audio or video tape demonstrating some learning points is an excellent way of helping them (and the trainer) to monitor their level of progress and understanding of the content of the work. Because this approach depends on the creativity and involvement of the group, it tends to be much more fun than the traditional examination methods of testing learning.

Here are some examples of how this approach has been used on different types of courses:

(1) *On a counselling skills course*: 'Make a 15-minute tape which shows the diffeences between at least three different styles of counselling.'
    'Film or tape a section of a counselling session which demonstrates the use of listening and empathy skills.'

(2) *On a welfare benefits course for advice workers* 'Imagine you have to instruct a new worker in the structure of the welfare benefit system. Make a short (not more than 20 minutes) tape which would help you put over the main points you want this new worker to understand.'

## A WORD OF WARNING

The technology available to trainers is increasing and improving all the time. In our experience there is no audiovisual aid which can take the place of the relationship between the trainer and participant when they are engaged together in the development of skills and attitudes. Audiovisual aids can enhance a training session greatly if they are skilfully and appropriately used. On the other hand they can stand in the way of learning if they are used as a cover for lack of confidence or competence in the trainer.

# SECTION 5
## Sample Course Designs

This section comprises examples of courses using a mixture of inputs and exercises selected from the manual. Each example uses material which can be modified to fit the needs of different professional groups.

## EXAMPLE 1:   ONE-DAY BASIC INTRODUCTION TO CLIENT CONTACT SKILLS

The course is intended as a very basic introduction to the helping process, and would be useful for new trainees, or for people who want to find out whether they wish to be helpers. It could also be used as the first day of an extended training course.

## Course Objectives

At the end of the course participants will be able to:
(a)   identify and list client contact skills;
(b)   define the three-stage helping process;
(c)   apply the process in a series of practical exercises in: (i) assessing the problem, (ii) active listening, (iii) goal setting.

| | |
|---|---|
| 9.30 a.m. | Session 1: Starting the course |
| | Exercise 1e:   Hopes, fears and expectations (page 36) |
| | Exercise 1h:   Learning contract (page 37) |
| 10.00 a.m. | Session 2: Client contact skills. |
| | Exercise 2e:   What happens in an interview? (page 40) |
| | Exercise 2a:   Why do they come to me? (page 39) |
| | Exercise 2b:   What kind of help is needed? (page 39) |
| 10.45 a.m. | Refreshment break |
| 11.15 a.m. | Session 3: The three-stage helping process |
| | Tutorial input (page 42) |
| | Exercise 3c:   Identifying helping skills (page 44) |

12.30 p.m.   Lunch

1.30 p.m.    Session 4: Assessing the problem
             Exercise 4f:   Practising assessment (page 50)

2.00 p.m.    Session 5: Listening
             Exercise 5d:   Cocktail party (page 53)
             Exercise 5i:   Mirror listening (page 56)
             Exercise 5k:   Putting it together (page 58)

3.00 p.m.    Refreshment break

3.15 p.m.    Session 6: Decision stage
             Tutor input (page 81)
             Exercise 10d:   Goal-setting scenarios (page 84)

4.00 p.m.    Session 7: Evaluation and end of course
             Exercise 32a:   Evaluating the course (page 158)

4.30 p.m.    Course ends

# EXAMPLE 2: TWO-DAY INTRODUCTION TO COUNSELLING SKILLS

This course would be appropriate for any group of professionals who use counselling skills as part of their work such as nurses, managers, community workers, advice workers, personnel officers and doctors. It would be a good introduction for people who were assessing whether they wished to train as counsellors.

## Course Objectives

At the end of the course participants will be able to:
(a)  identify and list skills required for counselling;
(b)  relate the three-stage helping process to counselling in practice exercises;
(c)  define and demonstrate specific skills: i.e. assessment, active listening, empathy, questioning, focusing, giving and receiving feedback, summarizing, goal setting, evaluation.

Day one:
9.30 a.m.    Session 1: Starting the course
             Exercise 1b:   Name game (page 35)
             Exercise 1f:   Best and worst (page 36)
             Exercise 1h:   Learning contract (page 37)

10.30 a.m.   Session 2: The counselling process: an overview
             Exercise 2c:   Different expectations of client and helper? (page 40)
             Exercise 2d:   What skills are required? (page 40)
             Tutorial input relating the three-stage process specifically to counsell-
             ing (page 41)

11.15 a.m.   Refreshment break

11.30 a.m.   Session 3: The first contact
Tutorial input (page 46)

Exercise 4e:   Client clues (page 49)
Exercise 4f:   Practising assessment (page 50)

12.15 p.m.   Session 4: Active listening
             Exercise 5a:   Active listening (page 51)
             Exercise 5b:   Listening as a four level activity (page 52)

1.00 p.m.    Lunch

2.00 p.m.    Session 4 (contd)
             Exercise 5f:   Barriers to active listening (page 54)

2.15 p.m.    Session 5: Empathy
             Tutorial input (page 59)
             Exercise 6a:   Empathetic understanding (page 60)
             Exercise 6b:   Barriers to self-exploration (page 60)
             Exercise 6f:   Practising empathy (page 63)

3.15 p.m.    Refreshment break

3.30 p.m.    Session 6: Getting information
             Tutorial input (page 64)
             Exercise 7f:   Open, leading and closed questions (page 67)
             Exercise 7g:   Exploration and focusing questions (page 67)
4.20 p.m.    Session 7: Evaluation of day:
             Exercise 32f:   Feedback circle (page 159)

4.30 p.m.    End of Day 1.

Day Two
9.30 a.m.    Session 8: Thoughts about day 1
             An opportunity for the group to share any thinking they have done
             about the course so far, and to clarify any issues left over from the first
             day.

9.45 a.m.    Session 9: Focusing
             Tutorial input (page 69)
             Exercise 8b:   Objectives for focusing (page 69)
             Exercise 8e:   Negotiating the focus (page 71)

10.45 a.m.   Refreshment break

11.00 a.m.   Session 10: Feedback
             Exercise 9a:   Giving feedback (page 73)

11.45 a.m.   Session 11: Summarising
             Tutorial input (page 75)
             Exercise 9d:   Practising summarizing (page 76)

12.45 p.m.   Lunch

1.45 p.m.    Session 12: Setting goals
             Tutorial input (page 78)
             Exercise 10d:   Goal setting scenarios (page 84)

3.00 p.m.    Refreshment break

3.15 p.m.    Session 13: Evaluation
             Tutorial input (page 98)
             Exercise 15f:   Self progress evaluation (page 102)

4.00 p.m.    Session 14: ending
             Exercise 32d:   Course journey (page 159)
             Exercise 32j:   Continued learning (page 160)

4.30 p.m.    Course ends.

# EXAMPLE 3: THREE-DAY COURSE ON MANAGING STRESS

This course can be offered as part of a continuing training programme, and is suitable for people who experience their work as stressful. It is also a good way of providing insights into the effects of stress on clients in order to increase the helpers' empathy and understanding.

## Course Objectives

At the end of the course participants will be able to:
(a)  identify and list sources of stress in their work situation;
(b)  connect different reactions to the causes of stress;
(c)  define their personal support system;
(d)  relate patterns of stress behaviour to five personality types;
(e)  respond to specific conflict situations with less stress;
(f)  practise relaxation and meditation techniques;
(g)  make decisions regarding long-term stress reduction

Day one
 9.30 a.m.   Session 1: Starting the course
             Exercise 1a:    Introductions (page 35)
             Exercise 1e:    Hopes, fears and expectations (page 36)
             Exercise 1g:    Group contract (page 37)
             Exercise 1h:    Learning contract (page 37)

11.00 a.m.   Refreshment break

11.15 a.m.   Session 2: What is stress?
             Exercise 27a:   Sources of stress (page 135)
             Exercise 27b:   Stressful life events (page 136)
             Exercise 27c:   Signs of stress (page 136)

12.30 p.m.   Lunch

 1.30 p.m.   Session 3: Reactions to stress
             Exercise 27d:   Identifying the threat (page 138)
             Tutorial input (page 137)
             Exercise 27e:   Escape mechanisms (page 138)
             Tutorial input (page 139)
             Exercise 27h:   Defence mechanisms (page 140)

 3.00 p.m.   Refreshment break

 3.15 p.m.   Session 4: Personal support network
             Tutorial input (page 140)
             Exercise 28a:   Identifying support groups (page 140)

|  | Exercise 28b:   Personal support network (page 141) |
|---|---|
| 4.15 p.m. | Session 5: Evaluation of day |
|  | Exercise 32f:   Feedback circle (page 159) |

4.30 p.m.    End of day 1.

Day two:
   9.30 a.m.    Session 6: Thoughts on day 1
                An opportunity for participants to share any thoughts or deal with any unfinished issues arising from the first day.

   9.45 a.m.    Session 7: Identifying and reducing stress
                Tutorial input (page 148)
                Exercise 31a:   Beginnings of stress (page 149)
                Exercise 31b:   Driver questionnaire (page 149)

10.30 a.m.    Refreshment break

10.45 a.m.    Session 7 (contd.)
                Tutorial input (page 151)
                Exercise 31c:   Back seat driving (page 156)
                Exercise 31d:   Motivating others (page 156)

12.45 p.m.    Lunch

   1.45 p.m.    Session 8: Dealing with situations which create stress
                Tutorial input (page 115)
                Exercise 20a:   'Five R' Script (page 117)
                Tutorial input (page 117)
                Exercise 21a:   Responding to criticism (page 118)

   3.00 p.m.    Refreshment break

   3.15 p.m.    Session 9: Relaxation and meditation
                Exercise 30a:   Choice of relaxation techniques (page 144)
                Exercise 30b:   Choice of meditation techniques (page 146)

   4.15 p.m.    Session 10: Evaluation of day
                Exercise 32f:   Feedback circle (page 159)

4.30 p.m.    End of day 2.
Day three
   9.30 a.m.    Session 11: Thoughts on day 2
   9.45 a.m.    Session 12: Practical ways of coping
                Exercise 29a:   Coping with stress workshop (page 142)

10.45 a.m.    Refreshment break

11.00 a.m.    Session 12 (contd.)

12.45 p.m.    Lunch

   1.45 p.m.    Session 13: Long-term changes
                Exercise 30e:   Changing lifestyles (page 147)

3.15 p.m.    Refreshment break

3.30 p.m.    Session 14: Evaluating the course
             Exercise 32c:    Checklist (page 159)
             Exercise 32g:    Goodbye messages (page 159)
             Exercise 32h:    Future plans (page 160)
             Exercise 32k:    Group hug (page 161)

# SECTION 6:
## REFERENCES AND RESOURCES

# SECTION 1: THE RATIONALE

## Chapter 1: How skills can be taught

1. Clayton, T. E.: *Teaching and Learning*: Prentice Hall (1965)
2. Wiman B. and Nierhousy, J.: *Education Media*: Merrill (1969)
3. Dewey, John: *Experience and Education*: Collier-Macmillan (1938)
4. Lewin, Kurt: *Field Theory in Social Sciences*: Harper & Row (1981)
5. Kelly, George: *The Psychology of Personal Constructs*: Norton (1955)
6. Rogers, Carl: *Client Centred Therapy*: Houghton Mifflin (1951)
7. Rogers, Carl: *On Becoming a Person*: Houghton Mifflin (1961)
8. Tennenbaum, Samuel: Carl Rogers and non directive teaching (in *On Becoming a Person*, Ch. 15): Houghton Mifflin (1961)
9. Maslow, Abraham: *Toward a Psychology of Being*: Van Nostrand (1962)
10. McLuhan, Marshal: *Understanding the Media — the Extension of Man*: Sphere (1964)
11. Kolb, David: *Experimential Learning*: Prentice Hall (1984)
12. Buzan, Tony: *Make the Most of Your Mind*: Pan (1977)

## Chapter 2: What are client contact skills?

1. Rogers, Carl: *Client Centred Therapy*: Houghton Mifflin (1961)
2. Bolton, Robert: *People Skills*: Spectrum/Prentice Hall (1979)
3. Bergman, D. V.: Counselling method and client responses, *Amer. J. Consult. Psychol* (1951, **51**, 21–224)
4. Source: Anti Defamation League of B'nai B'rith Rumour Clinic; quoted in *People Skills*, Robert Bolton; Prentice Hall (1979)
5. Egan, Gerard: *The Skilled Helper*; Brooks/Cole (1975)

# SECTION 2: BASIC TRAINING

## Chapters 3–5:

Bond, Tim: *Games for Social and Life Skills* Hutchinson (1986)

Brandes, D. and Phillips, H.: *Gamesters: Handbook* Hutchinson (1985)

Brandes, D. and Phillips, H.: *Gamesters' Handbook* (Book 2): Hutchinson (1982)

Brearley, G. and Birchley, M.: *Introducing Counselling Skills and Techniques*; Faber & Faber (1986)

Carkhuff, Robert; *The Art of Helping*; Holt, Rinehart & Winston (1983)

Egan, Gerard: *The Skilled Helper*; Brooks/Cole (1975)

Egan, Gerard: *You and Me*; Brooks/Cole (1977)

Egan, Gerard: *Exercises in Helping Skills*; Brooks/Cole (1982)

Feldman, Dr S. S.: *Mannerisms of Speech and Gestures in Everyday Life*: International Universities Press (1969)

Inskipp, Francesca: *A Manual for Trainers: Resource Book for Setting Up and Running Basic Counselling Courses*: Alexia (1985)

McKay, M., Davis, M., Fanning, P.: *Messages*: New Harbinger (1983)

Maslow, A. H.: *Motivation and Personality*; Harper & Row (1954)

Pfeiffer, J.W. and Jones, J.E.: *Handbooks of Structured Experiences for Human Relations Training*: University Associates (1973)

Maris, Peter: *Loss and Change*; Routledge & Kegan Paul (1974)

Nelson-Jones, Richard: *Human Relationship Skills*: Cassell (1986)

Nelson-Jones, Richard: *Practical Counselling Skills*: Holt (1983)

Pease, Allen: *Body Language*; Sheldon Press (1984)

Priestly, P. and McGuire, J.: *Learning to Help*; Tavistock (1983)

Rogers, Carl: *Client Centred Therapy*: Houghton Mifflin (1951)

Spier, M. S.: Kurt Lewin's Force Field Analysis, in *Handbook for Group Facilitators*; Pfeiffer & Jones, University Associates (1973)

Wilkinson, J. and Canter, S.: *Social Skills Training Manual*; Wiley (1982)

# SECTION 3: CONTINUING TRAINING

## Chapters 7–12

Berne, E.: *Games People Play*: Penguin (1967)

Bolton, R.: *People Skills*; Spectrum (1979)

Bond, M. and Kilty, J.: *Practical Methods of Dealing with Stress*: Human Potential Research Project; University of Surrey (1982)

Bowyer, S.A. and Bowyer, G.H.: *Asserting Yourself*: Addison Wesley (1980)

Cox, Tom: *Stress* Macmillan Press (1978)

Cox, G. and Dainow, S: *Making the Most of Yourself*: Sheldon (1985)

American Psychiatric Association; *Diagnostic and Statistical Manual of Mental Disorders*; (1985)

Dyer, Dr W. W.: *Your Erroneous Zones*; Sphere (1979)

Hughes, B., and Boothroyd, R.:*fight or Flight?*; Faber & Faber (1985)

Ernst, S. and Goodison, L.: *In Our Own Hands*: The Women's Press (1981)

Houston, Gaie: *The Relative Sized Red Book of Gestalt*: Rochester Foundation (1982)

Kahler T, and Capers H.: The Miniscript, *TAJ* **4**(i) 26–42 (1974)

Klein, Mavis: *Discover your Real Self*: Hutchinson & Co. (1983)

Klein, Mavis: Ten personality types, *TAJ* **(15)**224, 231

Klein, Mavis: How to be happy though human, *TAJ* **17**(4), 1988

Nelson-Jones, Richard: *Theory and Practice of Counselling Psychology*; Holt, Rinehart & Winston (1982)

Steiner, Claude: *The Other Side of Power*: Grove Press (1981)

# SECTION 4: TRAINING TECHNIQUES

## Chapters 12–14

Argyle, M.: *Social Interaction*; Tavistock Publications (1973)

Bion,W. R.: *Experiences in Groups*: Tavistock Publications (1961)

Douglas, T.: *Group Work Practice*: Tavistock Publications (1976)

Houston, Gaie: *The Red Book of Groups and How to Lead them Better*: Rochester Foundation (1984)

Napier, R.W. and Gershenfeld, M.K.: *Groups: Theory and Experience*; Houghton Mifflin (1973)

Randall R. and Southgate J.: *Co-operative and Community Group Dynamics*; Barefoot Books (1980)

Satow, A. and Evans, M.: *Working with Groups* (with video available from concord Video & Film Council; see Visual Aids) HEC/TACADE

Shaw M. *et al.*: *Role Playing: A Practical Manual for Group Facilitators*; University Associates (1980)

Stewart, V. and Stewart, A.: *Managing the Manager's Growth*; Gower (1978)

Thompson S. and Kahn, J.H.: *The Group Process as a Helping Technique*; Pergamon (1973)

## VISUAL AIDS RESOURCES

Concord Video and Film Council, 201 Felixstow Road, Ipswich IP3 9BJ (Tel. 0743 76012/ 0473 715754).
A major source for video and films. Ask for the catalogue called *Videos and Films for the Caring Professions*. These include material on issues like: Working with Groups, Approaches to Group Therapy, Supervision, Carl Rogers on Therapy, Counselling Techniques, Aggression, Violence, Crisis, Working with Disabilities (Mental and Physical), Issues around Race and Racism, Healthy Living, Alcohol and Drug Abuse.

The Audiovisual Aids Department, University of Leicester.
   Tapes on approaches to counselling.

Video Arts Ltd., 68 Oxford Street, London W1.
   A series of films and training material on various interpersonal skills relating to organizations.

## RESOURCE ORGANIZATIONS

**British Association for Counselling**, 37a Sheep Street, Rugby, Warks. **Scottish Association for Counselling**, Queen Margaret College, Clerwood Terrace, Edinburgh EH12 8TS. The central source for information about all aspects of counselling and counselling training.

**Standing Conference for the Advancement of Training and Supervision (SCATS).**
Further information from Caroline Bailey, 15 Liberia Road, London N5 1JP. A network for all those involved in interpersonal skills training. Activities focus on an annual trainers' conference.

**Centre for the Study of Management Learning**, University of Lancaster, Lancs LA1 4YX.

**Trainers**, 9 Marsili Court, 22 Palace Road, SW2 3NQ. Provides training courses for trainers.

**Training Unit, London Voluntary Service Council**, 68 Chalton Street, London NW1.
Publishes a regular *Training Directory* of organizations and course in London.

**Institute of Training and Development**, 5 Baring Road, Beaconsfield, Buckinghamshire HP9 2NX.
   The UK professional body for trainers.